The Education of a
WASP

Wisconsin Studies in American Autobiography

WILLIAM L. ANDREWS
General Editor

The Education of a

WASP

LOIS MARK STALVEY

The University of Wisconsin Press

The University of Wisconsin Press
2537 Daniels Street
Madison, Wisconsin 53718

3 Henrietta Street
London WC2E 8LU, England

4   6   8   10   9   7   5

Printed in the United States of America

Originally published in 1970 by William Morrow
and Company, Inc.

Grateful acknowledgement is made to Twayne Publishers,
Inc., for permission to quote from the poem, "If We
Must Die," from *Selected Poems of Claude McKay*.

Library of Congress Cataloging-in-Publication Data
Stalvey, Lois Mark.
The education of a WASP.
1. United States—Race relations. 2. Discrimination
—United States. 3. WASPs (Persons)
4. Stalvey, Lois Mark. I. Title.
E185.61.S77   1988   305.8'0973   88-40444
ISBN 0-299-11970-X
ISBN 0-299-11974-2 (pbk.)

Dedicated to the memory of
Malcolm X (1925–1965) . . .
who told white people to
educate themselves

AUTHOR TO READER—1988

When this book was first published, I hoped that it would soon become only a history of what racism used to be. I feel profound regret that it has not.

The book is the story of my family's education, of the racism I found in my heart and head, how it got there, and what I did about it. Some of the national events and names may be unfamiliar to a new generation, but the emotions, myths, and fears are, tragically, still alive in society today.

Last spring, seven *northern* campuses erupted with racist attacks once seen only in the South; last summer, a white baseball executive proclaimed publicly that black men did not have "the necessities" for front-office jobs; last week, a famous sports commentator revived ancient myths about the "in-bred" athletic abilities of black people. This week, ugly racism was revealed within the FBI. My black friends still experience snubs. Their children are still harassed by police solely because of their color.

In rereading this book before its reissue, I felt a personal despair. So little has changed. Must we indeed, I wondered, start all over again? Then I knew I would feel even more despair if we did not start over again at all.

So, in 1988, I again share my family's story with you, sadly aware that my education—and yours—is not yet complete.

AUTHOR TO READER

There are many books by experts on America's racial crisis; this is not one of them. This is simply the testimony of what happened to one WASP family—my family—inside us and around us.

It is not offered as The Solution. Indeed, I wonder if anyone, expert or not, can prescribe one solution for something as complex as relationships between human beings, each of us as different from each other as are our fingerprints. Instead, I have tried to tell only what happened to us, what we learned, and how we learned it. From this, the reader may come to conclusions different from mine.

An education should not have an end, but a book must. By the time this book reaches you, the reader, many unpredictable events may have occurred in our country. Perhaps these events will bring us closer together instead of increasing the distrust between black and white Americans. My most fervent hope is that this book will prove to be more a case history than an autopsy.

All the events related here are true. In order to speak frankly I have changed the names, physical descriptions, and backgrounds of all the people involved with the exception of my family. Unfortunately, in order to maintain consistency, this meant disguising people whose acts of great kindness I would like to acknowledge publicly. For this reason, I list some of the patient and honest "teachers" to whom my husband, our children, and I owe a tremendous debt of gratitude: Samuel Barnett, Fred Bonaparte, Rev. and Mrs. Leonard L. Smalls, Dr. and Mrs. Claude Organ, Joan McGuinn Jenkins, Mr. and Mrs. John Martin, "Bud" Outlaw, Horace Williams, Winifred Peterson, Dr. Leo Freeman, Katherine Fletcher, Raymond Pace Alexander, Sadie T. M. Alexander, Mr. and Mrs. Gerald Vallery, and Mrs. Randolph Brown.

For the critical encouragement and honesty she handed over our back fence, I owe thanks also to Eleanor Olkes Lavin.

LOIS MARK STALVEY

Philadelphia
January 3, 1970

x

INTRODUCTION

by U.S. Congresswoman Shirley Chisholm

Lois Mark Stalvey's experiences vividly recount to the reader the author's harsh, rude awakening to the realities of America's racist society. The extent and depth of racism is rendering America vulnerable to the attacks of opponents here at home as well as those abroad. Mrs. Stalvey's soul-searching, supplemented by her personal experiences in Omaha and Philadelphia, dramatically portrays the inherent weakness and sickness of this potentially vibrant nation which stands no longer at the crossroads but instead on the brink of the precipice.

It may sound like a trite, overworked phrase, but this book is a "must" for white America as it serves to reexamine many of the existing attitudes and prejudices. I would like to add, though, that *The Education of a WASP* ought to be required reading for every American with an interest in the future of this country. As one reads through this book one is faced with the ultimate realization that the equality, the justice and the freedom of which the American dream is composed cannot be realized unless the problems of which Mrs. Stalvey has become so vitally cognizant are resolved. As she so adequately and clearly points out, many of the basic values of white America are meaningless to the large black, brown, red and yellow segments of America's population for the simple reason that those values often intentionally exclude other than white Americans.

This book is not a polemic; it is instead a straightforward account of the education of one American white woman to both the real and the potential dangers contained in the day-to-day life of every American, dangers that may indeed preclude an American future.

The author does not attempt to seek scapegoats but rather artfully and objectively articulates one of the ills in America's cities and communities, an ill which has inevitably resulted in the racial polarization of our country.

Unlike many whites, Lois Stalvey does not stick her head in the sand like the proverbial ostrich but rather faces and penetrates through often painful and embarrassing incidents.

Unlike many black (and white) radicals, she does not allow her painful awareness of injustice to lead her into fits of outrage that would consequently cause her to lose her objectivity. But she does nevertheless leave one with the feeling that she is extremely committed to somehow finding ways to change the status quo.

She has not presented us with a blueprint to solve the problems, but by the time you have finished reading this book you will realize that she has helped you to come that painful first step.

She will have pointed out the "lie of democracy" in America, not with statistics and figures, but with personal insight and pain. And it is this recognition within each of us that is necessary as the first step toward progress through understanding in the United States.

Chapter One

A young black man, his shaved head revealing ugly scars on his skull, stood in my living room in Philadelphia.

"It's too *late* for talking, white lady," he screamed at me.

I reached out my hands to him instinctively. He backed away, shaking his head, and walked to the door.

Then he swung around. "You *know* it's too late, lady. Jesus Christ, you *gotta* know it's too late now."

Eight years ago I could not have seen the fear behind this young black man's anger or felt a frantic wish to reassure him. But I had had eight years of a painful education. My husband Ben, our three children, and I had moved inexorably from white middle-class serenity to the disturbing fear that this young man was right.

And if he was right, our three small children would suffer in ways it had taken me too long to understand.

This, then, is the story of a step-by-step education, begun by accident and continued often with reluctance. Its main value may be that it happened to such an average family in so many gradual steps. At the beginning, we would not have believed how much our lives would change and how much we would each change as people. As a family, we have received incomparable rewards; I also learned much I didn't want to know.

We are WASPs, my husband and I, lifelong members of the white Anglo-Saxon Protestant majority group, and some people say that it is primarily our group who created and continue "white racism" in America. In 1961 I would have denied this hotly. To me, my friends and I were thoroughly unprejudiced. But in 1961 we had not yet been tested. Black voices of complaint were heard only in the South, and it was easy for me to sit complacently in Omaha, Nebraska, detached from and deploring the white outcries against school integration in Little Rock, Arkansas, or the angry whites who harassed Negro college students attempting to occupy white-only restaurant seats in North Carolina.

For Ben and me, in Omaha in 1961, our lives were untroubled and serene. After six years of marriage, we seemed to have reached the happy ending to the national American Dream. We even looked like a magazine ad for the typical American family. A photograph would have shown us standing in front of our suburban ranch-style house, surrounded by an acre of pampered lawn. Ben, tall, lean, and craggy-featured, would be surrounded by our three blond, blue-eyed children. Five-year-old "Spike" (Bennett Odom Stalvey, III), slim, active, had inherited my impulsive curiosity and his father's quiet reflective moods. Noah, then three, was the mischievous, affectionate family clown, and Sarah, only two, had already discovered, and delighted in, the fact she was a girl.

As the mother in the family photo, I would probably show up slightly blurred as I tried to keep Spike still while watching for Noah's next antic or for a slipping bow in Sarah's hair. But I would be smiling happily and holding Ben's hand.

Our standard of living far surpassed what Ben and I had

known as children. We were proud of what we felt we had accomplished through hard work, careful planning, and the good luck of having married each other. Our marriage had weathered the first years of two different temperaments trying to adjust. I was learning to appreciate Ben's cautious, reflective nature and to count on him to temper my impulsive enthusiasms. Ben contended I had taught him to enjoy people. But our backgrounds were so nearly identical that most of our other adjustments were minimal. Ben's family was Baptist, mine Lutheran. We had both been brought up in the Midwest. Ben was born in South Carolina but had grown up in Detroit. I had been born and raised in Milwaukee. Most of the men in Ben's family were blue-collar workers while in mine they were at the bottom of the white-collar rung (frayed white-collar workers might be the term). I was the grandchild of European immigrants while Ben's ancestors were early American settlers, but security was the goal for both our families. We had inherited their nest-building tendencies. Our home, our family, and each other were our main interests.

Ben had gone to college on the G.I. Bill after service in World War II and then worked his way up to an excellent job as advertising-promotion director of a large, Omaha-based corporation. He was praised often by his superiors and had been told that future advancements would come quickly. Ben planned to stay with the corporation so that we could settle permanently in Omaha, right in the center of America.

I was supremely content with my job as a housewife. For me, homemaking offered more important challenges than my pre-marriage career in advertising. Because my parents had been divorced when I was three years old, a secure happy marriage was my most fervent childhood dream. Now, I prized the privilege of staying home (as my mother couldn't) and being with my children. Looking up into Ben's face each night when he came home from work and watching his deeply carved features soften into relaxed lines was a deep satisfaction. True, his square, stubborn chin could also jut in determination over what I considered "trifles," but that same chin was a resting place under which I could sob out an occasional domestic frustration and hear Ben's patient reassurances. Once frightened of repeating my parents' mistake, I delayed marrying until my late twenties. The wait had proved worthwhile. Often I would sit at our picture window, looking out at the hills across the valley, and reflect happily that "Yes, dreams did come true." Perhaps not all of them; the novel I had once hoped to write would probably never get written, but maybe one of my children would write it. Ben's job too was possibly a far cry from the heroic dreams of a young man, but, I suspected, he might hope one of his sons would fulfill those dreams for him. Wasn't this how life moved from generation to generation; the dreams of the parents passed hopefully on to the children? And wasn't accepting one's limitations a reassuring indication of maturity?

And so, for the six years of my marriage, when I blew out candles on birthday cakes or saw a falling star, the wish I made was that my world would stay exactly as it was. In 1961, I was not to get my wish.

Meanwhile, for the past four years, a large part of my world was represented by our Omaha neighborhood. We had chosen our suburb, Rockbrook, as the best among what realtors showed us when we moved to Omaha from another suburb in Chicago. I had asked about houses in the city, but we were told that there was nothing available to meet our needs. Rockbrook, realtors said, had the best schools, and so when we walked into a glass-enclosed living room with a magnificent hilltop view, we decided this was the house we wanted.

For the past four years we had had no reason to regret our choice of a neighborhood. Ben grumbled occasionally that golf scores and the stock market took over most conversations at parties, but I liked talking about housewifely things with the women. With three small children taking most of my time, *any* adult conversation was a pleasure.

In the late fifties and early sixties, there were few serious topics that were likely to come up, and in our neighborhood, even politics and religion were rarely talked about. During the Kennedy-Nixon campaign I found myself the lone Kennedy supporter and had no intention of taking on the entire neighborhood. single-handed. As for religion, I discovered that everyone was Protestant, and there was simply nothing to discuss.

The same atmosphere and attitudes pervaded parties given by people with whom Ben worked. We had formed few close friendships among company people. None of them lived in our neighborhood and also, as I lamented to Ben, I liked all the "wrong" company people. According to corporate protocol, you socialized with your office equals; unfortunately, the two women I really liked were the treasurer's wife and Ben's secretary. "Maybe I'm no good as a company wife," I said to him. He grasped by shoulders in mock anger. "Don't you think I'm good enough to get ahead without your social-politicking?" he demanded. I knew he was, and since I'd heard him introduced recently at a big company dinner as "the most promising young executive we have," I gratefully forgot about our relative social isolation from company people.

But if anyone had accused our neighbors or company acquaintances of bigotry, I would have defended them. True, one woman in our neighborhood praised a certain resort saying, "It's lovely and quiet. They discourage Jews." I quickly told her that I had worked with many Jewish people, had many Jewish friends, and found them no different from the rest of us. She dropped the subject immediately, and I thought I knew why the other neighbors considered her difficult and unpleasant.

At a company Christmas party, another woman made a similar remark; I made the same reply. She too was an unpopular person among corporation couples and, I believed, not typical.

In February 1960, the first lunch-counter sit-ins by Negro college students began in North Carolina. Neighborhood sympathy must have been with the students. Mine was and I can remember no arguments. I was glad I didn't live in the South where cruel customs of separation existed. I knew, however, that all Southerners were not Ku Klux Klan members. Ben's father and mother were native South Carolinians who moved North to Detroit only after Ben was nine years old. His parents were gentle people, not the type who would fight Southern bigotry, perhaps, but neither would they approve of it.

But with no Malcolm X or ghetto explosions to contradict me, I was able to believe that black people in the North were free and more or less content. In fact, events in the South only seemed to emphasize the freedom in the North. Northerners had no separate facilities marked Colored and White; we enforced no segregated seating on our buses; we did not build two different school systems. I may have been dimly aware of big-city slums and that they were primarily peopled with Negro families, but in the free-and-equal North, I believed, you could pull yourself up through hard work as Ben and I had done and as my grandparents had done before me.

I wonder how long I could have continued in this insulated cocoon without Harriet Fischer, my one friend outside the neighborhood. She began my education, but in the beginning I thought I was educating her. Harriet and I met through Ann Howard, the realtor who sold us our house. She and her husband, Irv, and Ann were Jewish. When Harriet teased me about living in an all-gentile area, I asked Ann if this was true of Rockbrook by coincidence or if Jews were kept out. Ann assured me it was coincidence. In fact, she said, housing was so open that a Negro undertaker owned that beautiful home at the other edge of our suburb. Because Ann was both Jewish and a realtor, I believed her. Harriet, I felt, saw bigotry where none existed. In a way, *she* was prejudiced against WASPs.

But in all other ways, Harriet was my much-admired friend and oracle. She and her husband had moved to Omaha from New York. Irv resigned a highly paid but hectic job with a TV network to buy a small local radio station, and Harriet, a tiny woman with sterling-silver hair, told me often how she enjoyed small-town living after the pace of a big city. Harriet had rejected what she called the "Golden Ghetto," a suburban section predominantly Jewish, and they had bought a large, roomy house from Ann Howard in an older section of the city. I liked Harriet immediately and admired her expertise in decorating, clothes, and cooking. She affected a big-city cynicism, but her warmth was forever surging through it. She casually served elaborate French dinners, shrugging off compliments, but would spend hours patiently teaching me how to duplicate dishes I raved over.

I remember a day in her kitchen when our conversation turned to the subject of prejudice. Harriet told me of being the only Jewish child in her neighborhood and how, each day after school, she would sit in the bathtub, crying and scrubbing herself because she'd been called a "dirty Jew." I felt a wave of personal pain. Still, I was sure the world had changed since Harriet's childhood. People had learned where anti-Semitism led in Germany.

So when Harriet invited me to a Brotherhood Week program at her synagogue, I nearly refused. A group from Kansas City, Missouri, called Panel of American Women was to speak; four women—a Catholic, Jew, Negro, and white Protestant—would talk about Brotherhood. I could hear the platitudes in advance. Finally I agreed to attend the luncheon, but only because I enjoyed Harriet's company.

A week later on an April afternoon the synagogue auditorium was filled with fashionably dressed women. A sprinkling of Negro women seemed to have been strategically scattered at the luncheon tables. As Harriet and I took our seats, she whispered to me to move down a few chairs. Why the whisper? I glanced to my right and saw there were three empty chairs between me and a Negro woman. Embarrassed by my thoughtlessness, I moved. When I asked the brown-skinned, middle-aged woman where she lived, my face must have revealed I had never heard of the street. She asked where I lived and probably labeled me.

When the program began it was not as boring as I feared it might be. The Catholic woman spoke first, with more humor than I expected. Still I wondered why she isolated her children in parochial schools instead of sending them into what I believed then was the melting pot of the public school. When the Jewish panelist talked, she told of leaving Germany because of Hitler and then, in America, being told by a realtor that Jews weren't welcome in a section of Kansas City where she had wanted to buy a house.

The Negro panelist spoke next. She began by saying with a smile that most people saw her as a Negro first and a woman second. My cheeks felt warm. Yes, I did see her as a Negro rather than as a woman. Only now did I let myself notice she was tall, slim, and wore glasses. And I had talked to the Negro woman sitting next to me differently than if she'd been white; not with dislike, but with a self-consciousness, a special tension I would not have felt with a white woman.

The Negro panelist then talked about her early life in Missouri. She was not allowed to buy concert tickets, attend a downtown theater, or borrow a book from a department store lending library.

I wondered why she stayed in a state like Missouri. If I were in her place I would move to some enlightened area like Chicago, New York, or Omaha. My grandparents had crossed an ocean to find a better life. All she needed was the energy and common sense to cross a few state lines.

I was still reflecting on the Negro panelist's lack of initiative when a sweet-faced blond woman began to speak. She was a member of the American majority, she said, a white Anglo-Saxon Protestant. She talked of the unearned privileges her family enjoyed; the freedom to choose a resort or hotel without wondering if they would be accepted. Her children, she said with a gentle smile, would never feel the hurt of being rejected because of their race or religion. When her family moved into a neighborhood, no one panicked. "Of all the women on the Panel," she said with a sad ruefulness, "I alone receive all the privileges of the American Dream."

To my surprise, I found myself listening intently. The impatient cynicism I brought to the luncheon had gradually been peeled away by the other panelists, and now this Protestant panelist seemed to be speaking directly to me. She ended with, "Because of the open doors I enjoy, I feel I must try to open them for others. If I do this, then when I bow my head in church I will not wear the face of a hypocrite."

Suddenly, I felt the chilling impact of memories I had avoided for years. The other panelists—the Catholic woman saying her rosary all alone in a Protestant summer camp, the Jewish woman rejected at a hotel, the Negro woman feeling different and unwanted in so many places—had stirred up old hurts. I was once the only child in my school with divorced parents. I knew *exactly* how it hurt to be different and to feel rejected by my absent father. For me, that pain was gone now. I had Ben. Together, we had created the close, happy family life I had wanted so much as a child. Now the Protestant panelist's words reminded me that I had taken my new security too much for granted.

The chills that came, I think, were the result of some pagan superstition, that if I didn't share all I had, divine retribution would take it all away from me. The only problem was how to do it. At that moment I felt like the Boy Scout anxious to help little old ladies across the street, but with no little old ladies in sight.

From what I could see, things in Omaha were going along well. Our popular Jewish Mayor had retired after several terms; Ben and I had recently seen an obviously affluent Negro couple at a fashionable Omaha restaurant; the Negro cleaning woman who worked for me had never mentioned any problems.

The Negro panelist's story had seemed the most poignant, but since none of the restrictions she mentioned existed in Nebraska, I was still unsure of what to do.

The program was over now and the spring hats of the women in the audience made pretty flowered circles around the various panelists. I decided to join the group around the Negro panelist. When her attention finally came to me, I asked, "How can I help?"

I am sure that panelist simply handed me the top file card in her mind. Did we have any Negro teachers in our school, she asked. No, we didn't. She suggested I bring this up at the next PTA meeting.

The large auditorium in the synagogue was nearly empty now. Harriet was waiting for me at the doorway. I can remember how she teased me for being absorbed by a program I had attended so reluctantly. But as we walked through the doorway together, there was no premonition that I would re-enter this room, just 364 days later, shorn of beliefs I had held all my life and about to leave—unwillingly—the community I loved.

Chapter Two

Introducing the idea of a Negro teacher for our school was to be deceptively easy. Ben, who often found the flaws in my enthusiasms, had listened, smiling, as I described my feelings after the Panel luncheon. I half expected him to ask some question I hadn't considered or to urge, as he had at other times, that I wait, that I think it over.

Instead, he nodded when I told him I thought our school should have a Negro teacher. He thought so too, but for reasons different from mine. "I've been a little concerned," Ben told me, "about our children growing up in this neighborhood." Even though our realtor friend, Ann Howard, assured us it was coincidental, Ben reminded me that our neighbors were all white, Christian, and even of the same income level as ours.

"I drove past Westside High School the other day," Ben said, "and it struck me for the first time that all the youngsters there come from neighborhoods around here, just exactly like ours." This meant, Ben said, that our children would grow up in a kind of isolation until they were college age. How much damage could it do to Spike and Noah and

Sarah, waiting that long before they met people who were different from themselves?

Ben's heavy eyebrows had pulled together in a familiar expression. He was carefully considering all sides of a deep concern. Then he smiled at me. Perhaps one Negro teacher couldn't solve the entire problem of our children's isolation, he said, but it could help.

At the board meeting of our school parents' committee, I simply quoted Ben's remarks. I had joined the parents' group before Spike entered kindergarten and now, as editor of the newsletter, I was a member of the board of directors. When I made my suggestion about the Negro teacher, our young, innovative principal immediately expressed his approval.

Lester Wheed, president of the parents' group, looked cautiously around for other opinions. My closest neighborhood friend, Bibi Van Dorp, cited child psychology specialists on the handicaps of suburban isolation. The only non-WASP her child saw, she said, was Bessie, their cleaning woman. She didn't want her child to grow up with a stereotyped idea of "colored people."

Jim Gibson was the only person at the meeting who failed to join in the general enthusiasm. I had always felt a vague pity for Jim. He was the denial of the "jolly fat man" myth. The folds of his fleshy face fell into the lines of a petulant infant and his puffy hands were often tightened into fists. I knew he had had several different jobs in the past few years and probably many disappointments. His answer to Bibi was: "We don't have a cleaning woman—so our kids aren't contaminated by that stereotype!" He had pulled his chin deeper into his collar as he said this.

But even Jim Gibson finally agreed with a shrug that a Negro teacher "couldn't hurt anything." Lester Wheed, the always-smiling thin little man who was our president, asked for a vote and seemed relieved that no one disagreed with the majority opinion that we should try to find a Negro teacher for our school.

Lester said since it was my idea, he felt it was my responsibility to talk with our district school superintendent. I said I would.

The superintendent of our suburban school district was younger, friendlier, and easier to see than I had expected. He quickly became enthusiastic over the idea. "Frankly," he smiled, "I'm a little ashamed I've never thought of it. My only excuse, I guess, is that no Negro teacher has ever applied to our district."

I said perhaps they thought they would be turned down.

The superintendent and I shared a smile over the suspicions of minority groups. Then, full of self-congratulations over having opened a door so easily, I volunteered to take another step. If he wanted me to, I would help find a Negro applicant. Somewhere I'd heard of the Urban League. Should I tell them our district wanted a Negro teacher?

The superintendent said "Great!" and we shook hands as if we'd just completed a mutually profitable business deal.

Driving home that spring day I felt satisfaction at having dispatched my obligations to other groups so easily and pleasantly. I had done what the Negro panelist suggested in spite of my friend Harriet's pessimistic predictions. "Prejudice has existed since man began," she said. "Why do you have to leap into a losing battle?" But the battle had been won, I thought, more effortlessly than I'd expected. WASPs were simply not as bigoted as Harriet believed.

In later years I was to explain over and over again how I could have been so incredibly naïve. I was not, after all, an inexperienced girl who had married right out of school. For seven years before marriage I had successfully operated my own advertising agency. In business, I considered myself realistic and aware of all sides of human nature. Yet in 1961 I was absolutely ignorant of the complex relations between blacks and whites.

Talking now with WASP friends of the same age and background, I know I was not unusual. The black and white communities in the North were separated by an unseen barrier, as soundproof and unyielding as a pane of glass. We could see each other, dimly, but we never came close enough to touch the barrier to know it was there. And so until the 1960s we could believe that silence from the black side meant contentment with things as they were.

The barrier behind which I was raised may have been more soundproof than some. After my parents were divorced my brother, mother, and I lived with my maternal grandparents, immigrants from Germany, in Milwaukee, Wisconsin. In Milwaukee the mayor and all the prominent citizens had German names, and I suspect my family was so secure in what they believed was their obviously superior heritage that they needed no scapegoats. My immigrant grandparents were also unschooled in the traditional American racial myths and so I was never told unpleasant tales about Negro people. Instead, my grandfather had imported his prejudices from Europe. I remember him telling me in his unique accent (acquired through having learned his English in Brooklyn) about the lazy, dirty, sneaky *British*. They had loose morals and should never be trusted. I neither believed nor disbelieved. I was aware only that I had never met enough Englishmen to find out for myself.

I grew up in a neighborhood at the opposite end of the city from Milwaukee's Negro section. Our neighbors, who were mostly railroad workers, clerks, and city employees, did not employ servants in their small houses and so there was no reason for Negro people to come into our area. The only place I could see brown-skinned people was downtown. I must have asked, as most children do, why their skins were dark and knowing my family's approach to such things, I was probably told, "God made them that way." Generations of us were told that, and I think we assumed He knew what He was doing and it was no business of ours.

I know that the first black face I saw was in a picture that hung at the front of our Sunday School room. It showed Jesus looking lovingly at a group of children, one of whom was brown-skinned. During the eight years of Sunday mornings that I faced this picture, my child's mind slowly absorbed the idea that if Jesus loved all these children, then we must all be the same. But I never asked why the only brown face in our church was the one in that picture.

My Saturday afternoons taught me no more about Negroes than my Sunday mornings. At the neighborhood movie I watched Bill Robinson happily tap-dancing with Shirley Temple. His only problem seemed to be whatever dimmed Shirley's dimple. "Our Gang" was integrated, Steppin Fetchit was funny, and Jeannette MacDonald had a procession of loyal, loving Mammys.

But the beautiful dancing girls were all white and mostly blond. The cowboys, the soldiers, and even the gangsters were white. Now watching these movies on TV, with the all-white crowd scenes, parades, and chorus lines, I realize how black people could begin to wonder if they really existed in America. For me, those Saturday afternoon movies emphasized what I had already absorbed—that my all-white world was natural and normal.

Later and for only a short time, an aunt lived in an area beyond the Negro section, and to visit her we rode a trolley through blocks where I saw only people with varying shades of brown skin. But through those same trolley windows, I also saw blocks and blocks where all the store signs were in Italian or Polish or strange letters that must have been Hebrew. When I asked questions I was told that people *wanted* to live with their own kind. I never got off the trolley to ask.

In elementary school, nothing challenged the impressions I had been gathering. Instead, I was conditioned *not* to notice who *wasn't* there. My school books, from Dick and Jane through eighth grade geography, showed people who looked just like me. Little Black Sambo didn't, but he lived in Africa among tigers.

In our all-white high school, American history, economics, and sociology were the names of courses I was exposed to, but when we studied the Civil War I came away with the impression that Abraham Lincoln had taken care of things nicely. In economics, I learned about the free enterprise system and I liked it. With this system there was no excuse for being poor, I decided, unless you were too lazy to work—or not very smart. I loved the compassion with which America had opened its arms to "all the huddled masses yearning to be free." We were not only the refuge for homeless people, but the beneficiaries of all the world-wide talents each group contributed.

In high school I enjoyed visiting the homes of my Greek, Polish, or Serbian friends who were scattered among the mostly German children in our school. I liked the food, the cadence of the foreign language, and the fun of trying to say foreign words to the amusement of my friends' parents.

If my sociology teacher tried to tell us anything about feelings between groups, I missed the point. I expect I was more concerned with the important issues of boys, clothes, and hairdos. And nothing penetrated those hairdos to shake my belief that this was a wonderful world, full of opportunities, built by whites but operated with fairness to all.

World War II began in my early high school years. Suddenly we had such enormous international villains that any local inequities would have seemed mild. Hitler's mass murders in concentration camps overshadowed anything I might have read about a Southern lynching; the rumored treatment of American citizens of Japanese descent passed me literally unnoticed.

The war only increased the intense patriotism I absorbed from my immigrant grandparents. Singing "America, the Beautiful" always made me cry and I recited the Pledge of Allegiance with proud fervor, sure that "with liberty and justice for all" was true then and always would be. When the war was over, we were too busy catching up with our disrupted lives to find out if "justice for all" meant anyone but us.

These were the conditions under which, I believe, most WASPs of my generation grew up. This should not excuse us, only explain us. The people I knew didn't practice discrimination; none of us suspected we were co-operating with it. We were like first-class passengers on a ship; comfortable with our privileges. We didn't know—or perhaps want to know—what went on below the decks on which we danced.

But for me, in addition to a typical WASP conditioning, there were three other influences that might explain what happened later: my grandfather's indifference to public opinion, an uncle who gave me a prejudice *against* prejudice, and my mother who inadvertently made me a tester of hot stoves and wet-paint signs.

My grandfather, a short, round man with large bushy mustaches, was a traditional, single-minded German patriarch. I suspect he was not so much tolerant of other races and religions as he was simply uninterested. While warm and indulgent with me, he ignored the opinions and actions of others. I can still hear the squealing brakes when Grandfather decided to cross the street. He would walk, eyes straight ahead, positive he was right. Occasionally the cursing of some irate motorist might catch his attention briefly, but then Grandfather would send him a quizzical glance of superior puzzlement and walk on. In the same way, Grandfather lived within his strict moral code, marching relentlessly toward heaven where a German-speaking God would judge him. Others could do as they pleased, live as they chose. God and Grandfather had their own understanding.

For this reason, I suspect, he never took issue with my uncle, at least not in my hearing. This uncle was a red-faced, peevish, unsmiling man who snarled at his own children and ignored my brother and me. He had faded blue eyes that darted suspiciously at people. The closest thing to pleasure I ever noticed in him was when he spit contemptuous words like "wop" or "kike" or "Polack." Then his washed-blue eyes would glint for a moment and I would feel frightened by something I couldn't explain. I grew up believing that bigoted people looked like this and avoided them as carefully as I would avoid drunken drivers.

But it was from my gentle, disappointed mother that I acquired a strong suspicion about myths and experts. Mother tried valiantly to speak well of my absent father. However, from family comments, it was obvious that my father was a fast-talking, easygoing dreamer who swept Mother into a short, disastrous marriage. To Mother, men got up each morning and went to work; to Dad, rainbows led to pots of gold. Mother went home to her mother. Dad left town, unpaid bills and his children behind. From this, Mother seemed forever after to expect new calamities that seldom happened. "If you don't get down from there, you'll break your neck"; "God will punish you for hitting your baby brother." I didn't, and He didn't.

She also handled my outsized curiosity with all the standard myths. I was told about the stork, but the rise and fall of Aunt Helen's waistline coincided suspiciously with the appearance of Cousin Nancy. I was told carrots would make my hair curl, dentists didn't hurt a bit, and all Irishmen were drunkards. So, carrot-filled and straight-haired, I suffered the drill of cold-sober Dr. Casey—and disillusionment with childhood's first expert: Mother. I grew up unwilling to accept anything completely that I hadn't investigated for my-self. Luckily, most of the hot stoves during my life proved to be only delightfully warm and most wet paint merely a little sticky.

So, against Mother's pessimism, I developed a devout belief in Happy Endings. If you told the truth and acted honorably, all obstacles fell. Anything was possible if you just tried hard enough, long enough. And for most of my life it seemed as if things happened just that way.

This philosophy resulted in my outrageously unique first meeting with a Negro person. As editor of my high-school newspaper, I optimistically telephoned the downtown theater where Duke Ellington was appearing to ask for an interview. Perhaps my nervous treble struck a sympathetic chord in his manager, but in happy-ending style I was granted the inter-view. I remember arriving in Mr. Ellington's backstage dress-ing room at the Riverside Theater, overawed and shaking, and I remember this kind, great man treating me as seriously and politely as if I represented *The New York Times* instead of the Bay View High School *Oracle*. It was my first conver-sation with a Negro person and if a stereotype was set then, it was a stereotype of sensitivity and gentleness. But while I sensed Mr. Ellington's compassion for a nervous high school reporter, I had no way of knowing that this gracious, impec-cably groomed gentleman was considered unacceptable as a guest in most of Milwaukee's hotels.

In my late teens, a light brush with prejudice seemed to confirm my Happy Ending theory and reinforce my belief that "nice people" quietly fought bigotry which then neatly disappeared.

As a high school senior during the early 1940s, I was dating Mike, captain of his college football team and president of his fraternity. Two members of the football team were Negro. Someone proposed them for Mike's fraternity. Someone else objected. I heard Mike tell a fraternity brother that unless his Negro teammates were accepted he'd resign. At the next fraternity dance, the two Negro students were there. Good people, I believed, quietly saw to it that justice prevailed.

As far as I can remember, Mike's Negro fraternity brothers never asked me to dance and I never had a conversation with them or their Negro dates, but it was around that time that Mike gently suggested I stop using certain phrases. "A nigger in the woodpile" and "Who was your nigger *last* year?" were not in the best of taste, Mike said. I remember blushing. Certainly I'd drop those clichés. But I hadn't meant any harm. To me, a "nigger" was an impersonal word; an almost mythical figure from a minstrel show. No, I didn't realize this word *hurt* Negro people. That made me feel terrible; too much like my unpleasant uncle.

Perhaps because of this experience and Mr. Ellington, I began to practice a kind of trolley-car liberalism. A few times, I noticed, all the seats on the trolley would be filled except for the seat beside a Negro passenger. Some whites were actually standing instead of sharing that seat. My "Do Unto Others" training made me ask myself how I'd feel, sitting so pointedly alone and I would take that seat, probably with a flourish. But in all those years of young-womanhood, my Do-Unto-Others empathy never extended beyond sharing a trolley seat.

The next conversation I remember with a black person was in the employees' cafeteria in the large department store where I worked after graduation from high school. An attractive, light-brown-skinned, well-dressed young woman and I talked over our coffee. She mentioned she was going to college at night. It seemed odd to me that, with part of her degree already earned, she was a stock girl while I, with only a high school diploma, was a copywriter-trainee in the advertising department. I asked why she hadn't taken a more interesting, better-paying job. There was so much this young woman could have told me in her answer. She didn't. Why?

Was it impossible to talk of hurt and humiliation and anger to a stranger? Or did she believe I didn't really want to know? She said only that she was merely working part time until she got her teaching degree.

Something about this young woman's answer must have bothered me or I would never have remembered it so long. But, humanly, my career problems were more pressing to me than hers. At nineteen, I decided to test the free-enterprise system by opening my own advertising agency and, once again, my Happy Ending theory proved true. Most people were helpful, pleasant, and kind. Mother predicted I'd starve; I didn't. Instead, I was soon in a position to practice what is now called "equal employment opportunities." One employment service asked if I would accept a Jewish applicant. I was indignant that they felt they had to ask. Certainly I would! I was no Nazi!

But in the early 1950s no employment agency would even have asked about a Negro applicant, and in the banks, stores, or other offices there were no brown faces to remind me that my own office staff was needlessly all white.

And so my world bounced serenely along as I got to know myself and my profession. Little outside of the world of business interested me. I read *Advertising Age* and *Vogue*. There were enough unpleasant, greedy, and dishonest people I had run into to teach me humanity was not all sweetness and brotherly love, but the problems I saw seemed easily solved. I had several Jewish employees and when a printer made an anti-Semitic remark, I simply changed printers, believing that someone with these attitudes was not to be trusted.

Then, as I got to know myself better, I found that the business world was not as satisfying as I expected. For a woman I felt that creating babies was more fulfilling than creating another advertising promotion.

When I met Ben it was only a matter of time. His prominent chin and bushy brows over determined eyes suggested he got what he wanted. Luckily, he wanted me. We became friends first. I liked his rough-carved features and his brown eyes that crinkled over funny incidents I reported. But I noticed too that two deep lines of concern bracketed his mouth when he listened to whatever worried me. We lived in the same apartment building and I came to depend on his large square hands to open stuck jar-lids or windows—and on his careful analysis of elections or leases or people. In a year, Ben proposed unexpectedly and forcefully. He surprised me into an impulsive Yes that I have never regretted.

We married in June 1955 and conceived a honeymoon baby. We bought a small house in Park Forest, Illinois, but I was much too fascinated with what was going on *inside* me to wonder why Park Forest had no Negro families. As usual, I didn't notice who wasn't there.

And neither did Ben. Except for his first nine years in South Carolina, Ben's life in Detroit had been as isolated as mine in Milwaukee; the same kind of all-white neighborhood, the same school books. His army life during World War II had been subtly segregated, and later, at the University of Michigan, Ben had had the same deceptive experience of seeing that "nice people aren't bigoted." The head of his dormitory was a Negro student and Ben was his assistant. The caution and the many interviews that accompanied this arrangement was, to Ben, simply overdone concern about problems that never came up.

Ben had known only as much about Southern segregation as a nine-year-old boy could absorb. Most of his questions were answered with "shh" and he grew up believing that the unexplained rules about bus seats and drinking fountains applied only to field hands and servants and were the result of class- rather than race-discrimination. The rest of his life was spent in Michigan and, like me, he was too busy building a career to notice his Midwest world was all white.

I did, however, notice the Negro nurse at Chicago Lying-In

Hospital where our son Spike was born in April 1956. She was belligerent, rough, and abrupt. When I learned she was from Haiti, I proclaimed feelingly to my hospital roommate that she must have trained under a witch doctor. I tensed whenever she entered the room. Her nearly black face reflected satisfaction when I showed confusion over her sarcastic answers to my questions. She made me feel stupid and inept with my seemingly fragile new baby.

One night, my anxieties and her sarcasm collided and I burst out tearfully that she was the most rude, sadistic, horrible person I'd ever met. With as majestic a gesture as those hospital gowns allow, I pointed to the door and shrieked "GO!"

She went and, to my confusion, returned later, smiling and friendly, with helpful advice about handling my baby. It took almost five years before I would understand her abrupt change in attitude. And that, until Ben's new job brought us to Omaha and his increased salary allowed for a cleaning woman, was the extent of our contact with Negro people.

But even with Mrs. Robbins, who came once a week to clean our Rockbrook house, my experience was deceptive.

Because we were so nearly the same age, Inez Robbins and I talked about common feminine interests and one day she mentioned to me that she was having difficulty getting pregnant. I suggested she see my gynecologist. Since then I have heard often of white doctors refusing Negro patients, but again the world lived up to my expectations. My doctor accepted Inez as a patient and a few months later she confided that she was pregnant. I was delighted. It was my best friend, Bibi, who wryly reminded me that I had lost myself a good cleaning woman through my "helpfulness."

When Inez's daughter was a year old Inez returned to work. I waited for Inez to invite me to see the little girl in whose existence I had played some part. She didn't, and I finally suggested she bring her daughter to our house some weekend.

At first she accepted eagerly, but weeks passed and excuse followed excuse.

One day Inez said, "I think I can tell *you* the truth. My husband won't let me bring the baby out. I told him you were different, but he says he doesn't want anyone looking at his child and saying, 'What a cute little pickaninny.' "

It seemed unfair that Mr. Robbins would have this opinion of me when we had never met. Inez said she would talk to him again.

She did bring her daughter the next weekend, but Mr. Robbins had now become a challenge. I took home-movies of little Debbie Robbins playing with my daughter Sarah and suggested Inez invite her husband out to see the film. I had been right that no father could resist this bait, and Alex Robbins did come with Inez to our house. He was at first quiet and reserved, but as he gradually relaxed he proved to be interesting and highly articulate, much more informed on local politics than Ben and I. I began to wonder why this obviously intelligent man was a parking lot attendant.

When Inez came to work a few days later, she told me Alex had admitted we were different. I was annoyed. We weren't "different"; he was prejudiced about white people and wouldn't admit it. Inez remained silent. She also gave me vague answers about why Alex didn't try for a job that suited his intelligence. Her quick, brief excuses, her rapid change of subject told me she didn't want to discuss this topic. But whatever the truth, part of it, I believed, was Alex Robbins' bitter distrust of white people.

Now, three years later, in 1961, I drove home from the school superintendent's office, convinced white people were further proving themselves. With no opposition, I had just opened the door for a Negro school teacher and in less than three weeks from when the Negro panelist suggested it. The superintendent, our principal, Bibi, and several other neighbors had been not only in agreement but enthusiastic.

Once home, I dismissed the sitter and looked up the Urban League in the phone book. The director, Ken Hancock, sounded reserved but willing to give me an appointment for the next day. It was, I told him, about teachers and I would explain when we met.

Omaha's Urban League office was in a rundown building just off the main street. I opened the door and then almost stopped in surprise. Everyone—the receptionist, the secretaries, Ken Hancock himself—was black! It was a strange visual shock. Until now I had never seen even one Negro office worker. Confronting a familiar office setting but with brown faces in place of white was like seeing Hamlet in blackface.

Ken Hancock, a short, stocky man in his fifties with very dark skin, led me into a small private office. He may have sensed my discomfort; his manner was formal, slow, soothing. He nodded gently as I talked. And talk I did. I explained that our school district wanted Negro teachers and, with what must have been a patronizing air, ordered one as I would have ordered a plant at the florist's. Ken Hancock nodded. I talked on nervously, full of good intentions and utter ignorance. I asked Ken Hancock if there was anything else I could do.

Ken's emotions must have been mixed as he sat listening to me. I was obviously inexperienced, but he probably could not afford to turn down any willing volunteer. He excused himself to get the Community Affairs director, Justin Christopher, and for all I know may have said to him, "Wait 'til you meet *this* one!"

When Justin Christopher shot into the room I immediately felt more comfortable. This tall gregarious man looked very much like a brown version of my younger brother. He talked fast, moved fast, and appeared to be running while sitting down. He told me immediately that, yes, there were a lot of areas where help was needed, employment for one. "My husband could help with that," I said. Perhaps we could all get together at our house and Ben could hear what they had to say. Could they bring their wives? I had decided that it would be good to get Ben involved in something besides his job and the yard. He couldn't get interested in the school committee and I felt he needed some community activities as a change of pace. Ken Hancock continued nodding. Justin Christopher said yes, he would like to bring his wife. Impulsively, I set a date and Ben agreed later that he would be interested in meeting the two men.

When Ken Hancock and Justin and Grace Christopher arrived at our house, I got the instant impression that this tall, slim woman preferred to be elsewhere. Ken nodded as I introduced him to Ben; Justin Christopher uttered a fast, friendly stream of talk. Grace Christopher was stunningly attractive. Her skin was the same golden-tan I sunbathed to achieve in summer; her hair sparkled with highlights like a dark diamond. But her expression was as severe as her black silk dress.

Grace chose the orange chair in the farthest corner of our living room. Ken Hancock settled in the dark brown chair and I immediately wished he hadn't. It was exactly the same color as his skin and he seemed to disappear, leaving only white eyeballs and flashes of pink when he talked. There were, I decided, some things you had to get used to with Negro people. But the discussion about employment began.

Even now, Jewish and Catholic friends seem unable to believe Ben and I could have been so oblivious to discrimination in employment. But I contend that, for WASPs, it was easy. We had never needed to develop the sensitive antenna of minority groups. I had filled out employment blanks asking for Race and Religion. I assumed Race was a part of my physical description, and Religion was to tell employers whether to call a rabbi, priest, or minister if I were seriously injured at work. When you could write Race-white, Religion-Protestant, you never found out what happened if you couldn't. I saw no signs saying "WASPs only." They were invisible.

Now Justin Christopher and Ken Hancock were telling us that Negro men were not hired for responsible jobs, even though they might be as qualified as white men. For the first time, I realized that Ben's company had no Negro employees. But could it be that Negro people had never applied? That's what the school superintendent said. Justin Christopher flashed me a quick, cynical smile.

All right, even if the school superintendent was lying, which I doubted, I *knew* I would have hired any qualified Negro applicant who applied to my advertising agency. So what about a mailing campaign reminding people like me that they should make an effort to hire Negro people?

Ken Hancock gave one of his usual nods. Ben smiled encouragingly at me, and Justin shrugged quickly, verbally galloping off into the problem of mailing lists. Only Grace Christopher remained still, her long legs arranged gracefully, her head down.

Suddenly she cut into the conversation. "It's hopeless," she said. "This country will never give our men decent jobs. My son will have to fight the same bigotry his grandfather fought. The only solution is leave this country."

I stared at her, hoping to see some sign that she didn't mean what she'd said. Her brown eyes met mine without wavering. But certainly, I said, her son could find opportunities here. How old was he? David was three, the same age as our middle child, Noah. Cheerfully, I suggested, "Why, David could go into advertising! Advertising people are very unprejudiced."

Quietly, but biting off each word with undisguised anger, Grace said, "*Your* son's future is not limited to the fields that will *accept* him. I want the *same* freedom for *my* son."

I opened my mouth to reply and found I couldn't. Grace was right. My children could follow their abilities in any direction. Among their difficult decisions in choosing a life's work, the problem of acceptance because of color or religion simply did not exist. Yet I had expected her to accept this handicap for her son; I had even expected her to be grateful for my "sensible" solution.

In that moment when we two mothers stared at each other across generations of misunderstanding my initial confidence drained away. The men carried the discussion to its end, still optimistic about the mailing campaign, but I was now as silent as Grace had been. Suddenly, nothing seemed as simple as it had only a few minutes ago. I was deeply ashamed of what Grace Christopher had shown me about myself, but more than that, I was afraid. What else didn't I know? Who would teach me?

Reaching out to this angry young woman seemed impossible, but there was no one else and I had to try. When I asked her to bring her son to Noah's birthday party in two weeks, I expected her to refuse. But she hesitated only a moment.

I know now that if Grace Christopher had been a different kind of person my education would have stopped at this point or at least been delayed. If Grace had been anxious to cross over socially into the white world, she might have told me all the reassuring lies; if she had been utterly without hope of understanding by white people, she would have seen me as not worth the bother.

But because she had just enough hope left, she patiently answered my questions and began my education. Because she had so *little* hope, she wasted no time sugarcoating what she felt were the facts.

Chapter Three

Events moved swiftly for everyone, following my meeting with Grace Christopher on May 6, 1961. I mailed her an invitation to Noah's birthday party, hoping to reinforce my verbal invitation the night we had met. Noah's party was May 24. Between our meeting and Noah's party civil rights hit the headlines. On May 14, 1961, the first Freedom Ride took place. Negro people and sympathetic white Northerners defied bus segregation laws and were pulled from their buses in Alabama and beaten. A screaming mob of several hundred white men and women attacked twenty-one Freedom Riders in Montgomery, Alabama. The governer of Alabama refused to speak to the President of the United States on the telephone. By May 21, President Kennedy had sent six hundred U.S. marshals into Montgomery after a white mob attacked a Negro church whose members had merely cheered the Freedom Riders. National Guardsmen patrolled Montgomery. For the first time we learned how violently white people would fight to maintain segregation.

Reading the newspaper stories, I was moved by the courage of the Freedom Riders who submitted themselves to beatings

—and proud that nothing like this could have happened in the North. That federal troops would eventually be sent into Omaha—to Newark, Detroit, and scores of other Northern cities—was as inconceivable then as the fact that my sympathies would not be with the troops.

The day before Noah's birthday party, Ken Hancock phoned to say he had a teacher applicant for our school and did I want to interview her? Me? No. I couldn't judge her qualifications. Just ask her to see the superintendent, I suggested.

The day of Noah's third birthday arrived, warm and sunny —perfect for the outdoor party. I was pleased when I saw Grace Christopher walking across our lawn holding the hand of her little boy, David.

Whatever surprise the other mothers felt at seeing Grace and David there, they had the length of our lawn to adjust to it. Helen Carter strode over with her golfer's stride and shook hands with Grace; Elaine Mifflin smiled and took in every line of Grace's flawlessly tailored navy linen dress; Emily Wright, one of the most sweet and gentle women I knew, sat next to Grace and told her how handsome her son David was. The only jolting moment was when I saw Val Schmidt marching across the lawn, her features tensed in anger. For the first time the possibility of a scene occurred to me. But Val's anger was directed at her daughter, Janie, who she'd seen throwing sand at Noah. I chided myself for a suspicious, overactive imagination.

I realize now that Grace Christopher was the most acceptable kind of Negro woman for my neighbors to meet. Daily golfing had made Helen Carter's skin actually darker than Grace's, and Grace was beautiful by Caucasian standards. Her thin nose and only slightly full mouth were not much different from white features. Her crisp linen dress with its obvious custom touches told each woman there that it was expensive. (Only I knew, from Grace's "Thanks, I made it myself!" when she first arrived, that it wasn't a name-designer dress.) No white woman there could have found any objection to or felt unfamiliar with this attractive, well-dressed woman with her suntan skin. Or to little David, a shy, quiet child with a gradually growing smile.

After the day of the birthday party, Grace and I began to talk almost daily over the telephone. I learned that she was the daughter of a college professor. When she named the college my "Oh" must have revealed I'd never heard of it. It was an all-Negro college in Nashville, Grace said. She had been raised on campus, gotten her degree in social work, and then done postgraduate work at the University of Pennsylvania.

Her liquid, slow-paced voice had hardened mentioning the Philadelphia university. I waited, wondering. Only much later would Grace describe what it was like, going from the protection of an all-Negro college to the special "goldfish bowl" life as one of the few Negro students at a white university. "Daddy protected me," she said when we had become closer friends. "It was done with love, but I didn't know what I should have known. I went from being a *woman* at Dad's college to being a *Negro* at Penn."

We talked at first largely of children, sewing, books, and husbands. Justin was too mercurial to Grace; Ben was too stubborn, I said. Over the telephone perhaps it was easier for Grace to speak to me as just another woman—or perhaps Grace was testing me to see if I thought of her as "a Negro" or a woman. By the time we got into discussing social issues, I could be as unself-conscious and inquisitive as I had been while asking how she had helped David give up thumb sucking.

We began to talk seriously of prejudice only after I finally told her, one day, how her statement about leaving America had disturbed me. There was a long pause at her end of the telephone wire, then a sigh.

She had come to believe, she said, that perhaps this was the only way she could live freely—the only way her son could grow into an undamaged man.

From then on many of our conversations fell into a pattern. Grace would relate an experience and I would insist she had misinterpreted the episode. Women she met at Brotherhood Luncheons would pass her on the street pretending not to see her; well, I passed people when I was preoccupied. Salesclerks avoided waiting on her; salesclerks avoided waiting on *anyone,* me included. When Justin, Grace, Ben, and I went out to dinner together Grace would quietly point out the other diners staring at us. I laughed. Grace was a strikingly elegant woman, I said. The stares were compliments. At the time I believed Grace was telling me of the most significant incidents that accounted for her bitterness. They all seemed so trivial.

And usually, she answered my questions: *How* did employers avoid hiring Negro people? (Simple. The I'll-call-you-don't-call-me ending.) Why was she bitter over her years at Penn? (The social work supervisor who insisted she could not do case work with white families; the professors who "talked to me in one-syllable words as if I were retarded" or "made me a special pet.") Again, I believed Grace misunderstood kindness.

But we never talked of ghetto schools or intermarriage or housing. I wanted to learn but I didn't know what questions to ask. Grace may have interpreted my white isolation as a desire not to know too much.

Finally, all by myself, I smacked painfully into one of the invisible barriers I didn't know was there.

One day I suggested we take our children to a nearby (for me) amusement park and swimming pool.

Grace was silent. Then, "I can't."

"Why not?" I asked. Was she busy? Didn't she like the

place? It was perfect for children the age of ours and I'd taken my children there often.

"I'm not allowed to go," she said. Again a silence followed.

"But why?" I persisted. Had Justin forbade her to go? The place was safe and the prices reasonable.

Then, "Lois, don't you know they don't allow Negroes there?"

No, of course I didn't know Grace would be kept out of that park. I'd been there so often and, once again, I had never noticed who *wasn't* there.

I felt the pain of humiliation from two different sources: the humiliation Grace must feel from being declared unacceptable, unwanted, and at the same time I felt the deep shame of having participated, even unknowingly, in a white-only restriction. In that month, June 1961, America had voted in the United Nations to condemn Portugal's treatment of black people in its African colony, and now, here in Omaha, my friend was barred from an amusement park.

Grace told me later that my gasp actually stunned her. It must have had all my shock behind it. She said I sounded as if I were strangling when I asked immediately, "What can we do?"

I remember asking the question and I remember Grace's answer. "Nothing. We can do *absolutely nothing*."

I told Grace I was phoning the amusement park.

Grace was right. My phone call accomplished nothing except to give me my first defeat. A woman's voice informed me that Negroes were most definitely *not* allowed. "We couldn't have them in our pool, you understand."

"This is a privately owned park," the woman said. "We can make whatever rules we want." All I could do was sputter in potent rage that we would never, NEVER come to that park again.

The woman's voice had a shrug in it.

I was still holding the cradled phone in angry helplessness

when it rang under my fingers. It was our school superintendent. He had interviewed the Negro teacher, found her exceedingly qualified, and offered her a job. He had just received a note from her turning it down. Did I know why? Had he said something offensive? Could I find out?

I called Ken Hancock. Yes, he knew. The teacher felt she didn't want to be the first Negro teacher in our district.

Now I did want to talk to that teacher. Ken gave me her phone number. At first her reasons were vague, but finally she burst out, "Look, I know I can't take it!"

"Take what?" I asked. The Freedom Riders were being beaten with clubs and hauled off to jail; by comparison what was there to "take" in our school district? I'd been able to do nothing about the amusement park, but I had opened the doors in our school district. Why did she have to be pushed through them?

"You wouldn't understand," she said. No, I didn't. I believed she was a selfish, cowardly person, as bigoted against our school district as the amusement park was against Negro people.

I reported the conversation to the superintendent, adding that this particular woman seemed to have problems we didn't know about, but that we'd keep trying. To Ken Hancock I said the same.

That evening Grace called to say she felt I should know the truth. The actual job offer had surprised Ken, Justin, and the teacher herself. They had assumed the interview was a meaningless gesture given only to satisfy me. They believed that the teacher would be disqualified with some false excuse and the issue forgotten.

Grace laughed then. "But the biggest surprise to Ken Hancock was that you wanted to look for another teacher! He was positive you'd be irritated and say 'See—they don't *want* help!' and drop the whole thing!"

Grace seemed to have forgotten the amusement park incident and now her remarks drove it out of my mind too. Certainly I wanted to find another teacher. Why would one neurotic or paranoid type make a difference to me? But I was angry at Ken Hancock. Negro people seemed to be judging me and my neighbors a lot more than my neighbors were judging them.

A few days later Grace telephoned to say she wanted to ask me a favor. The "favor" was for Ben and me to come to their house to meet some friends, Dr. and Mrs. Paul Benson.

Well, sure, we would be delighted. But why was this a favor?

Grace explained she wasn't sure we would want to come to their all-Negro neighborhood. If we had any reluctance about it, she would understand.

I was deeply hurt and confused. Ben and I had both wondered why the Christophers had never invited us to their home; I had finally reminded Ben that we had avoided entertaining until we had gotten the house just the way we wanted it. Perhaps Grace felt the same way. But now it developed that the Christophers believed we wouldn't want to come. But Grace *knew* me. How long did it take for her to trust someone? If there were barriers, I was becoming convinced those barriers were by no means erected only on one side.

We never kept the date I made with Grace that day to meet Joan and Paul Benson. A few days later, Grace called to tell me that Justin had received a job offer in California. He'd accepted it and they were flying out there immediately. Grace Christopher left my life. There were a few letters and, over the years, letters from me full of gratitude for what she had begun. Perhaps Grace was not a letter writer; perhaps she was a more important part of my life than I was of hers.

She was, though, the link between us and the Bensons. When I called Joan Benson to introduce myself a few days after Grace left, I found Joan was as anxious as I to close the gap Grace had left in both our lives. I invited Joan for coffee. And through our friendship my education was to move faster in three weeks than it had in my three-month friendship with Grace.

When I saw a brown-haired, full-figured woman walk up the path from our driveway at the time Joan Benson was to arrive, I thought she was an unexpected stranger. When she introduced herself at the door as Joan Benson, I was totally confused. Grace had never mentioned that Joan Benson was white! Joan wasn't, as she let me know quickly by her cheery statement, "We Negro women have trouble with our hair in humid weather like this," as she removed a pretty white straw hat in our foyer.

But Joan looked startlingly Caucasian. She had creamy olive skin, actually lighter than my ruddy complexion. My mouth was fuller and my nose broader than Joan's. She was tall, Junoesque in fact, and carried herself with a quick grace I often saw in action later when she grabbed for one of her five small sons.

Joan was different from Grace in all possible ways. While Grace customarily sat back in a chair, languid and elegant, Joan leaned forward as I did, gesturing out, touching people as we spoke. Grace wore stark clothes; Joan wore soft colors and easy lines. And unlike Grace's initial reserve, Joan was bubbly, relaxed, and friendly. Grace had told her all about Ben and me, she said. I knew less about them, but we seemed to become friends instantly.

Joan talked about her children and about her husband, Paul, with the unmistakable radiance of a happy woman. We talked of getting our husbands together. I knew Paul Benson was a surgeon, but I knew nothing else about him. I found myself hoping he was as warm and wonderful as Joan, and that Ben would like him.

After my first meeting with Joan (followed by many phone

chats) there was a delay of several weeks before we met Paul. I had begun to wonder if, like the husband of Inez Robbins, the woman who cleaned for me, Paul Benson had a prejudice against white people. Finally, Joan called to say they could accept our invitation that coming Saturday.

Luckily, by the time Paul Benson strode into our living room, I was prepared. His first cool words were: "Sorry I haven't had time for you folks before." Ben's eyes widened at Paul's arrogance. Then I knew Ben remembered what Grace Christopher had once told us about the defenses black people need against possibly patronizing whites.

Paul Benson looked like a big brown cinnamon bear. There was no doubt about his being Negro, but the most striking first impression of Paul was his way of taking over a room completely. He was an enormous man, over six feet and muscularly bulky, but there was also an assurance in his demeanor that I would see later as he took over an operating room; Paul seemed to enter *every* room like a star making his first-act entrance and Joan's eyes always provided the applause.

Paul proceeded to tell us how busy he was; how seldom he took time for social visits; in short, how lucky we were to have him there. With someone else I would have wanted to tell him to take his precious time elsewhere, but somehow Paul's great need to protect his pride at all costs came through.

He finally saw we were smilingly unmoved by his imperious attitude. He began asking questions. What did we think of the Freedom Riders? How long had we lived in Rockbrook? Where did our children go to school?

Somewhere, hidden in these questions, was Paul's test to see what prejudices these new white friends had. In a way, I was as interested in the results as he was. Grace Christopher had exposed one blind spot in me—I expected her son to accept an obstacle mine didn't. Maybe I had other unconscious prejudices. It was better, I'd decided, to say what I thought without trying to censor myself and then let potential Negro friends uncover any of my unknowing prejudices. It was better for this to happen at the beginning of a friendship rather than later when someone could be more hurt by it.

But while I was willing to be judged, I intended to do some judging too. Ben and I were more involved now in interracial relationships than I'd intended. That Panel of American Women had moved me to find a Negro teacher for our school. Now we were about to form our second relationship with a Negro couple.

The Christophers and Ken Hancock had told us that white people created the problems black people suffered from, but was this true? The only white prejudice we'd seen so far was the amusement park incident; humiliating, but hardly a serious handicap.

On the other hand, it was true that white people held all the important jobs in business and government. Why? While the theory that "all men are created equal" sounded fine, I knew it wasn't entirely true even among white people; some were simply born with more intelligence and good health than others. But white immigrants had come to this country and managed to pull themselves up to those high positions in politics and industry. Why hadn't black people? They had been here longer than most immigrants. The Emancipation Proclamation had, I believed, made them free a hundred years ago. What had really held Negroes back?

Now I can smile at my naïve belief I could learn about black people through a few friendships, especially a friendship with people like the Bensons. For many reasons, they were totally different from average black Americans. But later, when our black friends were people with prison records or on welfare, it was only through those first groping steps with the Bensons that we were able to understand.

We must have tentatively passed Paul Benson's "test" that

first evening, for he suggested we have dinner out the following week. The busy doctor wasn't quite so busy, it seemed.

We met at Omaha's most fashionable restaurant the next Saturday and Paul's lordly manner with the white maître d' was as amusing as was the tender, loving care of the Negro waiters, most of whom, Joan told me, were Paul's patients.

If anyone stared at us, I was too involved in the conversation to notice. Paul had amusing stories to tell on a dozen subjects and I could see that Ben was enjoying himself as much as I was. With the Bensons we *did* discuss politics and religion; the Bensons were Catholic, and Paul had expert political knowledge. We disagreed good-naturedly about some things, but I reflected it was seldom two couples were so totally compatible.

The only moment a cloud crossed Paul's expansive mood was when the maître d' placed the dinner check squarely in front of Ben, reaching over Paul's shoulder to do it. I saw a flash of anger in Paul's eyes as he grabbed the check and refused to let Ben pay our share of it. Ben always checks the restaurant's addition, but Paul quickly shoved a fistfull of bills into the maître d's hand and waved him away.

Next week, Paul said, he'd like us to come to his house. We accepted at once.

But when Ben and I conscientiously followed Paul's directions for getting there the following week, we thought we had the wrong house. The address Paul had given us was one of a group of tiny wooden cottages, less than one-third the size of our house. Paul was a successful doctor. We assumed he earned much more than Ben. He couldn't live in a house like this, and with five children, too!

When Joan did indeed answer the doorbell, I hoped my surprise didn't show. We entered a living room smaller than my kitchen. The furniture reflected quality and taste, but my first impression was that the house looked like a beautifully decorated telephone booth. The dining room table seemed to extend nearly to the front door and off the living room I could see only two tiny bedrooms. Where did those five sons of theirs sleep?

From way back in my memory came a statement that Negro men spent their money on Cadillac cars and alligator shoes instead of more practical things. But Paul drove a Volkswagen. I glanced at his shoes as he took my coat; plain leather, like Ben's.

I covered my feelings by admiring the beautiful Queen Anne table that Joan told me she'd inherited from her great-grandmother. We sat in the small living room. Joan had decorated skillfully, using light colors and as many scaled-down pieces of furniture as she could, but no one could scale down Paul. He filled the largest chair in the room. Except for a coffee table separating us, I felt as if all our knees would touch. Paul served us drinks in beautiful, heavy cut-glass tumblers, but his elegance as a host was restricted by the precarious trip through the furniture.

My curiosity as to why a successful professional man would live in this undersized house pushed me into introducing the subject of housing in the only light way that occurred to me. I said, laughingly, that the drive out here was just plain too long. "If we're going to be friends," I went on, "I wish you'd move out our way."

My words must have seemed either a crude joke or the genuine naïveté they truly represented. Luckily, the Bensons gave me the benefit of the doubt.

"Anything for sale near you?" Paul asked quietly.

I hadn't noticed, but I'd keep my eyes open if they were interested. Interested? Joan burst out with how much she wanted a larger house, how crowded they were. Four of her sons had to sleep in the basement and she lived in fear of how they could get out in case of fire.

Ben and I began describing the virtues of Rockbrook. The

schools were excellent; the neighbors friendly and interesting; good road into the city.

Paul listened. Then, slowly and without expression he asked, "How would your neighbors feel if we moved out there?"

With warm feelings of confidence in the people among whom I had lived for five years, I told Paul, "Oh, please— our neighbors are too intelligent to be bigoted."

Our conversation that evening drifted to other topics, but as we left I reminded Paul and Joan that I would look seriously for houses and hoped they were really interested in our neighborhood. Joan glanced at Paul with what I read as wifely deference.

Then, strangely somber, Paul said, "You just call us when you see something you think we'd like."

The next morning I phoned Bibi Van Dorp to tell her that the Bensons were looking for a house. Bibi had met the Christophers and knew about our friendship with Joan and Paul.

Bibi felt this was wonderful; it would do the neighborhood some good. "Listen," she said, "what about the Kozarik house?" Mr. Kozarik had been the builder and had taken over the house when his customer declared bankruptcy. The Kozariks, Bibi said, were not happy in the neighborhood and would probably sell cheap.

This house was on upper Lindley Road, near Bibi, but four blocks from us. I knew nothing about it except that Jim Gibson lived across the street. As Bibi talked, I remembered seeing Jim one day, sitting in a lawn chair that seemed to sag under his obese body. But I hadn't really noticed the house across the street from him, except that it was slightly larger than the other houses around it.

"Go look at it," Bibi suggested, "then stop by for coffee later."

— 41 —

In a moment, Harriet Fischer called and I told her why I was rushing.

Harriet's first word was, "Don't!" With unusual concern in her voice, she said, *"Please* listen to me. How *can* you be so naïve?"

If anyone but Harriet had said this, I might have listened, but to me Harriet was prejudiced about my neighborhood and bitter from childhood scars. And perhaps out of my own pride I needed to prove Harriet wrong.

Hers was the only warning and I ignored it.

There were several reasons why both Ben and I were unaware of the possible reaction to a Negro family in a white neighborhood. In 1961, there was no open-housing legislation to cause discussion among people; there had as yet been no national headlines about Folcroft, Pennsylvania, where white neighbors rioted and nearly destroyed the home of a Negro couple.

Neither Ben nor I had ever lived anywhere near a Negro neighborhood and so had never heard the fearful talk of "them" spilling over into "our" area. In Milwaukee, where I had been raised, the Poles were the scapegoat group. If a Polish family had moved on our block, I believe my German grandparents would have been distressed. Lodged way down somewhere in a childhood memory was Grandfather, in his heavy accent, saying that "those foreigners" (the Poles) should stay with their own kind on the South Side and out of Bay View. But the possibility of a Negro family buying in our neighborhood was so remote, apparently, that I heard no speculation about property values or what "they" would do to a neighborhood. Later, when Milwaukee's Father James Groppi led a march in support of open housing through the Polish section near where I had lived, it was a strange sensation to find how violently the people my grandparents looked down on reacted toward those one step farther down our Milwaukee pecking order.

But another reason neither Ben nor I expected trouble over the Bensons being accepted by our neighbors was that our marriage insulated us more than we knew. We were close to each other: sometimes in close combat, sometimes in close agreement. It was to each other that we turned for violent arguments about moral values. Our temperaments were so different. My emotional instincts and Ben's careful ruminating approach made us believe that our arguments reflected both sides of an issue. They didn't. We were, I think now, arguing over procedures, not goals. Our marriage had reached the state where we were just beginning to recognize our unchangeable differences and trying to accommodate them into some workable arrangement for family harmony. I was working as hard as I could to understand this sometimes stonily stubborn man who failed to *feel* what I wanted him to; Ben was undoubtedly trying just as hard to understand a wife whose tears and moods never followed consistent "logical" patterns. The stormy marriage of Ben's parents and my own parents' divorce left scars that locked us both into a determination to understand each other and to work through our differences. When we reached points of understanding we were so delighted we must have believed we had achieved some universal truth. But in combat or mutual admiration, we were each other's best friend, and in this instance it was a handicap. Our closeness created a separateness from others. If either of us had needed to reach out for closer companionship with people around us, we might have found out that our feelings were different from theirs. If we had been less involved in knowing each other, we might have known others better.

Instead, I accepted what I thought were facts: my neighbors had expressed only enthusiasm over the idea of having a Negro teacher; my friends told me how much they'd enjoyed meeting Grace Christopher at Noah's birthday party. And so, sure that what I was about to do was no more controversial than collecting for the March of Dimes, I gathered Sarah from the sandbox and we drove along the four blocks to the Kozarik house.

If I had realized then this act would eventually lead to the end of Ben's career, I am sure I would have turned the car around and headed for home. I was willing to extend a hand to our Negro friends. I did not dream the grip would tighten and pull me in.

I walked up to a well-cared-for house across from Jim Gibson's and rang the doorbell. The chain-guarded door opened only enough to show a short woman with dark hair and eyes. I explained that Mrs. Van Dorp said the house might be for sale. When could I see it? A friend of mine might be interested.

There was silence. Then a voice said in a halting accent, "I think you may come—maybe—in now?"

The door opened and Mrs. Kozarik timidly motioned that I should enter. I lost some of my confidence. I thought I knew how my neighbors felt about a family like the Bensons, but this apprehensive little foreign woman might have quite different feelings.

She walked ahead of me through the house, apologizing needlessly for its meticulous appearance. The house was not as well finished or as large as ours, but it had four bedrooms, two more than the Bensons had now. I asked few questions; mostly, I was trying to decide how to bring up the Bensons' color. Mrs. Kozarik, I felt, must be told in advance or her surprise might hurt Joan and Paul.

Finally, all I could think to do was plunge. "I think my friends would like to look at the house," I told her. I said the husband was a surgeon; they had five children and needed a larger house. Then as quickly and casually as I could, I added, "By the way, this is a Negro family."

Mrs. Kozarik stopped in the middle of the living room, turned and stared at me. My heart sank. I waited for the words I now expected; that she wouldn't sell to Negroes.

The silence between us seemed endless, but then she said slowly, "Oh. Well, that is, I think, all right." I smiled, letting out the breath I just realized I'd been holding.

Before I could speak, Mrs. Kozarik continued: "But do you think the others—the neighbors—will be unpleased?"

Oh, no. They were all nice people. I knew them from our school parents' group. Mr. Gibson had voted in favor of a Negro teacher, and it was Mrs. Van Dorp from the next block who had suggested that I see the house.

Mrs. Kozarik seemed doubtful. These neighbors, she told me, were not as nice as I thought. But would I sit down? She would bring coffee. She would bring some toys for my little girl.

I felt Mrs. Kozarik was lonely and that her shyness, her difficulty with English had kept her from friendly relations with her neighbors. But she seemed so pleased to have a visitor now. She went quickly into her kitchen, bustling like a little mouse, and returned with steaming coffee and some delicious unfamiliar pastry; with milk for Sarah and some crayons.

She told me that she had been born in Lithuania, and when the Russians took over she had *walked* across Europe with what possessions she could carry. Through kind relatives she had come to America. The story of her courage was moving and I listened, feeling proud that she had found her happy ending in America.

Finally, I had to go. At the door, Mrs. Kozarik said softly, "You are a good person. You are helping your colored friends. Most Americans don't care about others."

Her words hit me like a slap. I don't remember what I

said; I do remember groping, feeling like a high school senior making a Fourth of July speech, but I had to try, as gently as possible, to make this disillusioned little woman understand that Americans *did* care.

I felt Sarah's little hand tighten in mine and I looked down into her two-year-old gaze. Sarah didn't understand what I was saying, but she must have felt my distress. I picked her up, smiling at her and at Mrs. Kozarik. Sarah was going to live and grow up in this country and it was a country full of good people. Mrs. Kozarik would find it out.

Chapter Four

My first act when I got home from the Kozarik house was to call Joan Benson. Describing the house in detail and enthusiasm, I missed her reservations about its four-bedroom size. Joan said she'd talk to Paul and call me back.

Just before Ben came home, my phone rang. The call seemed pleasant enough. It was from a woman I was never to meet face-to-face. She introduced herself in a thin, sweet voice with an almost imperceptible stammer as Marilyn Hanover. She said she lived next door to the Kozariks and that she had just heard from Bibi Van Dorp that a Negro family was buying their house. She wanted me to know she was pleased. A certain fervor in her voice surprised me, but I felt it was nice, if a bit unusual, for her to call. The house, I reminded her, was far from sold yet; the Bensons hadn't even seen it. Well, she wanted me to know she was in favor of it. Fine. I hung up with the warm feeling that Mrs. Kozarik was being quickly proven wrong.

Just before dinner, Bibi called. In a tone unlike her usual positive and assured self, she began, "I think we may have moved too fast. I don't think the neighborhood is ready for the Bensons."

When I asked what she meant, she was vague. "Some of the people up there weren't happy about the idea." Who? Oh, she'd rather not say.

I told her Marilyn Hanover had just called to say she was *very* happy.

Oh? Bibi thought that then maybe things would work out. Marilyn Hanover's husband, I knew, was in the same law office as Herb Van Dorp.

But I wondered how the news had spread quickly enough for Bibi to have known that "some" people weren't happy. I had only seen the house a few hours ago.

When Ben came home I told him everything that had happened. He shruged off Bibi's comments. He was much more concerned that I "just knew" the Bensons would like the house and buy it and be our neighbors. It might not be what they want, Ben reminded me, and I should be prepared for a disappointment. I promised to try and we went to sleep with no idea of what was going on just a few blocks away.

I woke the next morning to a lovely, quiet September day, with no premonition that, through the special offices of the telephone, this would be one of the most convulsive days of my life—that before I went to sleep that night the world would seem entirely different from when I awoke.

The first call came early. It was Mrs. Kozarik. She spoke in a voice bordering on hysteria, yet without expression, as if she'd memorized what she was going to say; wanted to say it and be finished. She was sorry, she said. She could not sell her house to my friends. The fat person, Mr. Gibson, said the neighbors would sue her if she did.

Mrs. Kozarik was obviously very upset; I felt sorry for her and responsible for having put her in this position. At the same time, I was almost positive no one could sue her. I felt a flash of anger at Jim Gibson and I could visualize this hulking, overweight man towering above this vulnerable little woman. Why hadn't Jim talked to *me?* If he knew this much, he also knew that I was the person who had talked with Mrs. Kozarik about the house.

But this was no time to question Mrs. Kozarik. Her voice blurred; she was apparently close to tears. It seemed best to reassure her there would be no trouble. Yes, I understood; she could not sell the house to my friends. It was all right.

When Mrs. Kozarik hung up I tried to absorb what had happened. Yes, I could imagine Jim Gibson as a bully. At school meetings I had heard him silence his wife with sarcastic, cutting remarks. It was Jim who had made the one sour comment about hiring a Negro teacher. Yet Jim always went along with the majority opinion in the end. Even if he objected to a Negro neighbor, it was hard to believe he would tell Mrs. Kozarik threatening lies entirely on his own.

Marilyn Hanover, the woman who had phoned to tell me how pleased she was at the thought of Negro neighbors, might know what was going on. I decided to call her; she lived next door to the Gibsons.

But the fervent, pleasant woman who had phoned me the day before had disappeared. Instead her voice was distant, formal, and her stammer was more pronounced.

"My . . . my husband says I'm not to . . . to discuss this, Mrs. Stalvey."

But, I told her, I only wanted to know what had happened. I didn't expect her to take sides, only tell me what was going on. Why had Jim Gibson threatened Mrs. Kozarik? Didn't he know my friends hadn't even seen the house yet? None of this made sense, I said, and I only wanted to understand.

Marilyn Hanover would answer none of my questions. Over and over, she stammered through the same sentence; she was not able to discuss the issue. Finally, in a tremulous voice she said, "I found . . . found out a lot about myself since . . . since yesterday. I . . . I wish I had your courage. But . . . but I don't."

What courage? Me?

But Marilyn Hanover was no longer at the other end of the line.

In the light of what has happened in America since 1961 I can look back now with a kind of awe at my continuing obtuseness. But I was in the unfortunate position of knowing both too much and too little.

Most of what I knew about integrated neighborhoods came from an article I had once read, and now remembered, in the *Saturday Evening Post*. It described the profitable racket of "block-busting." An anonymous realtor told how, in a Chicago neighborhood, he and other unethical realtors skillfully played on the prejudices and fears of white families in order to frighten them into selling their homes at low prices when a Negro family moved onto their street. The realtors would then re-sell these same houses to Negro families and pocket enormous profits. But, the author pointed out, if the white families refused to be frightened into fleeing, the neighborhood remained predominantly white, property values stayed normal, and his racket proved unprofitable. His point, I remembered well, was that white prejudice made his business blossom.

I was sure this white gullibility did not exist in Rockbrook. What then were Jim Gibson and, for heaven's sake, Marilyn Hanover's husband afraid of? If they had some strange belief that Negro families were slovenly or careless, all they would have to do is visit the block on which the Bensons now lived. The Bensons' house, tucked in among the other small cottages, stood out because of its neatness. I had had the sad thought that Paul felt he had to paint twice as often, to clip his hedges as skillfully as he sutured flesh in surgery *because* his family was the only Negro family there. Paul didn't have the luxury that Jim Gibson had; Paul couldn't sit in a sagging lawn chair and gaze lazily at his weeds.

But whatever silly fears people like Jim Gibson had, the fact remained that the Negro undertaker had lived at the outer edge of Rockbrook for years. There had been, as far as I knew, no problems there. Had the values of the houses around him declined? I didn't know. But wouldn't it have made more sense for Jim Gibson to find out rather than threaten a timid woman like Mrs. Kozarik with a lawsuit?

What I really wanted to do was talk with Ben, but there was no point to disturbing him at the office and, until he got home, I could seek out Bibi Van Dorp's ideas. She was probably as shocked as I was if she'd heard of the threats to Mrs. Kozarik.

When Bibi answered her phone I burst out immediately with everything that had happened: Mrs. Kozarik's call, Marilyn Hanover's strange change of attitude, all my questions about what could have gone wrong.

Usually, Bibi's reactions matched mine, but this time she only said calmly, "I told you the neighborhood wasn't ready."

Her odd calm surprised me, but I tried to ignore it and went on. Why would Jim Gibson threaten Mrs. Kozarik without talking to me first?

"Well, at the meeting last night . . ." Then Bibi caught herself.

What meeting?

Well, her husband Herb had said she shouldn't tell me, shouldn't get involved, but she thought I ought to know. There had been a meeting last night of all the neighbors on upper Lindley Road. The people were angry at what I had done and they had even talked of getting Ben fired from his job.

Her words about Ben's job made no impression. To me, these were silly childish threats, as foolish as Jim Gibson's threat of suing Mrs. Kozarik, but I was astonished that a group of intelligent adults would organize and then hold a meeting without Ben and me there. For, without us, they had no facts at all. Only slightly less astonishing was the fact that Bibi had not called to tell me. The last thing I expected from her was neutrality.

Bibi said she hoped I knew she agreed with me. The only problem was that Herb wanted her to stay absolutely out of it. Oops, there was her doorbell. She'd have to call me back.

For the rest of the day I did my housework, grateful for the mindless tasks that kept me physically occupied. I fed the children, dusted, vacuumed, and counted the hours until Ben would be home. My feelings were mixed, more shock and hurt than fear. But one thought kept returning: Mrs. Kozarik had been right about her neighbors. I had been wrong.

My last phone call of the day came just before dinner. It was from Joan who told me apologetically that they had decided not to look at the Kozarik house. It was too small. Before I could say a word, Joan gave what seemed a rather lengthy explanation. When they finally moved, she said, it had to be to a house large enough for the boys. Did I understand?

That was the only thing I did understand that day.

While Joan talked I tried to decide if it would be selfish of me to tell her what had happened. I needed to talk to someone, but I would be telling her that these people didn't want her. However, since she didn't want the house, perhaps she would be detached enough now not to feel too hurt. In the end it was impossible for me to hold it all in.

Joan listened as I told her about the day. When I finished, she was quiet for a moment. Then she said, "Can you and Ben come over tonight?"

Oh yes, we could. It would feel so good to air what had happened with people we trusted. And there were questions that Paul and Joan could probably answer for us. Feeling much better, I said good-bye.

All that was left was to tell Ben. But now I was even able to smile at the thought that tonight his usual question, "How did your day go, honey?" would have an attention-getting answer.

As usual, Ben listened silently until I had poured out the entire story while distractedly putting dinner on the table. Looking up from a pot or handful of knives and forks, I could see the three familiar lines forming between his eyebrows as he considered what I reported. When I said unhappily, "Maybe I just messed everything up," he walked over to me to hold me close. "No, you've done the right thing," he said.

Ben paid no attention to the threat to his job. What affected him most was that a neighborhood meeting had been held without either of us there. "What's the matter with those people?" he said. "How could they act without knowing the facts?"

He was glad I had made the date with Joan and Paul that evening. As we sat down to dinner, he smiled across at me. "Don't worry. You did all right. And Paul will have some ideas on what to do next."

Paul did. But when Ben and I finished dinner and drove across town to his house, Paul's advice caused us to do the opposite of what he suggested.

Chapter Five

The Paul Benson who greeted us that night was entirely different from the dynamic, debonair doctor we knew. We had never seen him without a suitcoat or without his amused assurance. Now he sat across from us in shirtsleeves, quiet and somber, asking me to repeat what I had told Joan.

I told him about Mrs. Kozarik's call and Bibi's report of the meeting. Ben interjected his angry comments and his amazement that adults would act this way. To Joan and Paul the story must have been as old and familiar as it was new to us. I know now that Paul's serious attention was not on what had happened, but on how Ben and I felt about it.

When I got to my questions, Paul answered them in a quick, offhand way, as if he had answered the same questions many times before. No, he said, property values did not go down unless dozens of white homeowners sold at once in a panic. In fact, studies showed that prices actually went *up* when the panic was over. No, there were not enough Negro families in Omaha who could afford to inundate Rockbrook; he only wished there were.

Paul was impatient. He had something else to say. He

leaned forward in his chair after glancing at Joan. Both of them looked at us intensely, with warm but serious expressions. Exactly, I thought, as if they were our parents about to tell us the facts of life. In a way they were.

Paul told us that we should stop trying to find a house for them. Then he sat back as if everything had been settled. I looked at Ben; he looked as confused as I felt. At first, I thought that perhaps the Bensons didn't want a new house; that for some reason they had decided they didn't want to move. I asked them.

Paul again looked impatient, as if he were dealing with some thick-skulled medical student. Of course they wanted a house; but they didn't want us to suffer for it. They couldn't allow us to.

"What do you mean, 'suffer'?" I asked Paul. "It's been disappointing to find some of our neighbors aren't as sensible as I thought, but that's not 'suffering.' "

Paul looked at us with genuine incredulity.

"Don't you two have any idea what those people could do to you?"

"But why would they want to do anything to us?" I said. Jim Gibson had apparently stirred people up with silly myths, but when they calmed down, they would realize how illogically they had all behaved.

"Well, your neighbors have already held a meeting and threatened to get Ben's job," Paul said bleakly.

Ben snorted. "That's proof that they're illogical, Paul. How can a bunch of hysterical neighbors affect my job!"

It was Joan's next comment that put the issue suddenly in a different light and affected much of what we did from then on. "You could lose all your friends over this," she said.

At her words, I realized who our friends were. Joan and Paul, whom we had known such a short time, were literally pleading with us to abandon them for our own good. Measured against Bibi Van Dorp's cautious neutrality there was no question of whose friendship was real. But even beyond that, I found myself comparing the Bensons, concerned over anyone suffering in their behalf, with Jim Gibson, bullying a frightened refugee woman. Suddenly I felt outraged that Jim Gibson believed the Bensons were not good enough to share his neighborhood. For the first time my emotions were becoming engaged in a new way. It was no longer merely a house for friends; other issues were expanding its scope.

Without realizing how far-reaching my statement would eventually be, I said to Joan that we didn't want the kind of friends who would keep her out of any neighborhood.

Paul rubbed his hands over his head in frustration. He was in an argument he hadn't expected. Joan told me later that after the night I'd offered to find a house, Paul believed he would never hear from us again. This had happened to them before with white friends. But because we had tried, Paul now believed we were friends and he wanted to protect us. He thought we would gratefully accept his asking us to stop. But now we were proving damnably difficult to protect.

His next argument came close to working.

"They'll hurt your children," he said.

Then I did feel fear. For a moment I was ready to recant everything. If Paul could show me how my children could be hurt, nothing else was important. What I visualized was that some physical harm could come to them.

"They'll call your children names," he said.

At first I felt anger at Paul for frightening me so badly and then coming out with this silly statement. But as I looked into his anguished face I knew what he had said was not ridiculous to him. The childhood chant, "Sticks and stones may break my bones but names will never hurt me," applied only to *me,* a white Protestant.

I felt the same gratitude as when I had heard the Panel of Women. Spike, Noah, and Sarah had been born with protection from ugly names. Now it was indescribably poignant to look across at Paul and Joan whose children did not have this immunity and see their concern for ours. Ben and I would find compassion like this often in the coming years. People who had never known safety would try to keep our family safe.

I heard Ben say gently, obviously as moved as I was, "Paul, don't you know there *are* no hurtful names for white Protestant children?"

Paul played his last card. The word he had to say came hard to him and he paused over it. "They can call your children . . . *nigger-lovers.*"

It felt good to smile and tell Paul that even six-year-old Spike could not be hurt by *that* name. He had never heard the word "nigger," and to Spike, loving someone couldn't be bad. Innocence, I realized, sometimes provided its own protection.

Joan had been quiet during most of the discussion, alternately watching Paul and then us. Her children slept in a basement, tried to play in a tiny yard. As a mother, I knew where my emotions would have pulled me: toward anything that might give my children the physical safety and comfort their father had earned for them.

Now she turned to us. Her face was soft and sober as she said that she believed we didn't know what a serious risk we had taken, but we should remember that our friendship did not depend on our helping them find a house. "As much as I want a better home," she told us, "neither Paul nor I expect you to make any sacrifices. Your friendship is more important to us than the house we will find someday, somehow."

I began to say that if we had had any doubts where our loyalties lay, we had them no longer, but Ben put his hand on my arm to stop me. We had all talked so much, he said, and we should make no decisions lightly. He reminded me that I had had quite a day and that I should sleep on this.

On the way home Ben and I spoke little. I sat close to him,

looking up at the strong prominent chin and smiling back when he glanced down at me. Along with everything else, tonight had shown me a new dimension to our marriage. We responded spontaneously and identically to issues we hadn't known existed twenty-four hours before.

Halfway home, I asked a question whose answer I felt I knew. "Do you think we should stop trying to find a house for the Bensons?"

No, *he* didn't, but I was the one who would be spending my days in the neighborhood, he said. "If there were snubs, you'll feel them most. I wanted you to think it over very carefully, honey, to be sure of how much you can take."

After we had gotten home and Ben was asleep, I sat in our darkened living room looking out over the view I loved, the dark valley and the tiny lights on the faraway hill. I tried to dig as deeply as I could into how I really felt. The people, the talk were all gone now; I was alone with me.

I didn't know how long the decisions I made that night would have to sustain me or where they would eventually lead our family, but I did know that this was the end to casual involvement. Whatever we did from now on would have to be with the knowledge that not everyone saw racial matters as we did, that indeed some people disagreed violently.

And though I'd brushed aside Paul's words about names hurting my children, I knew now that there *were* ways in which my children could be hurt. While there were no nasty names they could comprehend, they could understand being left out of birthday parties. Spike would understand kindergarten playmates who said, "I'm not allowed to play with you."

This thought was so painful I wanted to wake Ben up and ask him what to do. But I had to know my own feelings, thoroughly and honestly, before I could talk to Ben.

So, watching the lights across the valley go out one by one,

I tried to examine how I would feel if the Bensons' worst predictions came true. How would it feel to go to a school meeting where no one spoke to me? What if former friends passed me with icy stares? I liked people and needed them, but I meant what I said to Joan, that I didn't want Jim Gibson or anyone like him for a friend. Yes, icy stares would hurt, but under these circumstances they could be survived.

But what if Spike came home crying that no one would play with him? Even the thought of it brought a sharp pain. I could not make those three little children martyrs to my causes.

With this, I could feel all my high moral ideals crumble into so much hypocrisy. True, I was grateful that my children had been born with a white Protestant immunity to ostracism, but out of that gratitude I could not proceed to strip that immunity away. Well, I told myself, it didn't take long to find the limits of your idealism, did it? Anything that could put tears into my children's eyes was where my fight for justice stopped.

As my thinking changed course, I shifted my position on the sofa. Bending over now, I closed my eyes and began to think of what my reversal meant.

It would mean giving up the Bensons as friends. No matter what Joan had said, the friendship couldn't continue after I had (rightly, of course) put my children's interests ahead of hers. Even if she understood, my own guilt feelings would forever shadow our relationship. But we had lived happily in Omaha for five years without knowing the Bensons existed. They had been our friends for less than a month. I would miss them, but our lives would go on without each other.

So all that was left now was to call Jim Gibson and to tell him he had nothing to worry about. This was no problem. Early in life I had discovered I had less pride than I had a compulsion to correct my own mistakes.

I rehearsed the conversation I would have to have with

Jim Gibson. It was then I knew I had thought through only half the problem. If I said, "Jim, I was wrong," it would be a lie. The truth was, "Jim, I will go along with you because I am afraid my children will be hurt." And if I did this, would I truly be protecting my children—or would I do something much more damaging to them by agreeing, out of fear, with something I knew to be wrong?

That phrase "I will go along with you because . . ." began to echo through the years to when Spike, Sarah, and Noah would have to make their own decisions. The reasons they could add after "because" would seem as important to them as their protection was to me now: because I want to be popular, because I'm afraid to be different; because it's easier not to rock the boat. If Spike got drunk with his teen-age gang because he wanted to be accepted; if Noah raced a car dangerously because he didn't want to be called "chicken"; if Sarah had intercourse with a date because she wanted to be popular—how different was that from what I was feeling now?

What our children would learn would come not so much from what we told them as from what they *saw us doing*. I had to *act* as I would want them to act or risk infecting them with my own hypocrisies.

The answer I didn't want wouldn't go away. Ben and I would have to explain the missed birthday parties and rejections as patiently as we explained why they must brush their teeth or drink their milk. We would have to explain—and demonstrate—that people must try to do what is right, even when it hurts.

The next morning as I poured Ben's coffee I asked him if he thought Ann Howard might help us through her real estate company.

Ben smiled at me. "I think you ought to try, honey."

That night I told him of my step-by-step decision and, as I expected, he had been at the end of it, waiting for me.

Chapter Six

Helping the Bensons, I realized now, meant looking outside our immediate neighborhood. There were no houses for sale near us nor, I suspected, were there likely to be soon. Like Ben, most of the men in our suburb were executives in the main offices of their firms. Promotions could be expected, but not company transfers. As much as I wished Joan could live next door, I knew our house hunt had to be broadened. I was sure that Ann Howard, the realtor who had sold us our house and had since become our friend, would help me.

Ann was quick to make a luncheon date for the next day when I called. It had been *too* long since we had seen each other, she said. When we met for lunch she told me over the shrimp cocktail how much she had missed Ben and me. Over dessert, I knew we would never see each other again.

I had told her about our new friends who were looking for a house. With no intention to deceive, I described the Bensons as they were—Paul, a surgeon, five sons, Catholic— so they would like a suitable church nearby. I wanted her to know all about them before being distracted by their color.

Ann had bubbled enthusiastically about the many possibilities among her listings. The Greenfield section might be nice, she said; she had several lovely houses there. I was delighted. She hadn't even asked if they were white, and I was so sure she would feel exactly as we did when I told her.

"They have a problem, though," I said, "because they're Negro."

Ann was a sophisticated woman and her face showed nothing. At first she merely became evasive about when the Bensons could see the houses she had just glowingly described. Finally, as I pressed her, she told me that she could not afford to show a house to a Negro family.

At the end I was literally pleading with her and when she left for a suddenly remembered appointment, I knew her promise to "call you soon" was empty as the coffee cups we left on that restaurant table.

It was difficult to call Joan and give her news of a new rejection. But in this complex situation it seemed best to be honest. I preferred always to hear the truth. I had to hope Joan felt the same.

I need not have worried. Ann Howard's quick loss of interest had seemed cruel but among Joan's other experiences it was pathetically mild. She began to tell me of some of them.

When Joan began the chronicle of her house-hunting in her gentle, beautifully liquid voice, her soft tones contrasted sharply with the ugly facts she recited. Later, I learned that her story was commonplace among Negro families.

Their present house, Joan told me, was bought, sight unseen, five years ago. It had been purchased when the Bensons moved from Texas after Paul accepted a teaching position in the medical school of a Catholic university in Omaha. The white woman who owned the house was a patient of the doctor who had arranged Paul's job. When her neighbors found out she was selling to a Negro family, they hounded her. She changed her mind several times but finally, through the persuasion of her priest, agreed to sell.

But when the Bensons arrived in Omaha with their five small children, the woman had not moved out as promised. She had changed her mind again and wanted to give the money back. They had literally been turned away at the door.

This was the only time where Joan's matter-of-fact voice broke. They knew nothing about Omaha, she said, and had tried unsuccessfully to find a hotel to accept them until they could find another house. Finally, in desperation, they appealed to a Catholic orphanage to take the children, for only a few nights, they hoped. She and Paul found one room in a run-down ghetto hotel.

For the next three months Joan and Paul tried without success to find other living quarters while the woman wavered back and forth. There is *always,* Joan said, a housing shortage among Negro families and they would never have left Texas without believing they had the house. Meanwhile, the children stayed in the orphanage. In the end, the woman was besieged by anonymous phone calls and became so angry at her neighbors, Joan said wryly, that "she finally decided *we* 'served them right.' "

The week after the Bensons moved in For Sale signs were on every lawn on the block. One day, Paul marched out and planted a For Sale sign on their lawn to the complete confusion of the neighbors. While I could laugh briefly with Joan, I knew now that Paul's humor was his only outlet for his anger.

The Bensons had received threatening and insulting phone calls, too, but they had stopped now. The house, however, was just too small for the children and always had been. And so, for five years, Joan tried to find another home.

They looked in the all-Negro areas, but the houses there were all very old and in need of major repairs; also prices were far *above* what a comparable house cost in white areas.

"I know you'll understand this," Joan said, "but we don't really want to live in a white area. Unfortunately, it's only in white areas that we can find the kind of house we need and a decent school."

Joan continued. If real estate men recognized Paul's name, they would not call her back. After several calls she would do what they wanted her to do; give up. But occasionally, she said, she would phone about an ad she saw in the newspaper and a real estate man would be eager to show her the house.

"Many times they don't realize I'm a Negro because I'm so light. Then you should see how anxious they are to point out all the advantages of the house and how hard they sell!"

I knew what she meant. This was how realtors acted with Ben and me. I remembered the unctuous devotion with which we had been shown a dozen houses when we had moved here from Chicago. And I realized with a pang that it must have been at the same time that the Bensons were so desperately searching for a house.

"Then I make an appointment for Paul to see the house. Sometimes, in looking up our credit rating, they'll recognize Paul's college as an all-Negro school. When this happens the eager salesman is not in when I call and will not call back no matter how often I leave a message. If I can get him on the phone by accident, then 'The house is sold, Mrs. Benson. So sorry.' But when I pass the house, the For Sale sign is still there.

"Once we got as far as having a realtor make an appointment for Paul to see a house. The man insisted on picking us up. When Paul came out of the house with me, the realtor couldn't hide his shock. His mouth actually dropped open. But we got into his car. As the man drove he suddenly thought of a hundred things wrong with the house he was to show us; the plumbing was bad, the schools mediocre, and he'd just heard a highway might be put through there. He drove slower and slower. Finally he parked the car and said, 'I just can't show you the house.' He turned around and drove us home without another word."

Now I suddenly remembered the real estate salesman who had shown us a few houses when we first arrived in Omaha. Praising one house he said, "And another advantage, we keep Jews out of here." I had said haughtily that my brother's wife was Jewish, did this mean she couldn't visit us? Ben and I had then brushed this horrid little man and his all-Christian neighborhood out of our minds and bought our house from Ann Howard.

With this memory another one came back. In our deed I had found a paragraph limiting resale to "Christians of the Caucasian race." Ann Howard answered my objections by saying this was an "old" form; that these "restrictive covenants" had been declared illegal. "Don't worry about it," she said. I still couldn't bring myself to accept the deed to our house unless this paragraph was "officially" removed. "Just ink it out," Ann said. I did, feeling smugly moral—and forgot all about it. Restrictive covenants were illegal and I assumed people respected law and order.

Now I was finding that assumptions worked both ways. While I assumed realtors obeyed the spirit of the law against restrictions, they assumed I would not *want* them to obey it. They had decided I did not want Jewish or Negro families in our neighborhood. Without either Ben or me being aware of it, realtors had "protected" our white Protestant sensibilities without asking if we wanted that protection.

I began to see what my assumptions helped create: a climate where Joan's little boys had to spend three months in an orphanage, a world where Paul Benson's very appearance turned realtors whiter.

There was only one more question. I asked Joan about the Negro undertaker who lived at the edge of Rockbrook. She knew the family well. They had bought an undeveloped lot from an out-of-town owner, she said. Even then there had been nastiness: last minute attempts to cancel the sale; vandalism while the house was being built; a cross burned on the lawn. Also, Joan said, the property bordered a large piece of unzoned land on which anything—a factory, car dump, stockyard—could be built. But, yes, the family had lived there over eight years. The unpleasantness had largely stopped. Neighbors simply ignored them. No one had moved.

The Bensons were willing to buy a lot and build, too, but Joan told me that seeing lots through realtors was no easier than seeing houses.

At the end of our long conversation, I made what seemed to me a sensible suggestion. Realtors would show *me* property readily enough; what if I looked for Joan, then when something looked suitable, Joan could see it. If she liked it, I would talk with the realtor and the home owner and try to convince them that not all whites were bigots, that there were many, many other people like Ben and me who would welcome a Negro family. Perhaps even the homeowner's clergyman could encourage them? Joan agreed to let me try.

Our talk ended when my doorbell rang. It was my favorite neighbor, Helen Carter, and she strode into my kitchen looking worried and uncomfortable.

"I've come to tell you not to go to the sewing club tonight," she said abruptly. "Please don't tell the others I've warned you, Lois. But the girls are upset with you over the Kozarik house. They plan to be nasty."

Instead of concern, I could feel only relief. Now at last, the confusing events of the last few days could be discussed with women I knew and respected. I assured Helen I appreciated her warning, but I said, "It will feel good to talk about it. I want to know how the other women feel. Nothing has made any sense lately." Helen listened without comment as I described everything that had happened concerning the Kozarik house.

When I finished, she reported some of the rumors she had heard; that the Urban League had given me money to buy a house for the Bensons, that Mrs. Kozarik had "been forced" to sell her house to "Jews with twelve children."

I brushed these silly tales aside. "Helen, the Urban League doesn't have enough money to buy new typewriters, let alone houses," I laughed. And no one could "force" Mrs. Kozarik to sell her house. Had Emily and Val and Elaine believed this nonsense? If so, it would all get straightened out tonight. We had all been close friends for five years, I reminded Helen.

After dinner, I gathered the pile of mending I was taking with me to Emily's house where the sewing club session was to be held that month. As I left, Ben kissed me on the forehead. He didn't want me to go. Let some time pass, he urged. I couldn't. "But just remember," he said, "any friend you can lose, you never really had."

Three hours later, I knew he was right.

I had waited for the "scolding" Helen warned me about. Then I deliberately tried to open the subject by mentioning the Bensons. Finally, in a fascinated frustration, I began to wonder if anyone would bring it up at all unless I broke my promise to Helen and bluntly repeated what she had said.

No one did. Instead, eight women nervously played conversational basketball, tossing the talk as far as possible from housing, Negroes, and even upper Lindley Road. Each time I would inch toward any of these subjects, someone would suddenly remember a dress sale or a new recipe.

Helen sat silently, watching all of us. After coffee, I announced I had to go soon. When I left, everyone else seemed to be staying.

I walked home alone through the dark backyards. And, when I was inside my kitchen door, for the first time I cried.

Chapter Seven

Of all the dangers and difficulties Joan and Paul had tried to warn us about, they hadn't mentioned the one problem I would find most difficult to cope with—silence.

Yet I couldn't let the subject lie there, between me and the women who had been my friends for five years. If none of my friends would speak out in a group, perhaps they would talk about it individually.

With each woman, the same scene was replayed over and over. I began by describing our friends, the Bensons, told of their need for a new house. I reported everything that had happened at the Kozarik house, Jim Gibson's threats to Mrs. Kozarik, the meeting held by the people on upper Lindley Road. Then, trying to show my willingness to be contra- dicted, I said I didn't understand people's objections to a Negro family. Did they?

On Friday, over espresso coffee, Elaine Mifflin said every- one should have the right to buy the house they can afford, but it wasn't right to experiment in this neighborhood.

On Saturday, Val Schmidt, one of our neighborhood's few working wives, bustled through chores while she told me that she would be the first to welcome Negro neighbors, but she felt she had no right to *force* other white families to accept them.

On Sunday, after church, Emily Wright looked woebegone. Yes, she felt terrible about the Bensons' problems. She believed the silence at the sewing club was "because no one wanted to hurt your feelings." And, much as she sympathized with the Bensons, she felt it would be sad to split up the neighborhood over the issue.

No one was against the Bensons' right to buy a house—but not here and not now. The question of where and when simply dissolved in changed subjects and vague, unfinished sentences.

Helen Carter only shook her head. "Why don't you use your head and drop the matter?" she said. "No one can say you didn't try. Why not give up gracefully?"

Oh, how I wanted to. The only problem was that the Bensons *needed* a house. Four little boys were sleeping in a basement even though their father had worked for a medical degree and now earned enough money to give them comfort and safety. Whatever qualms my neighbors had seemed far less important.

Their fears, however, meant that they would not help find houses that the Bensons might buy. The obstacle of realtors who were reluctant to show property to Negro families remained. The only hope now was the plan I had suggested to Joan; I would see houses with realtors and then try to convince them to show the suitable houses to Joan. I had not told Joan about the sewing club women and when she called to tell me of an ad for a house in a new area near us, I pretended more optimism than I was able to feel. Yes, I would phone the McMann Realty Company and arrange to have their salesman show me the house.

A tall, angular woman with hair the color of lemon pie met me at the house site and introduced herself as Mary Ann

McMann. As she unlocked the door to the large, empty red-brick Colonial, I worried that her jangling bracelets would catch in the frilly chiffon cuffs spilling out of the sleeves of her plaid suit.

Inside the cool darkened house, she fanned herself and said "Whew! I've been working like a *nigger* today!"

I followed her into the kitchen. Its green wallpaper seemed to bring out Mrs. McMann's lavishly applied rouge. She flipped up the window shade, looked around the kitchen admiringly. "Classy, eh? And, honey, I'm almost sure I can *Jew them down* plenty on the price!"

Mrs. McMann's bracelets tinkled ahead of me, leading me through the remaining rooms, all spacious, attractive, and numerous. Five bedrooms—perfect for Joan—but I followed those bracelets as hopelessly as a dairy cow heading back to a dark barn after sunny fields. My hopes for the open-mindedness of the McMann Realty Company were so meager that I came to the point quickly. Yes, I thought my friends would be interested. This was a Negro doctor and his family, I said.

Mary Ann McMann's bracelets clanked as she brought her hand to her mouth. Oh. Well. She didn't know how the owner would feel. She'd have to talk to her husband. When she told me she had to rush to another appointment, I watched her drive quickly away. That, I believed, was my last sight of Mrs. McMann.

Even when she phoned that evening to ask if she and her husband could come out to talk to us, Ben cautioned me to expect only a long, conscience-salving explanation. When they arrived, Mrs. McMann and I both introduced our husbands; hers was a short, stocky man with a large cigar and an air of determination. He seemed uncomfortable in his gray pin-striped suit, as he squirmed into place on our sofa.

He wanted to tell us, he said, all the problems involved in "selling to the colored." Wouldn't our friends like a nice home in the "colored section"? Some of these old big houses weren't bad at all with a little fixing.

I felt spiritless. This seemed such a waste of time, but Ben said, No, the Bensons did not want to fix up an old house; they wanted a new one. Possibly the one I had just looked at with Mrs. McMann.

Brad McMann nodded. He was afraid this was how it was. Then he began to tell us how hard it was for realtors to sell "to the colored" in white sections. White families in the neighborhood got mad and wouldn't list their own houses with the realtor who had "busted" the neighborhood. Other realtors got mad too when a sort of "code of ethics" like this was broken. The realtors had put one man out of business a few years ago when he handled the sale to that Negro undertaker. "They all ganged up on him; wouldn't co-operate on listings and told customers what the guy had done."

"So," Brad McMann said, "it's a real bad problem. But it don't seem right for that colored doctor not to have a house. Somebody's gotta help the Doc and I guess it's gotta be me."

It took me a moment to realize what Brad McMann had just said. He looked at us, still obviously wishing there were some alternative, but his jaw, more firm and square than I had noticed, was set in determination. He said it and he meant it. Mary Ann McMann's bracelets were silent. Her hands folded in her lap. Mary Ann McMann was looking proudly at her husband.

I didn't know how to express the surge of gratitude I felt. My first impulse was to feed them something. "Let me make some coffee. Have some cake." Ben said later I bustled around as if I expected them to starve to death before they could show the house to the Bensons.

The next evening the McManns, the Bensons, Ben and I were in the empty living room of the red-brick colonial. Paul had shaken Brad McMann's hand with none of the cautious arrogance he had shown at our first meeting. "You are," he had told Brad, "a man I'm proud to know."

Brad McMann looked entirely different that night from the uncomfortable little man who squirmed on our sofa twenty-four hours ago; darned if he didn't seem handsome now and confident. He also seemed a little embarrassed by Paul's words. He was not making some patronizing gesture of helping "them," I felt. His manner was more like that of a man inwardly proud that he'd won a battle between his fears and his conscience.

It was Paul who was uncomfortable a bit later trying to explain to Brad and to Ben and me why this house wouldn't do. Was I disgusted with him for finding fault with this house? His apologies surprised me; Ben and I had looked at dozens of houses before we made our choice; the Bensons should have the same choice, no matter how long it took.

The "fault" was a pathetic reminder of how different house hunting was for a black family. Paul explained that the placement of the house on its triangular corner lot gave them a small backyard and little privacy. "Under the circumstances," he said, "we'll need a large backyard for the boys to play *at home*."

When I looked at Joan, she nodded. But her eyes went back to Paul and Brad, talking now in terms of sizes, prices, needs. "It looks so beautiful," she said, "just to see Paul *talking* with a realtor!"

When Brad McMann locked the darkened house that night, he had already made arrangements to show Joan several other houses. There were a few weeks of pleasant contentment after that. I returned to ordinary chores with relief. Life could get back to normal. Perhaps neighborhood friendships would never be the same, but at least the subject had been aired a bit.

Not enough though. A few days before, I had seen Jim Gibson's obese form waddling toward me in our suburban shopping center, his chins tucked down as he walked along watching his belt buckle. I was glad to see him coming. I wanted to ask him why he objected so strongly to a Negro family that he would threaten Mrs. Kozarik with a lawsuit. Perhaps now that time had passed and emotions had cooled, we could talk about it.

But Jim's eyes looked up, met mine for an instant, and then he turned with more speed than his bulk suggested. Suddenly, something urgent demanded his attention—in the opposite direction. He left, as if the devil, rather than one small housewife, were chasing him.

In that month, October 1961, Attorney General Robert Kennedy announced that three southern railroads had desegregated all their facilities. Racial problems were, I felt, gradually getting straightened out. Even Grace Christopher must be re-examining her depressing contention that she couldn't raise her son in America. Brad McMann was helping the Bensons; Ken Hancock had not yet found a Negro teacher for our school, but perhaps he would soon. By now I could sympathize much more with the teacher who "didn't want to be the first." There were also other problems, Ken said. Transportation was one. Because of housing segregation, a teacher must make a long daily drive from the opposite corner of the city. Very soon, I would learn of an additional obstacle, but that October I still hoped Ken could find someone.

Meanwhile, I wrote the newsletter for our school parents' group and, as usual, telephoned the president, Lester Wheed, to read it to him. Ordinarily, I would then have passed it on to the parent who mimeographed and distributed it. This time Lester's high voice said abruptly, "No. I'll pick up the newsletter copy." Still, I placed no significance on this. Lester was a tense man, terribly anxious to please people. He had a pathetic way of pulling his lips over his front teeth, and his glasses glinted as he looked around constantly at meetings to assess the majority reaction. He was short, partly bald, and looked, more than anything else, like an elf with aching teeth.

Even when Lester marched stiffly into my house the next afternoon, I was more intrigued than insulted. Without a hello, he grabbed the newsletter from my coffee table and read it, pulling his lips in even more tightly than usual.

"This one is all right," he said, "but from now on, I'll pick up your copy and take it to be mimeographed."

I stared at him, astonished at his stern tone.

Then he said, "Well, it wasn't *my* idea. Everyone voted. We just want to be sure you don't use the newsletter for *your own purposes.*"

Did Lester Wheed believe that I would read one version of the newsletter to him—and then have another version mimeographed and distributed? And who had voted on this? When? Had another meeting been held about me—without me? I couldn't reply to this unexpectedly belligerent little man. What he said implied more than I could grasp quickly.

Lester filled in my silence with, "And they vetoed your safety-route plan too!" His glasses flashed as he tossed his head.

He took a step closer and stood glowering up at me. "Everyone knows what you tried to pull with the Kozarik house."

Now nothing could hold back the fury and hurt that rose in me. The safety route had been worked out with our principal so that our school children could avoid several dangerous traffic areas. It hurt to be accused of wanting to sneak something (what?) into the newsletter, but I was furious that adults would scuttle a safety plan for children in order to hit at me. Lester Wheed lived far from upper Lindley Road and so did most of the other school committee officers, but obviously the feelings that started there had spread.

What I didn't realize then was that I was feeling what black people must feel—the hurt, outrage, and helplessness of being judged and penalized by strangers. At that moment, all I knew was that my emotions were erupting.

I could hold back my urge to attack Lester Wheed with my fists, but I couldn't hold back my tears. I loathed each one that began streaming down my cheeks. This was exactly what those people must have sent Lester to accomplish. At this moment, the most important goal seemed to be getting Lester Wheed out of the house.

I couldn't talk. All I could do was grab his shoulder and shove him toward the door. In retrospect, I can see how funny we must have looked. Tears were dripping down my face. His glasses caught the sun streaming through our picture window, and I pushed him as if he were a barrel I had to get up a steep hill.

Lester Wheed was talking frantically now, switching between indignation and concern. "Don't get so upset. But you brought this on yourself. Calm down."

I could hear him, but I could also hear something between a grunt and a mew. That was me. He was still talking when I got him over the doorsill, closed the door, and bolted it.

Immediately after Lester Wheed's visit, any emotional isolation I felt among my neighbors became physical. Suddenly, none of my friends needed a cup of sugar any more. I didn't tell Ben about the Lester Wheed episode. He would be angry and could do nothing. I went, as usual, to the parents' meeting at school alone and sat in the center of a circle of empty chairs.

All this was not as painful as I thought it might be. Much later, I developed a theory that at least seemed valid for me. It was sad to sit among empty chairs and old friends who looked away, but not unbearable. The secure acceptance with which I had grown up—a German-American WASP in a German-American-dominated city—gave me an immunity no minority group person may have. "Nigger," "dirty Jew," "wop," "Polack" were never meant for me when I was a child.

My unscarred ego assured me that if someone disliked me there was at least a fifty-fifty chance that *they* were wrong. And so I could sit, slightly ostracized, with the feeling that it was nothing really *personal* and that everyone would act sensibly eventually. Later, the anti-white words of Malcolm X and other black militants affected me in much the same way. The habit of feeling acceptable is, I think, a hard one to break.

These conditions, however, turned me more and more toward Joan Benson for companionship. Even Harriet Fischer was difficult to talk to these days. Harriet believed I should try to mend neighborhood relationships. "I'm so sorry I took you to that *damn* luncheon program," she said.

Only Joan offered a vicarious happiness I could share and enjoy. Brad McMann was showing her many houses. Some were inadequate; some had serious flaws that Brad uncovered and pointed out. But Joan was optimistic and thrilled with Brad's honesty and efforts. Joan offered the only pleasant, welcoming facet of life that fall. It was as if all other doors were closed. So I went through the only one that was open.

When Joan asked if I'd like to drive upstate to an Indian reservation where Paul performed charity surgery, I accepted immediately. Ben agreed it would be good for me to get out of the neighborhood for a day and that the sitter expense was well worth it. Brad McMann had arranged a night appointment for the Bensons to see a house when we got back to Omaha. Ben said he'd meet us there and take me home.

Joan, Paul, and I started out on a brilliant fall day. I'd come mostly to enjoy the companionship, but Paul had challenged me to watch his surgery. "You'd faint like any little first-year nurse!"

I laughed at Paul's baiting; I'd already decided to keep my eyes closed while he operated.

Paul talked about his wooing and winning of Joan; I described Ben's unexpected proposal. Paul teased about women "keeping their place"; Joan and I pretended indignation. We were three people enjoying a pleasant drive and each other.

When the car began to sway and bump with a flat tire, Paul's happy mood changed abruptly. His brown hands tightened on the steering wheel. We pulled to the side of the country road. Both Paul and Joan showed more concern than seemed reasonable. We were way ahead of schedule and while a flat was an inconvenience, it couldn't be as tragic as the expression on Joan's face.

But I was to have another glimpse into the world of black Americans.

Joan's first words were, "You're *not* going to change that tire, Paul. It would be selfish." She explained to me that the sensitivity of a surgeon's hands is a matter of life or death during an operation; one cut or scratch on them could prove disastrous.

Paul demanded angrily that she suggest an alternative. Surgery was scheduled for ten o'clock. The staff couldn't stand over a sedated patient waiting for him to show up.

Joan said, "You'll have to flag a ride back to a gas station." I couldn't understand Paul's disgust with this sensible idea.

While I sat with Joan in the car, Paul waved at one driver after another. All whizzed past him. Finally, he stuck his head in the window. "See," he said. "Give me the trunk keys. I'll be careful."

Paul bent over the trunk, hauling out tire tools. A small truck was coming up the road. I walked out and waved frantically. The truck slowed and stopped. I called up to the driver, "Dr. Benson is on his way to do an emergency operation. Will you drive us to a gas station?" Before the driver, a blond man in farm overalls, finished nodding, I jumped in the truck as a kind of hostage to the man's hesitation. Joan called out she would come along to phone the hospital.

Paul walked over and shoved a bill into the man's hand.

Paul's brown face stunned him, but he pocketed the money and drove us to a garage a few miles back.

Joan and I returned in the jouncing jeep driven by a burly garageman in grease-stained overalls who apologized frequently for the bumpy, dirty ride. I talked rather frantically about "surgeon's hands."

When we reached Paul, who had already started removing the tire bolts, I watched the garageman's quick frown. He looked contemptuously at Paul, spotless and impeccable in a dark blue business suit. "This'll come to ten dollars, bud," he grunted, holding out his hand, its white skin grayed with ground-in dirt. Paul gave him a ten-dollar bill and added an extra two dollars "to hurry." The man hesitated, shrugged, and went to work.

Paul hurled the car over the last miles to the reservation hospital. We were all silent. Perhaps Joan and Paul had been sharing my pleasant fantasy at the start of our trip, that the problems of prejudice were far away. Now my fantasy was finished. Racism waited in unexpected places. Unexpected, at least, for me.

When Joan supervised my dressing and washing for the operating room, she said apologetically that Paul always agonized over delays on his way to surgery. Just before she tied the suffocating surgical mask on my face she said, "Paul's mother died because of a surgical delay. They wouldn't admit her at the white hospital and she died on the way to the Negro one."

When Paul came through another door with the reservation doctor, he moved in a loose, relaxed manner, swiftly and confidently. The green surgical gown and mask were more becoming to his coffee-colored skin than they were to the pink skin of the man with him. Paul waved to me and began a stream of conversation with the other doctor and with the two surgical nurses that was at once jocular and instructive. Joan whispered that Paul was trying to ease the operating-room tensions. I could see the two nurses and the young white doctor gradually relaxing under Paul's gentle joshing. The patient was an anonymous and silent mound of white sheets with a small amount of tan skin showing.

I did close my eyes when I saw Paul's knife touch the patient's skin. I could hear his voice, calm and easy, explaining what he was looking for and how they would decide whether the woman's gall bladder was to be removed. I peeked through one eye. Once the stomach-churning link with reality—the incision through human flesh—was over, I found I could watch. But as I looked, timidly at first and then with absorbing interest, I was totally unprepared for the growing sense of awe at what I was seeing. Paul stood over the patient as reverentially as a priest offering Mass. A nurse handed him the wrong instrument; he spoke firmly, but paternally, as if admonishing an altar boy.

During the uneventful drive home I tried to tell Paul and Joan what a beautiful and awesome experience Paul's surgery had been for me. Joan smiled in understanding and pride for her husband. Paul, under his usual drollery with me, seemed amused, but pleased by my new deference.

We continued to drive to the house Brad McMann was to show the Bensons. Ben was waiting for us. As I got out of the car, he told me angrily that he had just found out the owner of this house insisted Paul come *only after dark*.

All day long Paul and Joan had carried with them the knowledge of this insult. Perhaps they accepted the terrible contradiction. I couldn't. I will never forget the sight of Paul, who had just given freedom from pain and death to another human being, being hurried up a dark path and into a shade-drawn house—especially since I knew a notorious white racketeer lived a few houses away.

I remember nothing about that house; I remember only standing in its kitchen, staring at grease-stained wallpaper and a sagging breakfast bar. And I remember Paul suddenly standing in front of me and pushing my chin up to make me look at his smile.

"Look," he said, gesturing at the splattered, dirty kitchen. "This proves what I've always heard! Those white people sure don't keep up their property. Do they, Lois?"

Chapter Eight

On November 18, 1961, President John F. Kennedy went to Bonham, Texas, for the funeral of Sam Rayburn. If any prophet had told us that two years, four days, and sixty miles away from Bonham, President Kennedy would be assassinated, you and I would have pronounced the prophet mad. On a television program that fall, Joan, Paul, Ben, and I heard another young man speak who was also to be assassinated. Ben and I would hear the news of his death in circumstances as unexpected as all the other events ahead for America and our family. This young man was tall, slim, and confident. His audience punctuated his words with cheers. Paul asked what I thought of Malcolm X.

At first I wasn't sure. Malcolm X talked about "blue-eyed devils" and said with ominous emphasis that "black men must do *whatever necessary* for their freedom." He predicted coolly that "blood will run into the streets before black men are allowed to *be* men."

He said that in the seven years since the Supreme Court ordered schools integrated, only seven percent had complied. Will it take ninety-three more years, he demanded, before all schools are integrated? Forget integration with the blue-eyed devils, Malcolm X said; give us a separate state.

I asked Paul what the X stood for. It was, he said, a replacement for the "slave-name" most Negro people bore from their former owners. The *white* Benson family, Paul explained, were large landowners in his native Georgia; Paul's ancestors had once been owned by this family. I could understand the X.

And I thought I could understand this tall, slim, bespectacled man who talked with calm, direct, honest hatred about doing "whatever necessary" for freedom. His violent words, I believed, were designed to get attention, to frighten us "blue-eyed devils" into the action our conscience had never made us take. I thought about Jim Gibson with his double chins and jowly jaws. Could Malcolm X frighten Jim into compliance as Jim had frightened Mrs. Kozarik?

I told Paul I was impressed with Malcolm X. Paul grinned mischievously. Did I know that this man—born in Omaha, incidentally—was a former drug addict, pimp, and convict? Oddly, in a way, I was even more impressed. If, from a life like that, Malcolm X had become what we saw now, challenging, articulate, intellectually skillful, then he was an exceptional man. He could, I thought, accomplish even more in what I assumed would be his long life.

But I also assumed his warning of blood in the streets was as empty as the threats of the upper Lindley Road neighbors "to get Ben Stalvey's job." Ben had snorted when I first told him of the threat and had never mentioned it again. And I too felt that Ben's job was secure—until a clear warning signal flashed to us.

In December we had dinner at the home of George and Mitzi Bell, our best friends among corporation executives. George passed on to me some remarks of the president about Ben's lunches with Paul, and later he reminded us both about various men who had been transferred to unimportant jobs in out-of-the-way places because of "misbehavior."

Ben protested that these men had had severe personal problems—drinking, marital scandals, and such. George said that to the corporation our friendship with the Bensons was at least as "scandalous."

I listened, feeling as if the silk-papered walls of the Bell living room were toppling in on me. George was a conservative, cautious scientist, not given to overstatement. If he was concerned, there was something to be worried about.

I turned to Ben, next to me on the sofa. He worked so hard; he fought so many self-doubts; his success meant so much to him.

"Why didn't you stop me?" I asked.

Ben said quietly and slowly, "Because I didn't want you to stop."

It would be years before I learned the difference between eloquent passionate speakers who unfurl brotherhood speeches like flags and the quiet, stubborn men who work silently doing what can be done, but that night mixed with my panic came a new view of the man I married. Lincoln Steffens once said, "Morality is only moral if it's voluntary." Ben's morality was. Mine hadn't been. I had impulsively bumbled my way along, sure I was risking comparatively little. Ben had let me bumble, knowing what it would cost him.

Ben's hand felt strong and warm and I just sat holding it, looking up at him and thinking to myself, "You know, this man is going to keep on losing the car keys and complaining about expenses, but I just don't think I'm ever going to be able to get really mad at him again over anything little." After four months of guessing wrong, I made, it turned out, my only valid prediction.

This was the last evening we were ever to spend at the

Bells'. New friendships would absorb us and our time in Omaha was so much shorter than we knew.

Until now the Christophers and the Bensons had been our only Negro friends, but now our circle expanded. I was glad. Highly educated, affluent Negro couples were hardly typical of their group; Inez Robbins who cleaned for me each week was an employer-to-employee (not a social) relationship. Between a cleaning woman and a surgeon there were many black Americans I knew nothing about. But without Joan Benson's jolting criticisms of white women, making my next Negro friend might have taken longer.

Joan asked one day whether I would join the Urban League Guild, the Women's division of the League which was involved in fund-raising and other projects. She explained that the group was supposed to be interracial, but that there were very few white women members. I told Joan I would be pleased to join.

Joan then went on to explain that she wanted the Negro members to meet someone like me. Some of the other white women had "unsavory reasons" for their interracial activities. Oh? Like what? Well, Joan continued, some had bigoted husbands and unhappy marriages. They hit back by irritating their husbands with their interracial interests. Some failed to get status in their own groups and enjoyed a feeling of superiority in Negro groups.

"And just watch," she said, "how quickly the white members disappear after refreshments. The black women are *always* left to do the dishes alone."

That night, at the first Guild meeting, held in a YWCA branch in Omaha's ghetto, the four white women did indeed leave first. But without Joan's comment I might have done the same. The Negro women began to leave, too. I waved away Joan's help and finally everyone was gone except me and a tall, thin, extremely dark-skinned woman named Janet Adams.

I collected the cups and cake plates scattered around the room while I thought over the evening. At first it had seemed odd to be in a room of brown faces. There were so many different shades of brown—from beige to the color of rich strong coffee. But gradually the oddness faded as these Negro women indulged in the same familiar, boring discussions I'd yawned through in white groups—endless quibbling about what food to serve on what plates at which fund-raising tea. Even the personality types as they emerged seemed the same—the dominant, the shy, the stickler-for-detail, and the sulker.

There was also the plainly unpleasant, a Negro woman named Connie Williams. She was fat, wore large round spectacles, and had tiny clawlike hands. She looked like a raccoon when she munched her cake greedily. Her husband was a doctor, she said to me, and he worked with Paul. She heard I was trying to help the Bensons get a house. She'd like one, too—four bedrooms, a big yard, and they'd like to move in before Christmas. She gave me her order as if I had a stockpile of houses and was notoriously slow on delivery.

While I gathered up the dirty dishes, I reflected that although I believed Connie Williams had the *right* to live next door, I hoped she never did.

The president of the Guild, an (apparently) white woman had disturbed me, too, but in a different way. Joan said, yes, Ruth McPhetridge was Caucasian and seemed to be truly sincere. She was a slim woman with red-turning-gray hair, deep lines in her delicately constructed face, and beautiful aquamarine eyes. But her hair was pulled severely, almost defiantly, back into a bun and her chin was raised as if expecting a blow. She had welcomed me with the same cool suspicion as Grace Christopher showed when we met. But Ruth McPhetridge was white. What could have happened to make her aquamarine eyes so hostile?

Ruth McPhetridge had crashed a mound of dishes onto a tray, looked at her wrist watch, and announced she was late to her next meeting. Now as I carried the last of the dishes from the empty meeting room, I wondered how I would make conversation with Janet Adams, the almost *black*-skinned woman scraping and stacking the dishes in the tiny kitchen.

Janet Adams had given a report during the meeting as chairman of something called the Special Events Committee. Her report was brief, concise, and businesslike. For the rest of the meeting, I noticed she sat unsmiling, her head cocked to one side, her hands clasped in her lap. She seemed cold and aloof, not at all the kind of person I would have chosen for a companion over a pile of dishes.

She was also the most African-looking person I'd ever met. Grace Christopher, my first Negro friend, had Caucasian features; a thin nose, lips no fuller than mine, skin the sun-tan color white women work to achieve in the summer. Joan Benson could pass for white. But Janet Adams looked like pictures I remembered from the *National Geographic;* she might have come from Kenya. Her nose was broad and flat; her thick lips parted over purple gums; her blue-black hair was straight, but there were crinkly-kinky strands at her temples and the back of her head. Her skin was the color of fertile soil making her white teeth a distracting contrast.

And I realized suddenly that this was my chance for an emotional experiment I felt I had to make. Janet Adams was pure Negro, as different from me as was possible. Were there, after all, other differences? I decided I would talk with her, deliberately freeing myself from any *obligation* to accept her as equal. From the stack of dishes around us, it was apparent we would be together for some time.

I picked up a dish towel and, while we made small talk, I tried to react unself-consciously and honestly to this woman next to me. Yes, by my standards, she was unattractive. Her broad nose had large nostrils; her black hair looked stiff and oily; I had the urge to touch her dark skin to see if the brown rubbed off. The palms of her hands didn't match the rest of her; they were pink. As she handed me wet cups, the contrast of her brownness against the white china was an optical shock.

The next shock was finding Janet knew much more about me than I knew about her. In her low, melodic, and (I decided) trained speaking voice, she said she had heard I was trying to find a Negro teacher for my suburban school. Ken Hancock had talked to her about taking the job; she was a school teacher. By now, her meticulous grammar and pronunciation would have made me guess her occupation, but she continued, "I feel I owe you an explanation as to why I said no. It was not an easy decision."

She agreed that white suburban children would benefit from an interracial experience; she commended me for trying to help provide it. "But I feel my place is in the ghetto schools."

"Ghetto schools are unpopular with most teachers," she said, smiling ruefully. "Our children come from homes where their parents have had third-rate educations themselves." Added to this handicap, most of the homes have all the problems that discrimination and poverty can bring—from emotional strains to poor nutrition. "Our children are much harder to teach than . . ." She paused and I finished for her: ". . . the well-fed children of well-educated parents?"

Well, yes. And unfortunately, Janet continued, ghetto schools usually got the "most unwanted" teachers, the inexperienced young girls just out of college or the inferior teachers that white parents had managed to get transferred out of white schools.

"But even potentially good teachers get discouraged by all the problems and take their frustrations out on the children," Janet said. Her brown forehead wrinkled and her eyes looked pained. "Too many of our children are slapped by their teachers." Then she straightened and smiled at me. "I may not be anyone's idea of a great teacher, but I feel I've got to stay and try. I sincerely hope Ken can find someone else for you."

This alien-looking woman was speaking with compassion, not only for children, but for me, a white woman who with no thought at all would have taken a qualified teacher from where she was badly needed so that our suburban school could have the "latest equipment," a portable lesson in race relations. Ken Hancock never found a teacher for our school and I never urged him again.

Janet was telling me now that she was a widow, with no children, that her husband had died two years ago from a heart attack. Suddenly, the result of my emotional experiment hit me with a startling impact. I watched Janet's brown hands place dishes into my pink ones and the rhythm built up to a crescendo of understanding. That brown color. That's all it was. Inside the color was a woman, much like me, who had loved her husband as I loved Ben, who struggled with her sense of responsibility as I tried to do. Yet to real-estate people, to my neighbors, it made no difference who was inside that brown skin—greedy, gross Connie Williams, the Bensons, or Janet Adams.

And what if I had been born—just as I was—but inside a brown skin that would make people forever judge me at a glance and turn away. What if—no matter what I did—no one ever saw *me*, the me I knew I was. I would have the same problems white people face and are sometimes overwhelmed by, worries over love or money or health, but in addition I would have the burden of the prejudice of others. For one brief moment I thought I knew what it must be like to be locked inside a prison by white people who would never let me out.

When Janet Adams and I finally finished the dishes that night, it was the beginning of many things, our long friendship included. Janet asked me to be on her Special Events

Committee and I offered to have the next meeting at my house. There, among five other Negro women, I made a suggestion for a Special Event. Any of the women could have told me it was an impractical suggestion, but I suspect they felt it would be good for me to find out for myself.

With Christmas coming, I suggested we compile a list of Stores-of-Good-Will, stores which practiced fair employment, so we could all shop at these places. Janet said fine. Would I compile the list?

When I telephoned the manager of the first store he assured me his store qualified. They'd always practiced equal opportunity employment. Oh, yes. Put us on your list, he said. I was delighted. How many Negro sales people did they have, I asked him, and how many Negro executives?

Oh. Well. None at present.

How long had it been since they had had Negro executives or sales people?

Um. Well. He didn't know, but they did have five Negro employees in "other areas."

The five Negro employees were cleaning women.

With naïve sincerity I told this man his store didn't qualify, but that we would call him next year.

My innocence lasted through about two more phone calls, then the familiar pattern became apparent. Like my neighbors, no one was *against* equality; they just didn't practice it. Each personnel director or manager assured me he hired "all qualified applicants"; each voice vibrated with brotherhood. Until I asked, "How many?"

One man, manager of a local branch of a national chain, gave me his passionate speech about open employment and then, his admission that there were no Negro employees. In his dismay he burst out, "But if I hired one, all the white salespeople would quit."

I didn't have an answer for him and I had no names at all for my list, until I walked through Omaha's largest department store, Brandeis, which I had yet to phone. A brown-skinned woman approached me in the Infants' Department and sold me the shower gift I'd come for. I headed immediately for the Personnel Department. This was why I had thought of the idea in the first place. I knew I had seen Negro salespeople. I had simply not noticed where—or how seldom.

The personnel director told me, "We have a Negro man who is an assistant buyer, a woman assistant, several office workers, and five salespeople." He seemed pleased to tell me the story behind their employment policy. The president of the store had been impressed by the efficiency of a Negro stock girl, had tried her at saleswork, then as an assistant buyer. Other Negro women had been hired, several Negro men. They were, he said, more conscientious on the average than white employees for the unfortunate reason that jobs like this were darn scarce for Negro people.

I told him about the store manager who believed his white employees would quit if he hired "one."

He grinned. Yes, when the first Negro secretary was hired, a white secretary marched in to say she wouldn't "work with niggers."

"I told her she didn't have to. I'd accept her resignation immediately," he said. He gave me a mock-quizzical glance. "For some odd reason we had no complaints after that."

No, he could not tell me why other stores didn't practice the same policies. I left pleased and somehow proud. I had no idea that this case history would soon prove a severe burden to me. My Stores-of-Good-Will list, however, would include Brandeis, a jewelry store, and a paint store in the ghetto. Janet invited me to come to her house with my report.

In 1961, no one told me it was "dangerous" to drive alone at night into the center of an all-Negro area, and so, standing on Janet's doorstep, my thoughts were not on criminals lurking in the shrubbery; they were instead on how similar this area was to the neighborhood in which I had been raised. The houses were small, neat, close together like the homes in my German-American neighborhood. Janet's house, two-story stucco with a glassed-in porch, produced a wave of nostalgia; it was so much like the one I had grown up in.

Inside, the similarity ceased. I knew enough about antiques to see that Janet's were valuable, but I did not yet know why modest Negro homes often had lavish interiors. It would take me a while to learn that Negro families who are not allowed to buy the better and more expensive houses can afford interior luxury.

But that night all I thought of was that my Special Event was a failure. As if I had discovered some new truth, I told Janet that merchants had *lied* about equal employment! To Janet's eternal credit, she didn't laugh. She said only that the project had served an important purpose; stores were at least questioned.

But as Janet poured cup after cup of coffee for me, we drifted off into other subjects until we had both slipped off our shoes and were chatting as if we had known each other for years. We found several common interests: Theodore Dreiser's books, Judy Garland's records, and Chinese food.

Janet was very different from Joan and I could understand later why they were not close friends. Janet was brisk while Joan was gentle; Joan was wrapped up in Paul, the children, and her house hunt, while Janet had her work and a house she was completely satisfied with. Soon, Janet confided her only problem—indecision over whether to marry Warren Platt, the black army officer she had been dating for over a year. I offered advice; I had felt undecided about marrying Ben until I realized my parents' divorce gave me a fear of deep, permanent commitments. Janet agreed that her husband's death might have caused this same fear in her. We were talking as comfortably and intimately as I talked with my oldest friends. Until we talked about her childhood.

Since then, I have often wondered about the strange silence Negro people maintained for years. Those I had met while growing up had allowed me to continue my fantasy about "liberty and justice for all." The stock girl at the department store where I had worked after high school, the Negro team-mates of my beau, Mike—none of them had tapped me on the shoulder to say, "Listen, things are bad!" My education would have begun so much earlier. Perhaps the reason for the silence was because human beings can share deep hurts only with friends.

That night I remarked casually to Janet that I had spent most of my teen years dancing in the park pavilions Mil-waukee opened to its teen-agers. Janet said that the state of Missouri hadn't even allowed Negro children in the skating rinks, movies or parks.

"We'd walk for hours to find a field where no one would chase us. And in the winter, we went to church. Not for pray-ing, particularly!" She laughed. But because church was the only place they could go. "We attended every and any meet-ing held in the church. I heard speakers on forestry, fudge-making, and Fiji! It had its advantages. Our parents knew exactly where we were and none of us got into any trouble."

Then Janet's face shadowed. "Except for Sammy," she said, almost to herself.

"Sammy," she said, "was a boy who would now be diag-nosed as retarded. He was big for his twelve years and very, very slow. I sat in front of him all the way through the first six years of school and tried to keep him out of trouble. Sammy trusted everyone. One day in 1936, he wandered over to a crowd of white people downtown who were gathered around . . . I never did know what . . . but as Sammy crowded in to get a look, a white girl yelled that he had touched her hip. I'm sure he hadn't. All young black men are taught not even to look at white girls and even Sammy knew that much."

Janet sat across the sofa from me, looking down at her skirt, smoothing it, talking to her own hands.

"The crowd turned on Sammy. I ran home as I was told to do when there was any trouble with white people. Mother called my brothers and sister and we stayed in the house with the shades down.

"That night, Sammy's parents and his eight-year-old brother came in our back door and hid in the basement. Sammy had been hanged from a tree outside his house. The mob set his body on fire. They said he should not be cut down. He was to hang there as a lesson. I remember understanding then why my mother had pulled down our window shades and why Sammy's family were hiding in our basement."

Janet continued, speaking very softly and slowly. "I remember Sammy's mother trying to stifle her crying, but what I remember most is Sammy's eight-year-old brother. He didn't cry. He just sat there with the coldest, hardest face I've ever seen on a child. The crowd had made him witness the lynching."

Janet sat silent for a minute. Then, as if to brush away the memory, she whisked her hand across her skirt and raised her head. "Sammy's family left town early the next morning. Later, some decent white people arranged to have the body cut down; they even paid for the burial. But I've always wondered whatever happened to Sammy's brother."

Janet filled my coffee cup and said, "You know, I never thought I could tell these things to a white person." I wanted to say that she should have told them earlier and often to whites, but all I could do was shake my head and say stupidly that I was sorry.

Janet plunged into the rest of her history to give me a chance to recover. With an attempt at gaiety, she said she had worked at a country club as a waitress to earn college tuition. "The clubwomen kept telling me, 'Why go to college? I'll pay you whatever you want as a cook!' " Janet said. "I saved some Missouri family from chronic indigestion—I'm an awful cook—by getting my B.A. at Omaha U. Met my husband and settled here." She missed him terribly, but had filled her life with teaching.

But no matter how gaily she talked, recovering from her story of Sammy was impossible. It had triggered half-buried memories of lynchings I had read about long ago—of Emmett Till, a fourteen-year-old black child lynched as late as 1955. No Negro mob ever murdered a white child. White people committed these atrocities and kept doors closed to neighborhoods and jobs. When Janet was a child, it was my people who kept her out of parks and movies and restaurants—and murdered her classmate. And yet it was *my* group who viewed *hers* with suspicion and fear.

I interrupted her with my question, "After what you've seen, why don't you hate white people?" I gestured at the coffee cup. "How can you even be civil to me?"

She was sitting straight now and she put out her feet in front of her, looking at her toes instead of me. "We can't afford to hate," she said. "If my people ever gave in to hate, we'd have room for nothing else."

It was not a satisfactory answer. The man I had heard on television—Malcolm X—had given in to his hate. Wasn't facing strong emotions healthier?

No, Janet said, this kind of hate would destroy the Negro. Things were getting better, she said, almost heatedly. Bitterness was too expensive. Had I observed Ruth McPhetridge, the white president of the Guild, Janet asked. Ruth McPhetridge had become so bitter that she accomplished little. Ruth's schoolteacher husband had been denied promotions because of Ruth's running battle with the school board and the mayor over discrimination. "She's a wonderful woman," Janet said, "but she's made herself useless through her own anger."

Janet looked at me with a level, direct gaze and said, "Ruth is a lesson for you too, Lois."

That evening, the gulf between my personality and Ruth's seemed so wide that I hardly caught Janet's implication. I had seen Ruth and talked with her several times since the first Urban League Guild meeting and found she was a brilliant woman. She would reel off statistics and dates on school discrimination; she had described the current fight for a Fair Employment Practices Ordinance as efficiently as an attorney. I could see no comparisons—now or in the future—between Ruth McPhetridge and me. Janet, I felt, was paying me a compliment by comparing us in any way at all.

Within a few days Janet paid me what I felt was a more realistic compliment. She invited Ben and me to a birthday celebration for her friend, Warren Platt. We were the only white people there and we had been invited without the Bensons. We were there as Janet's friends.

Her party, which turned out to be the official announcement of her engagement to Warren, was also another strange optical experience at first. In Janet's dimly lit recreation room, all those brown faces were nearly indistinguishable. But then I began talking to those brown faces. One woman was a lawyer, the first female lawyer of any color I had ever met; she was fascinating and friendly. An officer colleague of Warren's described his quartermaster duties in endless boring detail. Gradually, the strangeness of brown skin disappeared as personalities replaced appearances. When I glanced at Ben, talking with Warren Platt across the room, Ben now looked conspicuously pale. Then I passed a mirror and was startled by the other odd-looking pink blob among the tones of brown.

Later Warren Platt, a big, gently smiling man whose eyes seldom left Janet, showed me one stereotyped notion I still retained. Warren asked me to dance and I accepted eagerly. When 250 pounds of Warren crunched on my toes, I felt an additional crunch of disappointment. Then I could laugh at myself. Sammy Davis, Jr., and Bill "Bojangles" Robinson were apparently no more typical of their race than Fred Astaire was of mine—but I had truly expected all Negro men to be good dancers.

I smiled bravely up at Warren—and dodged his feet with my white-Protestant natural sense of rhythm!

Chapter Nine

The month of December 1961 was like a landslide for us. Small rocks I had dislodged months before gained momentum; now, inside and around me, everything was moving too fast to stop. In mid-December we heard the rumbles; when the month had ended, we felt the crash.

December began happily with a new friendship, Warren Platt, Janet's army captain beau. Warren and I had become instant friends, largely because I was his wholehearted supporter in his campaign to marry Janet soon. It was obvious that he worshipped her and, to me, Janet deserved no less. But Warren had other attributes in addition to his adoration of Janet. Like Ben, he combined strength and sensitivity. Warren looked like a recruiting poster (black version) promising exuberant physical fitness through army life; he was well over six feet tall and carried his muscular body with grace. But he treated all women as if they might break if he raised his voice full volume or shook hands too hard. His own hands were unexpectedly slender for such a big man. Janet told me he had wanted to be a violinist, but a music teacher in his segregated Texas school pointed out that there were no black members of symphony orchestras, let alone black soloists. And so Warren took one of the few possible routes out of Southern poverty; he had joined the army at eighteen, had finally been trained as an engineer, and was now one year from retirement.

Our friendship with Warren was to be pathetically short. After Janet's party we had gone to a jazz place in the ghetto. (We had all laughed at Warren's patient boredom; he preferred Beethoven.) In the next weeks we had gone out to dinner together and, one evening, to a movie. My last conversation with Warren took place at our house where we had come back for coffee.

That night's conversation was an example of the pattern we would find so often with Negro friends. There was always the testing of us at first—the silent observing, the oblique questions, the waiting for unconscious slips of the tongue or stereotypes of thought. When the tester felt satisfied, it was as if a dam suddenly burst. Caution changed into sudden confidences, personal and moving. Sometimes I worried that the confidences came too rapidly; many times I wondered if I deserved them.

Something like that was happening with Warren that night. He began describing his army life and told me, first, as a joke on himself, about his first trip home after enlistment. "Here I was, feeling big in my brand new uniform. I got off the bus in that Texas depot and walked right through the regular door—*not* the door marked 'Colored'—and I got grabbed and shoved right back out the door, brand new uniform and all."

Warren could laugh at the memory, but he talked with a special happiness of his duty in Europe—in France, England, Germany. "On those European streets I was just an American man. Nobody saw anything but the uniform." Only back in the barracks, he said, shyly now but wanting to express it, was he treated as a Negro.

Yet I knew he was planning to live in America when he retired from the army. Janet told me he had the promise of a job with a New York engineering consultant, but he had also been offered a job by a German firm.

I asked Warren why he didn't stay in Europe.

Warren hitched his chair closer as if to tell me a secret. I can never forget this big man, army-trained, trying to articulate his feelings. Oh, he said, he thought about staying in Europe, thought a lot about it. They needed engineers; they wanted him to stay; he could have lived real well there.

Then he said, "But you know, I got to thinking. America began because those people in Europe wanted something better than what they had. A whole lot of them came *here*. Well, what we've got—our ideas about democracy—maybe haven't worked yet the way they should. But they will someday."

He said maybe this sounded like a lot of flag-waving, but he added, "When we've got America going the way it was supposed to go, we're really going to have something here. Something a lot better than what they have in Europe."

This big, gentle man had shown me there was no comparison between his patriotism and mine. It was easy for me to love a country that loved me back; he loved America so much he could forgive it.

That night Warren deftly switched the conversation to happy memories of European cities. He named Karlsruhe, Germany, his favorite city. Why, that was my grandfather's birthplace! I'd never talked with anyone who had been there and now it seemed sentimentally appropriate that Warren loved it too. Warren was like my grandfather; stubbornly patient and sure that promises would be kept. Warren promised to find some pictures of Karlsruhe and give them to me.

For a while it looked as if December 1961 would be the happy ending to an eventful year. I saw a brand-new For Sale sign on a house I thought Joan might like. It was in an older, more expensive suburb that adjoined ours; a low red-brick ranch house with large grounds and mature shrubbery for attractive privacy. Brad McMann made the appointment and Joan asked me to come with them.

C. Courtney Sells met us at the door of his house. He was a handsome man in his fifties with extra pounds only beginning to blur his good looks. The rough silk shirt he wore was the same beige color as his light hair into which gray blended attractively. He had ice-blue eyes and his heavy gold signet ring caught the light as he smoothed his hair.

He was, Brad told us, a realtor himself, chairman of the realtors' ethics committee and also a member of the school board.

The room into which he graciously welcomed us was decorated with gleaming mahogany and brocade. It looked like pictures I had seen of rooms in Williamsburg, Virginia, with colonial candlesticks, Chippendale chairs, and a magnificent Oriental rug with intricately woven reds, blues, and yellow. In the middle of this period room was a modern upholstered chair with magazines—I could see *Fortune* and *Playboy* in the stack—piled next to it.

C. Courtney Sells introduced us to his wife, Martha, a thin, small woman who came out from the back of the house with tiny hurried steps. If Courtney Sells recognized Joan's name or color, it didn't seem to disturb him. He guided us, charmingly, informatively, around the house, explaining that "I built it to last my lifetime" but that, with the children married, it had become too large. Mrs. Sells trailed after us, injecting apologies for several bare rooms whose furniture had already been moved to their new apartment.

A disarming honesty made me feel that Mr. Sells was a nice person. He pointed out that the family room was hard to heat and after heavy snows one of the window wells leaked a bit. But I could see Joan loved this house. She was already deciding, I thought, where to place the Queen Anne table now squeezed in almost out of sight in her tiny living room.

Mrs. Sells felt Joan's delight. "And if you like them, I can leave all the draperies for you," she said.

Courtney Sells cut her off, smiling. "No, dear. They have to be extra. But I can give you immediate occupancy." They were moving next Tuesday whether or not the house was sold. At the door, C. Courtney Sells told us good-bye with a bland, neutral expression, but his ice-blue eyes searched Joan's face trying, I thought, to appraise her reaction. That was easy: Joan could hardly control her enthusiasm.

I remember the three of us—Joan, Brad McMann, and I—sitting in Brad's car outside the long, low, solid-looking house with its snow-coated shrubbery while Joan literally bubbled. I remember it because I sat in my car in the same spot just a few hours later, crying and pounding the steering wheel. But now, Joan told me how much she loved this house. Would I talk to them and explain so that Paul could come to see it?

Our plan—that I would talk with the owner, listen to any misgivings about selling to a Negro family and then, we hoped, persuade them—seemed unnecessary with a man like Courtney Sells. He hardly seemed like the kind of man to fear any bigoted neighbor; he was obviously civic-minded—he served as a member of the school board. And he was successful, affluent. Hadn't Brad said Courtney Sells was chairman of the realtors' ethics committee?

Brad thought it wouldn't hurt for me to talk with him; Joan said please let's not take any chances. I agreed to call the Sellses and, with the excuse of taking some measurements for a mythical grand piano, come back to see them alone.

That evening Courtney Sells welcomed me with an almost flirtatious warmth. He hoped Mrs. Benson would like the house, but he asked, smoothing his hair, where did I live? He held my arm as he led me to a wing chair opposite the incongruously modern chair that was obviously his. Martha Sells came from the kitchen.

I traced the pattern on the Oriental rug with my eyes, planning how to introduce the subject of the Bensons' color. I felt silly; it probably didn't matter to this self-assured, sophisticated man.

C. Courtney Sells helped me. "What does Mr. Benson do?" he asked.

Sitting across from him I could look directly into Mr. Sells's eyes and he didn't even blink when I said, "*Doctor* Benson— Dr. Paul Benson." With no change of expression at all, Courtney Sells said, "Oh, yes. I've worked with Dr. Benson on the Cancer drive."

I relaxed with relief. Courtney Sells showed no shock. His pleasant smile never dimmed. The Bensons' long search for a home was obviously over now. But as chairman of the realtors' ethics committee, perhaps this wonderful man would want to know how difficult it was for a Negro family to buy a house in Omaha. I told him some of the problems the Bensons had encountered.

Courtney Sells shook his head in sympathy, his signet ring gleaming as he resmoothed his hair. Prejudice, he said, feelingly, was certainly a deep cancer in our "land of the free." Had the Bensons tried out North?

Oh, well, they didn't have to now. Joan Benson was in love with this house and sure that Paul would be just as enthusiastic.

C. Courtney Sells's smile never lost its warmth as he said it was truly unfortunate that they were unable to sell the house. They just couldn't find a suitable apartment.

In total confusion, I turned to Mrs. Sells who was sitting in a small straight chair near the fireplace. Her head down, she was twisting her wedding ring. Her knuckles looked white.

Courtney Sells got up from his chair, still smiling pleasantly. He hoped the Bensons would find a house; terribly nice people. His ice-blue eyes looked directly into mine and

I thought I saw challenge. He knew I knew he was lying—and he also knew there was nothing I could do about it.

I don't remember being handed my coat. I remember only walking across the snowy street to my car and sitting inside, banging my fists on the steering wheel in impotent rage. I had been lied to as easily as if I were a child, and with a child's helplessness I had to accept the lie. Courtney Sells hadn't even bothered to make it plausible.

That night I was too full of my own frustration and Joan's disappointment to wonder why Courtney Sells refused to sell his house to Joan and Paul. I still wonder. He must have known nothing would happen to real estate values. He could hardly have believed any of the myths; he knew and worked with Paul on civic committees. He was a powerful, invulnerable man. The only conclusion I have ever reached is that he reacted instinctively with what was *easiest*. By refusing to sell he would save time—no explanation to friends, no setting of precedents, no possible complications. A smart man like Courtney Sells would never stop at the scene of an accident.

Breaking the news to Joan seemed so dreadful. I sat there, unable to drive away from the house she couldn't have. Finally, I realized that prolonging Joan's hopes could only make her disappointment worse and that I had to tell her now. At their house, Joan and Paul, ironically, comforted *me*. There would be other houses, they said; I should not get that upset over only a house. I couldn't explain my feelings. Humiliation and helplessness and grief were all mixing together; powerful Courtney Sells symbolized something other than one more house.

But I did feel we had played fair long enough. I asked Paul that night why Ben and I couldn't simply buy a house for them and turn it over. No. Paul wanted to do it "the right way." Other young black men watched what he did; he felt he had to do things "right." But why play fair when your opponent cheats? Paul said, "Someone has to keep following the rules."

It was only a few days later that Ben told me the strange story of a contract that had come to his desk to be co-signed. In reading it over he found that it was an agreement with a radio station in Oklahoma to promote a bowling contest, and it stated clearly: for *white* bowling alleys *only*. Ben had taken the contract to his immediate superior, Jake Suppan. This clause violated the new interstate commerce law, Ben told Jake. Also, keeping Negro bowlers out of the contest was not only illegal but poor business. Why not increase sales among Negro consumers too?

Jake Suppan was an elderly, cautious man serving out the last year until retirement. As usual, he made no decision and no comments. Ben saw him hustling into the president's office. When Ben asked about it the next day, Jake snapped, "It's out of your hands. Forget about it." Through his secretary, Ben learned that Jake's typist had mailed out cancellations for the entire promotion. Advertising material already prepared was being wastefully scrapped. Ben was irritated. No matter what his private convictions were, he fumed to me, this was an expensive, impractical business decision.

Much as my fears were growing over Ben's status at the office, I agreed that he had had no choice. A few days later I would make a choice, too. We have never known which one cost Ben his job. Janet Adams asked me to go with her to a City Council hearing on a proposed Fair Employment Practices Ordinance. White faces, she said, were needed in the audience. At the door of the hearing room in the City Hall, Janet introduced me to a short, chubby Negro man from the Department of Labor. He gave Janet the latest statistics on how many black men had lost their jobs because of the new automation at the packing plants. This hurt everyone, he said, glancing significantly at me. Janet must have sensed my puzzlement. Automation, she explained, eliminated the unskilled labor jobs largely held by Negro workers. Company profits increased through automation, but, as taxpayers, we paid for the company's "waste product," the unemployed men now on welfare rolls.

The stout little man from the Labor Department turned smilingly to me. "Now don't you forget that anyone can testify. If you think of something, you just walk right up and get recognized."

At that moment nothing seemed less likely than my speaking before the City Council. However, I was glad I had come; the crowded hearing room was indeed filled mostly with Negro people. Seated next to Janet now, I listened as heads of various civic groups read statements. Ken Hancock presented the Urban League statement; Ruth McPhetridge, president of the Urban League Guild, read hers. Her aquamarine eyes glinted angrily at a bland, disinterested-looking man who apparently represented the opposition. Several ministers testified.

Then, the president of the City Council, an elderly man, with a deep growly voice, asked for statements opposing the bill. The bland-looking man to whom Ruth McPhetridge had directed her caustic looks walked to the microphone to announce he was the legal counsel for a group of business firms opposing the FEPC law. He read a list of names; I recognized some of the stores I had telephoned during my futile Stores-of-Good-Will project. Ben's employer was also named in this list. The lawyer, a young man in his thirties, explained earnestly that his clients were sympathetic to fair employment and practiced it *without* an ordinance.

Janet and I exchanged cynical glances.

Then he continued, sincerely and smoothly, saying that any law *forcing* them to hire minority groups would bring about unbearable hardships. "This," he said, "would result, unfortunately, in the loss of white employees and, in many cases, of white customers."

While he talked on I whispered to Janet, "What about Brandeis?" Janet whispered, "Go ahead."

I wish I could say that I prepared to go to the railing to be recognized, but I didn't. Instead, I sat there, terrified. It wasn't the danger to Ben's job; Ben would want me to do what was right. It was simply that I was afraid of speaking unprepared and in front of the City Council. I would stumble and stutter and make a fool of myself. My legs were already shaking; I couldn't talk in front of lawyers and councilmen. I hadn't even known much about the FEPC ordinance until that night. I looked around desperately, hoping to see someone else approach the railing. The lawyer talked on. Perhaps the council president would just end the hearing after he spoke. Maybe the story of Brandeis wasn't important anyway; not important enough for me to risk making some humiliatingly inept attempt to tell it.

But I knew it *was* important. The plea on which this attorney based his opposition was proved invalid by the facts given me by the personnel director at the Brandeis store. And Brandeis was one of the largest, most successful business firms in Omaha.

The lawyer had stopped speaking now and I heard the City Council president ask for more testimony. In the pause that followed, my thoughts raced as fast as my heart. Was this where I stopped? Until now, none of the actions I had taken had been painful. The *results* had been, but the actions—looking for a Negro teacher, talking with Mrs. Kozarik about her house, phoning employment managers, approaching Courtney Sells—had all been easy for me to do. Did I stop when something became personally uncomfortable?

Suddenly, it was very lonely in that crowded hearing room. There seemed to be just two people there—me and the person I was going to find out I was.

The president's growly bass voice said, "Well, if there's no more testimony . . ." and I found myself on my feet, walking to the railing as if my body had taken over the decision. I can even remember hoping desperately that the president wouldn't see me in the crowd and would declare the hearing officially over.

But he saw me and suddenly there was a microphone in front of my lips and a wavering voice which I assumed was mine began to speak. I don't remember a thing I said. When I heard applause from the audience, I knew I must have finished. Only then do I remember turning to the lawyer and saying with a poise that came from knowing the ordeal was over, "*Now* . . . you can tell your clients that fair employment is *perfectly safe*."

I walked back to my seat through smiling faces that said nice things and hands that shook mine. I felt exactly as I had as a child when I rode my two-wheeled bike for the first time —astounded that I had done it and very, very pleased.

When Ben called from the office one afternoon three weeks later, I remember distinctly how I felt then, too. His voice sounded dazed. "Jake just told me I had to take a transfer to Philadelphia or resign," he said. Ben had interviewed men for this job with the newly-acquired Philadelphia branch and we both knew it was to last only during a two-year transitional period. It would not only be a demotion but a delayed dismissal. Yet hearing the shock in Ben's voice made me calm. I felt my stomach tighten, but my mind shut out everything except what to do five minutes at a time.

"I don't think we should discuss this on the phone," I said. "Can you come home?"

"Yes," he said.

When I hung up I realized it was nothing to discuss at home, either—not in front of the children. I got dressed, phoned a sitter, and while I waited for Ben looked up Philadelphia in the *World Book*. Over coffee in a drugstore, Ben told me what had happened. The three lines between his eyebrows were deeper than I had ever seen them and his face was gray.

"Jake called me in and said I could take the Philadalphia job or quit. Just like that." Ben shook his head as if to wake himself from a bad dream. "Then Jake asked if I wanted to quit. He acted as if he expected me to."

Jake Suppan would give no explanation for the abrupt demotion. "He said he 'was not at liberty' to discuss it. And he just kept asking if I didn't want to quit." Ben gazed through me as he spoke, trying to make sense of something that had no logic. "I told him I had to think it over."

Ever since Ben's phone call, I realized we had no choice. If Ben quit in indignation he would be stuck in a small town with limited possibilities. Philadelphia was a big city, only ninety miles from New York and much better for job hunting. Uprooting our family was something I would think about later.

That moment in the drugstore, however, Ben's dazed look of defeat was my biggest concern. "Why?" he repeated over and over. I think we had both expected some warning, some get-back-in-line-or-else. Suddenly, Harriet and Irv Fischer seemed to be the people we should talk with. If Harriet's predictions had indeed come true, perhaps she and Irv knew what we ought to do next.

Irv Fischer had grown up in the toughest section of New York. In his fifty years he must have seen things that made our dilemma mild. As a Jew, he knew the nuances of discrimination Ben and I had never had to learn. Irv was sympathetic as Ben described what happened, but far from shocked. He may even have felt a kindly amusement that it could happen to WASPs too.

"Well, they shot you down, didn't they!" he said, smiling

sardonically. Irv had not a minute's doubt as to what happened and why.

All right, but I still couldn't understand why they hadn't warned Ben . . . told him to stop and to stop me . . . or else.

Irv laughed. The corporation was handling it very cleverly, he said. They sold a consumer product and there was always the chance that Ben could create a public issue if he were threatened. No, someone was being very smart. This way they could fire him over refusal to accept an assignment, or, if he accepted the Philadelphia job, fire him there after "a decent interval." It would be quiet, neat, and unprovable. Ben should go to Philadelphia; finding a new job in the East would be easier.

Harriet did not say to me "I told you so!" But she looked at me as if I were her daughter, illegitimately pregnant. I had done what she warned me against. (A few months later she resigned in protest from a program for handicapped youngsters that excluded Negro children. Several of Irv's clients were on the committee; he lost their business; Harriet had stopped taking her own advice.)

When we left the Fischers' I began the most concentrated lying I had ever attempted. I *wanted* to move to Philadelphia, I told Ben. I chattered on about everything I had read in the *World Book*—Independence Hall, Benjamin Franklin, theaters, zoos, museums. It was a much better place to raise our children than this populated cornfield. I knew nothing about big city school problems or any big city problems. I knew only that if I talked enough Ben might believe me. I might believe me too.

Paul and Joan didn't. Paul shook his head when we told them about Ben's "promotion" to the Philadelphia job. "No," he said, "I know what happened." In that moment, Paul looked more brutally hurt than we could ever be. "I did this to you," he said. "Oh Lord, when will I learn that I only destroy my friends?" He sat in his living room, his head

— 109 —

in his hands. Joan was torn between comforting us and Paul. "Yes, it's happened before," she said. White friends were suddenly transferred out of town.

We made a strange scene; Joan with her arm around Paul, me gabbling away about Benjamin Franklin, big city museums, and Ben's "wonderful future."

The next day a newscast made Paul's anguish and Ben's job crisis seem minor in our lives. Over the kitchen radio I heard the calm impersonal voice of an announcer reporting that "Captain Warren Platt, age thirty-seven, tried to save the lives of two of his men at Offutt Air Base who had backed their crane into a power line." Captain Platt, the voice continued, threw himself at the men to push them out of the way of the falling line. The men were saved, but Captain Platt, a native of Texas, was killed.

I telephoned Joan, hoping there was some mistake. No, Paul had gone out there. He was with Janet now. Yes, the two men Warren saved were white.

In the mail, the next morning, I received the photos of Karlsruhe that Warren had promised to send.

Chapter Ten

Now, looking back, it is clear that I spent the last months in Omaha trying to make myself a moving target against my emotions; keeping too busy, physically and intellectually, to feel. All I could give Ben was my pretense of optimism. Over and over again, I predicted this would turn out to be the greatest stroke of luck we had ever had. I thought I was lying, but Ben began to act as if he believed me. Watching Janet Adams' gallantry in her grief over Warren's death drained off any of my self-pity. She had lost two men she loved and she went on. I could, too, but not passively.

Ben would be leaving for Philadelphia soon. I would remain in Omaha until Brad McMann sold our house. I knew then I wanted to organize the same kind of Panel of American Women I had heard nine months ago at Harriet's synagogue luncheon. This panel of housewives—Jewish, Negro, white Protestant, Catholic—had awakened me from complacency; it might be a small legacy to leave behind. I wrote to Esther Brown, the Kansas City housewife who created the panel. She would help me but before I left Omaha I would get one more lesson in prejudice. I would discover an old, venomous bigotry in myself and, finally, understand its construction.

Esther Brown answered my request for advice by coming to Omaha. A bubbly, beautiful brunette, tiny and dynamic, she was thrilled that her panel had moved me to action, but a bit dismayed that I had apparently managed to create a family calamity. She was nevertheless encouraging and helpful about my forming an Omaha panel before I left town. "You can do it," she said. The key was finding sincere women who could speak honestly about their own experiences and feelings. "Empathy, not expertise, is the important quality."

In that case, the Omaha panel was half completed. Harriet would be the Jewish panelist; Joan the Negro. When Janet's grief over Warren's death abated a bit it might be good for her to fill empty evenings alternating with Joan.

Finding a white Protestant panelist was solved when I met Jane Fuller. Jane was the kind of WASP I knew must exist all over America. Jane had heard about the events on upper Lindley Road. She had once called me to ask how she could help. Yes, she would be a panelist, if I thought she would do.

Until it came to selecting the Catholic panelist—until I was dressing to keep the appointment Paul had made for me with Sister Mary Rita—I had believed I was uninformed but also unprejudiced. Now there was something about my abrupt movements as I dressed, an impatience, and, when I looked in the mirror, a grimness around my mouth. So? At least I was doing it, wasn't I? The panel "required" a Catholic and I was "willing" to get one—*no matter how ridiculous and destructive the Catholic Church was.*

A year ago I would not have wanted—or needed—to examine my feelings about Catholics. And I might not have been able to. But now I remembered Esther Brown's words: "honest, sincere women" were necessary for the panel. If I were presumptuous enough to select them, I'd better be honest myself.

All right. How *did* I feel about Catholics? Joan and Paul were Catholic, but I "allowed" them the eccentricity. I felt pity toward individual Catholics; the Church brainwashed them young. Yes, my hostility was directed not at the people but at the Catholic Church itself. But my hostility, I believed that day, was no prejudice; it was knowledge. The Catholic Church demanded blind obedience to rules that could ruin lives; it locked people into unhappy marriages, forced women to have baby after baby, put ritual ahead of reason or humanity. As for nuns, they were maladjusted, unattractive women, afraid of marriage or unable to find a mate. And this wasn't prejudice; all this was fact.

My next question seemed harmless enough. It was only the second step in analyzing a thought: Where had I acquired these facts? Suddenly, I was blustering and sputtering. Why, I'd always known them! Everybody did. They were true because . . . Well, everyone knew they were true.

Good heavens! At that moment I felt like a temperance worker suddenly realizing she's drunk. This was exactly what prejudice was: "knowledge" based on beliefs "everyone" holds, on unexamined emotions solidly rooted in—nothing. I was as much a victim of prejudice as those people I deplored on upper Lindley Road. Their "knowledge" and dislike of Negro people came from the same source as my beliefs about the Catholic Church.

The only reason embarrassment or, worse, defensiveness, didn't stop me cold was because I knew I could be my own guinea pig. If I could dissect my prejudice about Catholics, the anatomy of prejudice itself might come clear. I might be able to understand what had happened in the past months.

But I was about to understand something quite different. Exploring my antipathy toward the Catholic Church was like opening a closet. Inside, I had hidden more than religious prejudice. It was all tangled up, the good with the bad. I had wanted to hide some thoughts and memories and in so doing I had had to hide them all.

First came my admission that I had not learned about Catholicism from Catholics. Yes, some-of-my-best-friends-were-Catholics, but, as with Joan and Paul, I avoided the subject. My opinions were too strong to risk exposure. My "knowledge" had come, I knew now, from my mother and my grandparents, in small pieces all my life. And my father, my absent Catholic father, was inextricably tied in.

That afternoon, staring out at the Omaha snowdrifts from our bedroom window, stories from my German-Lutheran childhood flooded back. The priest who married my parents had "forced" my mother to sign papers promising to raise her children as Catholics. I had been "dragged" to a priest by my paternal grandmother who "frightened your poor mother to death" by saying I looked sickly and should be baptized before I died. Later, I was told that my father "could commit any sin he wanted, confess, and go right back to sinning." After enough sins, Mother divorced him and, from the age of three, I was raised according to Martin Luther. To my grandfather, the German monk, Luther, had been right about the Catholic Church; my father proved it.

My father went back to his family in La Porte, Indiana. I was told that he stayed out of Wisconsin to avoid paying child-support for my brother and me; that he was "lazy, dishonest, and wanted to get rich without working." I had vague memories of having seen him when I was five or six. At eighteen I made the trip to La Porte to meet him.

We found each other in the La Porte train station only because we were the last two people left. An hour after I met this stranger who was my father, I felt I understood the divorce completely. Dad was a tall, red-faced man, uninhibited, profane, violently and loudly bigoted against Jews, Negroes, Democrats, and my grandfather. He apparently lived by his wits. As we drove through town he pointed out people on whom he had "put one over." "Sold that man some lake property in winter," Dad said. "Damn fool never knew till spring how far the water came in." He pointed to a farmer. "Sold him a *pedigreed* cow." Dad laughed and winked. Marriage to my quiet, conventional mother must have been like a mating between Billy the Kid and Emily Post.

Arguments between Dad and me began almost immediately. Dad was exuberant in his prejudices and when I fought back he would cheerfully expand his fables about "race," religion, or Roosevelt. On one of my visits he took me to Mass. The priest, an old man, preached a sermon that might have come from the anti-Semitic Father Coughlin in the 1930s. I refused indignantly ever to go to church with him again. It seemed logical, of course, to judge international Catholicism after listening to one Indiana priest.

My father died a sudden and lonely death in a car accident when I was twenty-five. After the funeral, at which I could not cry, the ancient priest said to me, "He was a good man; he came to Mass every Sunday." Oh, how I had tended my bitterness over those words for years! My father left two children, not knowing or caring what happened to us, but to the priest he was a good man: he came to Mass every Sunday!

That day in Omaha, sitting on the bed, all my hatred of the Catholic Church swelled up at the memory of those words. And then, of course, I knew where the hatred really belonged: it was the love-hate of a child toward the father who left her and didn't seem to care. I couldn't face my anger at my father; I locked it up in the closet with his Church.

But I had locked all my love for him up in that closet too. Suddenly and for the first time I could look at him and try to understand this man and, perhaps, parts of myself. Yes, we had argued heatedly, but Dad gaily accepted my opposition. He had those big dreams, none of which came true, but he could point with honesty to all his failures as he drove through La Porte: the restaurant, the movie house, the gas station that hadn't worked out. Maybe part of his dream was to come back to us with treasures, to prove to my mother that she was wrong. Pridefully, she had never asked him for money. Was it possible he thought we didn't need him? Did he think *we* were the ones who didn't care?

I had opened the closet to examine my prejudice toward Catholics and found that a childhood hurt could now begin to heal. That afternoon I did not rush to Sister Mary Rita ready to become a convert, but at least I *knew* I knew nothing about the Catholic Church. I had carefully preserved my immaculate misconceptions by "proving" them to myself whenever I could, probably in the same way people "proved" their beliefs about Jews and Negroes. Just as they "saw" only the Jews who fit their stereotype, I had done the same with the Catholic Church. While they saw and remembered unkempt, unreliable people who were Negro, I saw and remembered only the Catholics with large families and unhappy marriages. Was that what we all did? Remembered only what we wanted about groups we had *decided* to dislike?

Sister Mary Rita was probably the happiest accident in my first determined gesture toward the Roman Catholic Church. This merry little woman opened the convent door to me, clapping her hands together over "My very first chance to *really* talk with a Protestant girl!" Her tiny little feet did a kind of dance beneath her voluminous habit hem as she polka-ed me into the convent parlor, apparently delighted by an experience that had me tense and nervous. My nervousness completely dissolved when she pulled her chair up close to mine, clapped her hands again and said, "Now, dear, tell me. I've always been dying to know if Presbyterians get upset if their children marry . . . say, Methodists!"

I know our friendship began on February 20, 1962, because Sister and I chattered with one eye on the convent TV as John Glenn's historic orbit of the earth was being televised. Soon, other nuns heard us giggling over our mutual misunderstandings of each other's religions and joined us. One freckle-faced young nun admired my yellow wool suit and said I looked like "a canary among a flock of penguins." I was relaxed enough now to laugh and say how lucky *they* were, never to have to wonder what to wear!

I was also comfortable enough to say that my mother had told me Catholics were forbidden to read the Bible; Mother had seen it *chained* in the church! When the giggles died down a sweet-faced woman with creased parchment skin said that Catholics, of course, were encouraged to read the Bible, but that it was chained in the church for the same reason the pen is chained in the post office.

Sister Mary Rita bounced on the chair and said, Now, could I please tell them about Protestant methods of birth control. She knew nothing—just nothing—at all about it. I glanced over at John Glenn's triumphantly glowing face on the TV screen. Somehow his orbit of the earth seemed more credible than my sitting among a lovely group of women who were nuns, about to explain birth control!

As I left Sister asked my father's name. Aloysius. "I thought so," she said. "You were named for him." Lois was the feminine form of St. Aloysius, she said. If I had ever been told, I didn't remember—or want to—until then.

With Sister Mary Rita the Omaha Panel of American Women was complete. We prepared for our first appearance. At the office Ben prepared his assistant to handle details until a new advertising director was hired. My determined optimism had begun to affect Ben. He told me, laughing, that some of the other executives seemed as bewildered by his cheerfulness as he had been bewildered by his transfer.

Ben left a few weeks later for the Philadelphia office. I stayed busy with the Omaha Panel of American Women and keeping the house straightened for Brad McCann to show to potential buyers. We had offered to sell it to Joan and Paul, but

Paul said, "You're *lucky* I don't like your neighborhood." He had, he said, gotten us in enough trouble already. When I protested, Joan took my hands and said that our house and our neighborhood were lovely, but that they really did need five bedrooms and they did need to be closer to the hospital where Paul did most of his work. Really, honestly.

In Philadelphia, Ben was looking at new houses for us. When he came home one week end he named the areas his co-workers recommended—Paoli, Bryn Mawr, Whitemarsh—all suburbs. One man said, "But stay away from Elkins Park. It's all Jews!"

I don't remember the moment we decided to buy in a racially mixed neighborhood or even which of us suggested it first. It was just so logical. Long before knowing the Christophers or the Bensons we had been vaguely disturbed that our children were growing up in an all-WASP area, but it had been difficult to do much about it. All right, now we could try to find a neighborhood where Negro families already lived. The whites in a neighborhood like that would have to be the kind of people who felt as we did. We were, however, not so much choosing an integrated neghborhood as trying to avoid another all-white, Christian, segregated community.

Ben went back to Philadelphia and to house-hunting adventures that were both amusing and depressing. Some realtors told Ben abruptly, "We don't sell in mixed neighborhoods." Some real estate agents he phoned never called back. Much later, we suspected why. Hearing only Ben's voice, they must have decided that anyone asking for an integrated neighborhood *had* to be black.

A bright young realtor recommended by a man in Ben's office recoiled instinctively. "Oh, I couldn't do that to a nice family!" Didn't Ben know that real-estate values dropped to nothing when Negroes moved in? Ben said, well, then we ought to be able to pick up a bargain. The young man stared for a moment and then said, "Jesus, I never thought of *that!*" He seemed reassured, however, when he thought of an answer. "But you wouldn't want your children to go to school with . . ." and he lowered his voice to say the awful word . . . "colored."

This realtor, as did others, had an area he pronounced "safe" and "the right place for a family like yours," and each area was the same: suburban. Ben's stories were sometimes funny, but they gradually made an ugly, depressing point. Our family, because of our experiences, was determined to buy in a mixed neighborhood; realtors were determined we would not. Any white family less stubborn would have been scared off long ago.

Finally, Harper Thorpe, an insurance salesman, called on Ben at the office. Ben described "Harp" as having a face full of freckles, a wide-open grin, and a lounging manner. "By the way, chum," he said to Ben, "My sister sells real-estate, so if you haven't bought yet. . . ." When Ben told him of our search for an integrated neighborhood, Harp's feet came down off the chair on which he'd propped them.

"Hey, you're a real liberal," Harp had said. "Glad to have you aboard. This city needs guys like you."

Ben told me that Harp glanced around, then advanced toward Ben's desk, hand out, as if welcoming Ben to some fraternity of liberals, complete with password and secret handshake. Harp's freckles congealed into an even broader grin. Sure, his sister would find something for us. The Thorpes lived on the Main Line. Was Ben *sure* he didn't want to move out there with them?

Ben told him we didn't think we did. By now we'd learned more about Philadelphia, and Ben said we'd like to see houses in a section of the city called Mt. Airy. I had learned about Mt. Airy through an ex-college roommate of Joan Benson's.

Joan had introduced me to Barbara Hamilton through the mail. We had already exchanged several letters and I was

— 119 —

looking forward to meeting this friendly, informal woman whose dark-brown face smiled out of Joan Benson's class pictures. Joan told me that Barbara had an outstanding soprano voice and had studied opera at Julliard. She was married to a minister, had two small children, and lived in Mt. Airy. Since Barbara was a Negro woman, Mt. Airy must be integrated. Ben and I agreed that we would ask to see houses there.

By March, Brad McMann had sold our house—to a white family. The horde of black buyers just waiting to inundate our neighborhood never materialized. A blond woman about my size with an Anglo-Saxon name would be taking over my kitchen and perhaps looking out of our picture window late at night at those lights across the hill. Ben had several houses for me to look at in Mt. Airy. None of them, I was sure, would be like our own home.

When Ben met me the next weekend at the Philadelphia airport, our new real-estate agent, Harp's sister, Marjorie Willis, was with him. She had Harp's freckles and wore seasoned, rumpled tweeds, and well-preserved loafers. She looked about my age and walked as if following a golf ball on a fairway. Ben had been told that Harp and Marjorie came from one of the most socially prestigious Philadelphia families, but Marjorie was apparently serious about her work. She was brisk, businesslike, and knew all the facts about the houses she showed us. Her unfamiliar Eastern accent was hard for me to understand at first; she melted words together as the British do: "Wisikin" Avenue was Wissihickon Avenue on the street sign. Easterners, like Negro friends, would take a little getting used to at first, I decided.

Marjorie Willis was openly curious about our insistence on an integrated neighborhood. She and Harper were active in several civil rights organizations out on the Main Line, she said, as we drove through the gas-storage-tank area near Philadelphia's airport. This bleak approach to our new home looked like some futuristic moon colony instead of the historic city I was planning to love. But Marjorie's descriptions of all the civil rights groups she "knew" we would be interested in distracted me. "Harp will want you on many of his boards," she said. I wasn't sure I wanted to be on anybody's boards, but, after Omaha, it was reassuring to find that socially prestigious people were involved in civil rights.

The first houses Marjorie showed us that day were, for one reason or another, not appealing. Finally, we waited in a charming Victorian house for the realtor who had the original listing. He arrived, a tall, thin, red-haired man, with the same rumpled-tweed look as Marjorie. He led us through the house, pointing out the fireplace in the master bedroom, the interior wooden shutter blinds. Back in the living room I asked him, "What is the neighborhood like?" curious about whether young families with children lived there.

"Oh, don't worry, Mrs. Stalvey, it's all white-Christian!" he beamed.

It was both sad and infuriating. He interpreted my question quickly and as if he had answered it often before. I remember looking up at this tall red-headed man with a malicious sweetness and saying, "Oh, that's too bad. Our children have lived in WASP ghettos too long as it is." I smiled as I watched his face turn as red as his hair.

Suddenly, there "may be a few Jewish families across the street" and "there are some Negro families a few blocks away." The "all white-Christian neighborhood" was now only partly Christian and temporarily white. Marjorie Willis looked out the window.

In the car, I asked Marjorie to please show us only houses on blocks where Negro families already lived.

It meant nothing to Ben or me that the next three houses Marjorie showed us were all on one block. We were naïve about signs of panic selling. When Marjorie led us up the walk to a beautiful stone house in the middle of the block, I hardly noticed the enormous For Sale sign on the lawn across the street. Marjorie pointed out a low, ranch-style brick on the corner. A Negro family owned that, she said. Fine, but this house we were approaching was obviously over our budget. I was astonished when Marjorie told me what the owners, the Schusters, were asking. Why, it was the same price we had gotten for our house in Omaha!

Marjorie's comment that "They're a Jewish family, but very civic-minded" explained nothing. I only regretted her "but."

Standing before a magnificent mahogany door I was prepared to find a shambles inside. Instead, a beautiful white-haired woman, Mrs. Schuster, opened the door and we walked into the best maintained house I had ever seen. The Schusters' furnishings were luxurious, but so were the impeccable walls and floors. Straight in front of me, leading upstairs from the large entrance hall, was a broad polished mahogany stairway down which I could see three-year-old Sarah gliding as a bride someday.

I had fallen so immediately in love with the house that I was afraid to look closely. There must be some serious flaws to account for the low price. We could see nothing; no water stains on the basement walls, and the copper plumbing was new; snow still covered the roof, but inside the house was draft-free.

Outside, Marjorie suggested we hire an independent architect to inspect it if we were in doubt. We asked about schools. Oh, it was close to several good private schools—Penn Charter, Stevens, Springside, Chestnut Hill Academy. No, what about the *public* school? Marjorie said she knew nothing about it except that it was three blocks away.

We drove past the school, closed now for Easter vacation. It was a large, darkened-brick building. It looked old, but businesslike and reassuringly similar to the elementary school I had gone to in Milwaukee. I would have liked to visit, but when I had phoned Joan's friend, Barbara Hamilton, that morning, she said, "Try to buy in the Henry School district." This was the Charles W. Henry School. In 1962 big city school problems had not been widely publicized; Spike was in kindergarten and I had no experience in judging schools; Barbara's children went here. There were no other factors on which to decide.

That day we continued our drive around the neighborhood. Later, when the trees leafed out, this would be the most beautiful spot I had ever seen, but even then, with a late April snow covering bushes and lawns, I loved the sheer variety I saw: big houses and small, modern, Victorian, and Colonial. I had forgotten how dull the look-alike suburban houses had been. And if there were large and small houses, this meant there would be people with different incomes. I knew there were also Jewish families; several houses we had looked at were owned by people with Jewish names. And Marjorie told us that Mt. Airy "was around twenty-five per cent Negro as of now." We had found the kind of American melting-pot variety we wanted. If an architect pronounced the Schuster house free of any serious flaws, we might have found just exactly what we had hoped for. My pretended enthusiasm for Philadelphia had now become real.

I went back to Omaha with my fingers crossed. Ben phoned in a few days; the architect said if we didn't buy it at that price, *he* would!

Ben told me laughingly that *after* he had signed the agreement of sale. Mr. Schuster mentioned "the lovely Negro family on the corner . . . very fine people." Mr. Schuster, a gentle-faced, pleasant man, looked surprised when Ben told him we knew about the Negro family and that we had purposely looked for an integrated block. Mr. Schuster first peered sharply at Ben and then became even warmer and friendlier.

"This morning," Ben chuckled, "Dar Lewis, the vice president in charge of the office here, called me in." Mr. Schuster had phoned to congratulate him on "your fine, civic-minded new executive" who intentionally bought in a "changing" neighborhood. Ben said Dar Lewis looked at him searchingly for a few minutes and then said, "Schuster is one of our leading Jewish citizens, but a real gentleman."

Paul Benson frowned when I told him Ben's story.

"You realize, I hope, that you're telling the corporation to go to hell," he said. "What if this was only supposed to be a temporary exile for Ben? You would have been much safer settling down with Ben's co-workers in a suburb."

We hadn't thought about the corporation, only the children, in choosing where to live. But as I listened to Paul I wondered if any suburb would be truly "safe" for us. Some other racial issue would come up eventually and then, unless we tried to forget everything we had learned and everything we believed in, we would be right back where we were in Rockbrook. I tried to explain this to Paul. All in all, I said, we were probably "safer" in a mixed neighborhood among people who felt as we did.

Helen Carter, who had been fondly shaking her head over me since she had tried to warn me away from the sewing club meeting, asked her question: "But how will you feel if the neighborhood goes all black?"

Ben and I *had* considered and discussed this. Once, the idea of being surrounded by unfamiliar black faces might have frightened me, but now, we were lucky. We had known people like Paul and Joan and Janet and Warren; living among similar people would be good indeed. Surely there would be black people in Philadelphia like our friends in Omaha. We had been accepted; our children would be too. I said, and believed, Ben and I were panic proof.

Finally, in late spring of 1962, the only tasks left were packing and moderating the last appearance of the Omaha

Panel of American Women. The Panel of Women had been created as easily and successfully as its Kansas City founder, Esther Brown, had predicted. At our first appearance, in the high school where Sister Mary Rita taught, we found that the personal stories of the four women did indeed open up free, honest discussion. Teen-agers got up to say they had never felt able to discuss racial and religious differences before. Many wanted their parents to hear us. Soon we got calls from Sodality groups, Kiwanis Clubs, inner-city PTAs. The magic worked there too. Audiences questioned us with much less self-consciousness than they would have questioned "experts." The answers that Harriet, Joan, Jane Fuller, and Sister Mary Rita gave from their hearts were certainly more moving than theories and statistics. As Esther Brown predicted, sincere women speaking honestly from their own experiences could communicate across all barriers.

I was to moderate one more Panel before I left Omaha. It would be at the same annual Sisterhood luncheon that Harriet had taken me to almost exactly one year ago.

When I sat on the stage I felt as if a circle had closed. Just twelve months before I was one of those faces out there in the audience. I had been smug, serene. My life seemed full of everything I could possibly want or reasonably expect: a happy marriage, healthy children, comfortable home, and close friendships with my neighbors. Now I was leaving Omaha. The Bensons had no new home, our school no Negro teacher, and Ben had no future with the corporation.

Then, as I peered out into the audience, I suddenly felt sorry for the woman I had been when I sat among them last year with my head full of platitudes and petty problems. Now my life was insecure by some standards, but by others I had never felt so safe. I had discovered in Ben new strengths and protectiveness. I had been forced to test myself; I was not as wise as I hoped, but neither was I as weak as I feared.

When I smiled from the stage, genuinely pitying the untried woman who had once been me, I didn't know that my education was less than half completed. In Omaha I had merely glimpsed the depth of white antagonisms; in Philadelphia I would learn how wide and complex they could be.

As the program chairman began to introduce the Panel, I knew only that the past twelve months had changed me more than any year of my life. When the Panel program began, my first words were, "I owe the women of this synagogue a tremendous debt of gratitude."

Chapter Eleven

In late spring of 1962, as I dismantled, discarded, and packed up five years of accumulation in a house we never expected to leave, the newspaper headlines were not of crime-in-the-streets, but of crime-in-the-executive-suites. Billy Sol Estes and James Hoffa made the news. No one speculated on the long hot summer ahead; riots were unthinkable then.

I used my excitement about our new house in Philadelphia to dull any other feelings about leaving Omaha. It worked until the night before I left. Paul and Joan came to say good-bye. We'd see each other again; Joan promised to come to all the Eastern medical conventions. But in our driveway, while Paul, muttering imprecations, carried the enormous rubber plant I was leaving for Joan, I suddenly clung to Joan and sobbed.

It was not my good-bye to her or to our house or to our neighborhood that hurt; it was some much more final and forlorn ending. I remembered Joan, walking up this same driveway the day we met. My optimism and my belief that Americans—all of them—did care about others was so unshakeable. Joan had gradually and reluctantly let me see the real world. Now I was sobbing on Joan's shoulder because I had wished so hard that *my* world had turned out to be real; Joan was crying, too. Maybe for the same reason.

In Philadelphia, Ben carried me across the threshold of our new house to the amazement and hilarity of the children. Together, we explored each room. Few things live up to our memory or expectations, but this house, empty now and all ours, was even lovelier than I remembered. In this home only good things could happen.

As soon as we had finished exploring the house I telephoned Barbara Hamilton, Joan Benson's friend who had become mine. Barbara's frequent letters were strewn with enthusiasm and exclamation points. Her voice on the telephone had been rich with friendliness and full of plans for the things we could do together with the children once we were in Philadelphia. I hadn't written to tell Barbara that we had bought a house three blocks from hers; I wanted to save it for a surprise when we moved in.

Now I dialed her number to tell her the good news.

Barbara's voice raised in excitement that we were so near. Our children would go to Henry School together! Then, "But I didn't think you could buy west of Wayne Avenue."

At first I thought she believed the park began there. No, I explained, we were a block away from the park. Yes, she knew that, but she thought you couldn't buy the houses there. Our conversation was getting more and more confusing. I said Well, we had and there were two other houses for sale here.

Barbara must have put my denseness down to my having come from a place like Omaha. Finally, she said, patiently, slowly, "Yes, but I thought *we* couldn't buy them."

An unbelievable thought came into my mind and I hesitated helplessly before I asked, as I had to: "Barbara, do you know I'm white?"

There was a soft gasp and a silence at the other end of the

line. During Barbara's silence that seemed so long I struggled with feelings WASPs seldom need to cope with. I was saying, in my mind, "Barbara, please see *me*. Don't just see my color and close up." For the first time in my life I was being judged on something I couldn't help.

But there was no mistaking the difference in Barbara's voice when she spoke again. Her voice was formal now. No, she hadn't known I was white. I plunged ahead asking when she could come to see our new house. Stiffly, she said, "Well, when would it be convenient for you?" (This was, I learned later, her first "test" of me; most white people, she believed, "tell us to come at a specific time so we won't run into the wrong people.")

I said come anytime, but come soon. Now?

Barbara did agree to come that day. My first view of her was from an upstairs window. A woman, her dark skin emphasized by a yellow dress, got out of a Volkswagen in front of our house. She was followed by two children, a boy who, I knew, was Jimmy, six years old, midway between the ages of Spike and Noah, and a little girl, Paula, just a few months older than our three-year-old Sarah.

At the stairs leading up from the street I saw her stop and deliver what I could guess was the same behave-yourselves-or-else lecture I gave so often to my children before a visit. And I went downstairs to welcome Barbara.

Barbara's children disappeared into the yard with mine almost at the doorstep. Barbara followed me into the living room and sat, white gloves in her lap, her feet close together like a good little girl in Sunday school. Once, I would have failed to notice her attractive coloring. For most of my life, brownness was so unfamiliar, so different that I missed its variations. Then my eye had actually changed after Ken Hancock seemed to disappear into our brown chair in Omaha. However, it had taken time.

When I first began reading *Ebony* magazine, the dark-skinned figures in familiar advertising settings made me blink. On our first visit to the Bensons' house, it was a visual shock to see family portraits with brown faces instead of white. When Janet Adams took me to the *Ebony* fashion show, I was at first uncomfortably distracted by one African-featured model. Her black-coffee skin and pure Negroid features clashed, I thought, with the Balenciaga and Givenchy originals she wore. But as the fashion show continued, I could feel my vision gradually adjusting itself as women, beige and black and in-between, modeled beautiful clothes. By the end of the show it was astonishing to me that I now saw the African-featured model as the most elegant and attractive of them all.

From then on I thought I could understand why some white people claimed, "All Negroes look alike to me." Brown skin had immediately signaled "Not one of us"; our eyes and minds stopped right there. If we had no friends with brown skin, why search brown faces for recognition? Why notice variations in features? It had taken many friendships to retrain my eyes.

Now I was able to appreciate Barbara's pretty color. Her skin was as dark and soft-looking as wild mink and her features had the same rounded suppleness. Wide, expressive eyes looked at me, seriously and directly. Her full, sensitive mouth said the polite things—"I hope you'll be happy in Philadelphia; how is Joan Benson's family?"—in the voice of a trained operatic soprano—modulated, liquid, controlled.

That first day, Barbara looked like the perfect minister's wife. She sat primly, her hands folded gracefully in her lap, her body erect. Even her linen dress was too well-bred to have wrinkles.

She had caught me in shorts and shirt, hanging bedroom curtains, but I didn't mind. She could see me as I was. Hopefully, she would tell herself that she had been my friend *as I was*—in letters—on the phone—before she knew I was white.

All we could do now was trade histories. She didn't talk of the trips to Philadelphia's zoo, the drive to Pennsylvania Dutch country, or the tour of the historical houses she had said we would take together when she wrote to me in Omaha. Instead, Barbara told me she had been born and raised in New York. At the time it didn't strike me that all of our other Negro friends had grown up in the South, but I would not have understood the differences then. Leland, her husband, was a minister, and he now held the job of chaplain at a penitentiary. "The first Negro chaplain in any state institution," she said, with pride cutting through her formality.

Gradually, Barbara's prim posture relaxed. We talked about our children. Her brown hands left her lap to gesture; they clenched over Jimmy's mischief-making, clasped over the delights and dilemmas of having a daughter. When I matched her stories with Noah's mischiefs, Spike's head-in-the-clouds personality, and my own identification with my little daughter, Barbara's hands moved more freely. Her gestures completed themselves instead of halting halfway.

Later, our husbands would tease us both for "talking like two semaphore signals," but to Barbara and me things were "this high" or "this wide" and people were to touch. We would also find out later that we wore the same size clothes and that, incredibly, the same colors—yellow, blue-green, and beige were our best. Somewhere beneath Barbara's dark brown skin and my pink one there was an undertone that matched.

That first afternoon Barbara and I had begun to reach out to each other. Her white gloves were tossed on a table now. My legs were curled up under me in my chair. Just then our daughters, Sarah and Paula, came into the living room seeking the reassurance needed by three-year-olds that Mommie was around. They clambered up on the sofa together while Barbara and I watched. Paula reached over and ran her little brown hand down Sarah's long straight hair. She giggled. It must have felt slippy and slidy to her. Then Sarah put her hand to Paula's hair. She giggled too as she patted its springy bounciness. They jumped down from the sofa and toddled off, holding hands, thoroughly delighted with each other. When Barbara and I looked across the room with the identical maternal smiles and with no words, we began a long, permanent friendship.

As she was leaving Barbara told me that they were beginning a three-week vacation the next morning. When they got back she would show me the city. But my family couldn't wait. During the next few week ends Ben, the children and I made friends with the city on our own: the Franklin Institute, the Art Museum, the Fels Planetarium, the waterfront. I had been determined to like Philadelphia, but unprepared to be overwhelmed by it. These museums, the concert halls, the theaters were going to be an important part of our children's education. Already Spike was wide-eyed at the Greek, French, Swedish sailors in their fascinating uniforms; Sarah watched spellbound as we skimmed the Schuylkill River in a sight-seeing boat; Noah was up, down, around, in and under every inch of the Children's Zoo with its ark named after him.

Omaha, I said to Ben, was never like this!

Just meeting Ben each night was an adventure. I watched a wonderful conglomeration of people spill out with him at the Upsal Street Station. Not only were they black and white, but all ages and conditions. A dowager in outdated clothes shuffled gamely along behind a long-haired youth in jeans; two laughing young black women swung gracefully past a preoccupied gray-bearded man with a worn brief case. In Omaha's suburban shopping center any one of these people would have attracted stares.

During our first month in Philadelphia, I thought we had found a happy ending to the upheavals of Omaha. It was, of course, just a beginning. Spike's day camp was my initiation into big-city life, its vocabulary, and my next misconceptions. I had learned that most of the neighborhood children went to one of the local day camps during the summer—the Y, Allen's Lane Art Center Camp, or others. Allen's Lane had room for four-year-old Noah but their six-year-old group, Spike's group, was already filled. I began telephoning other day camps. Finally a pleasant-sounding man at Germantown Settlement Camp said, "Yes, we have room for your son."

The term "settlement house" had been no part of my Middlewest, middle-class experience. I visited the camp, a pretty Victorian house surrounded by large grounds and well-equipped playground. The blonde woman director was warmly informative; the children were taken on trips around the city, on nature hikes, visits to farms. The other counselors seemed mature and responsible. I noticed a Negro man working at one of the desks in the office. Good. This place was integrated. The fee struck me as extraordinarily low, but the directress said they would have room for Spike and I could drop him off early and pick him up late to enable me to get Noah to and from his camp.

Because of this arrangement it was two weeks before I saw the other children at Spike's camp. Each morning I had left him in the care of the blonde woman; each afternoon she waited with him until I arrived. Spike talked happily about his camp friends: Lenny, Johnny, Bryan. Lenny's father could wiggle his ears; Bryan's mother sent cookies to camp. Tomorrow they were going on a big bus to visit a real farm!

That day I waited for the bus to return, trying to chat with a not-very-friendly Negro woman who waited, too. When the bus came and the children romped out, I remember saying to her, "That's my son in the green shirt." She gave me an odd look. Then I knew why. Spike was the only white child in the entire group.

When Spike rushed over to me, pulling two little boys with

him, I felt dazed with guilt. How could I have carelessly put a sensitive six-year-old into a situation like this? He'd been uprooted from his Omaha home, taken to a strange city, and then, because of my stupidity, made into a pitiful little minority of one. This wasn't American variety; this was Spike and about fifty Negro children.

But something else was coming through to me, even more upsetting. As Spike danced around me, introducing his friends, I looked at the other children more closely. They were as neat and clean as Spike—as neat and clean as children can be at the end of the day—but their clothes all bore the frayed and faded look of poverty. Spike had pulled me around the corner of the building to find his friend Bryan, and now I could see a huge sign in the next block: Urban Renewal Project. Most of the children were trooping toward the red-brick buildings of a public housing project that had recently replaced their slums. Good heavens! In addition to being the only white child, Spike was also in a camp for underprivileged slum children.

As a child I had been taught nothing about Negro people. I was, however, taught about poor people. The run-down house of a poor white family across the street was an insult to my grandfather and out of bounds for me. To Grandfather, being poor was not only voluntary but sinful. In America, no one had to be poor unless they were lazy. Poor people were dirty, evil, and had diseases—indescribable diseases.

When I sent Spike to play in the yard and headed toward the director's office, I didn't know I was responding to such old emotions. All I knew was that I wanted Spike out. The blonde camp director—*social worker* I realized now—said "I thought you knew about the camp." But it was not for underprivileged children, she said; they wanted a diversity. Spike, obviously, was the only diversity that had come along. Too bad, but in my mind I decided my child was not going to be someone's social experiment. Before I could put this kindly, she asked, "Has Spike enjoyed himself?"

I knew he had. He left me each day, eager and excited, and returned happy and full of tales of his friends. So he had never noticed he was the only white child. But the other children must have noticed. I had read that as early as four children were aware of ethnic differences. *He* couldn't see how different he looked, but *they* could.

The blonde woman continued: "Frankly, we've been interested by how well Spike has been accepted in the group." Could she ask me if my husband and I had peer-group relations with Negro people? Yes. Well, she said, that explained it.

By six, she said, children were well indoctrinated with the racial attitudes—spoken and unspoken—of their parents. If Spike observed *us* in interracial relationships, he saw them as normal and proper. His unself-conscious acceptance of Negro children resulted then in his being welcomed.

Very interesting but . . .

She asked if I had noticed how neat the children were. Yes, I had. The carefully mended rips and the wash-faded colors caught my housewife's eye.

Well, the children who came to the settlement house had parents who cared very much about them and, among the upward-striving poor, it was a fact that standards of cleanliness and morality were even more rigidly enforced than among the middle class.

What she was saying was that I needn't worry about dirty kids or dirty words or dirty habits. But I wondered if she had children. If she did, would her theories convince her to put them in this group of poor children?

We were standing at the window now, watching Spike and his friends zipping down a slide. Yes, Spike was enjoying himself. In fact this would be one of the problems—taking him out of camp and explaining why. If I told him the truth, I

would have to say that it was because he was the only white
—and the only middle-class child. Then the rest of the truth
came to me. I would be taking him out of the camp, not because he was uncomfortable, but because I was. I would not
be protecting my child, I would be reacting to my own fear
of poor people.

That day I realized only that I knew little and felt much
about the poor. I wasn't even sure why I feared them. The
"indescribable diseases" could obviously be caught just as
easily on a public bus or in a zoo washroom. We had said
that it was important that our children learn about the world
as it was. Well, there were poor people in the world and I
had inadvertently put Spike among them. There was no
logical reason to take him away, there was only my discomfort.

Spike stayed in the camp. By the end of the summer I had
picked him up at the homes of several playmates; some had
come to our house. In the homes I visited, the furniture
sagged and the floors were bare, but they were indeed almost
painfully neat. I didn't realize then that these were "upper-
class poor." Children who came to our house were unim-
pressed. One child seemed to feel we were eccentric—"You
live here all by yourself?" Another child said proudly, "My
mother cleans for a lady with a bigger house than this!"

The day camp experience, however, prepared us for our
neighborhood school when I registered Spike for first grade
in the fall. It was like wading in a puddle after swimming in
a stream. By comparison, the Charles W. Henry School, which
was 65 per cent Negro, seemed racially balanced.

On September 4, 1962, I sat in the corridor of Henry
School, waiting to register Spike for first grade and reading
from the morning paper. White crowds in New Orleans were
reported demonstrating around thirty schools and jeering the
handful of Negro mothers attempting to register their children in the formerly all-white Catholic schools. It was strange

to look around me at the white and black mothers, serenely seated on the small wooden chairs while in another state white crowds went wild at the thought.

Registering Spike in this school took no great moral commitment. By now, it was primarily selfish. Way in the back of my mind was the suspicion that no school was likely to turn my child into—or prevent his becoming—a genius. Buying some guaranteed-perfect education would be wonderful, but I felt it was a fantasy. Harriet Fischer, who had taught in New York's public and private schools, supported this belief before we left Omaha. She had said, "A school is as good as the teacher your child has *that* year." In her experience, there were as many good and bad teachers in the private as in the public schools. "Parents can dodge responsibility by paying for an expensive school," she said, "but usually all they get is a balm for their conscience."

This seemed depressing, but true. Spike's seven years of observing Ben and me were probably more crucial than a parade of paragon teachers. If he saw we valued knowledge, displayed self-discipline in our tasks, prized accomplishment over appearance, his attitudes would be set. School, I suspected, was where he learned to work with a group and to accept the authority of a non-parent for the first time. If this were as true as it seemed, then the variety of the group was an advantage; it represented the same variety he would meet in the world.

And in the corridors of the Henry School, as I waited that day, the variety was certainly there. Among these children were the well and poorly dressed; the bright-eyed and lethargically dull; there were children with soft, gentle faces, and some with hard-eyed assurance.

When I walked the three blocks to school, I had seen other advantages Spike would have going to this school. In the suburbs, he had walked along roads without sidewalks, among houses that looked much like his own. He had had to cross a highway to get to school. Here he'd have broad sidewalks, quiet residential streets, and a fascinating view of tiny row houses and gingerbread Victorians. But most important, he would have the benefit I had almost forgotten from my own childhood. Clustered near the school were a barber, a dry cleaner, a real estate office, drugstore, candy shop; there would be windows to look into, work to watch, adults to question. I could remember my own sense of independence and privacy, chatting with our neighborhood barber or druggist on my way to school. It was a vital part of my growing up, and now Spike would have it, too.

These were the thoughts interrupted when a tall, elegantly dressed white woman in a red suit came out of the principal's office and called my name. She introduced herself as Evangeline Peters, the principal, and reminded me that she had telephoned me the day we moved in to tell me "about our wonderful school." To me, her call was an example of extraordinary Eastern friendliness.

Now she wanted to show me the school "and all the unusual things we're doing." She paused at a coin-operated milk machine, as we walked along the corridor. In one swift movement she deposited a coin and handed me a carton of chocolate milk. This was my first experience with Mrs. Peters' chocolate milk therapy. In the years to follow, Spike, Noah, and Sarah would report that injured knees, feelings, and possessions were "all right now. Mrs. Peters gave me a chocolate milk and then . . ."

That first day, my chocolate milk in hand, I merely trotted obediently behind this overwhelming woman, into and out of classrooms. Vangie Peters was unquestionably more Madison Avenue than Board of Education. I had seen advertising campaigns presented to clients with less passionate salesmanship than Vangie Peters presented the Charles W. Henry School to me. She showed me seventh grade biology projects and fourth grade French classes as P. T. Barnum might have presented Jenny Lind. "Notice," she said in her voice that could go from maternal mewing to bull-horn volume, "that the school is rebalancing itself racially. Did you see that the lower grades have more white children than the upper?" Later, I'd find out why, but after Spike's day camp experience, color balance at Henry School was not my major interest.

My interest centered around the three first-grade classes I had seen. Spike would be in one of them. All the children were adorable; intent little faces struggling with words and numbers. Of the three teachers, one was old and looked cross; the tall red-headed teacher had a nasal voice and fluttered; the third, and only Negro, teacher was a softly smiling woman with precise diction. In the corridor Vangie Peters asked which teacher I preferred. All were excellent, she said unhelpfully. I chose the Negro teacher only because of her attractive voice; if Spike was to learn phonics from someone, it would be best from her. Two children later, I learned that the teacher, Mrs. Grant, had more than impeccable diction, but—also later—I heard white parents object to Negro teachers because "they all have that terrible drawl." Mrs. Grant was from Boston and sounded like a female version of John Kennedy.

That fall of 1962, with Spike settled happily in first grade, the optimism I had once pretended to feel about Philadelphia seemed to have been a prophecy. In a few months I felt more at home in our neighborhood, Mt. Airy, than I had ever felt anywhere in my life. To Ben's total bewilderment I had even become interested in gardening during the summer, but I explained that working in the fertile soil beneath towering oaks and elms and yellowwoods was a lot different from getting baked along with the Nebraska clay in our suburban yard. Ben had even won his five-year war with crab grass. It didn't grow in the lush green lawn in our yard with its screen of evergreens, rhododendrons, and enormous azalea bushes.

Philadelphia and our neighborhood proved to have all kinds of bonuses we had never expected and never missed in the Omaha suburb. The children had a wonderful wide-zooming swing Ben made for them in the branches of an enormous oak—older, I insisted, than the state of Nebraska. And all summer these same ancient trees cooled the house. In Omaha I had flipped on the air conditioning in July and stayed imprisoned inside while the prairie sun broiled Rockbrook. In Philadelphia, I could read a book to the children on our terrace or prune privet or just watch the big purple rhododenron blossoms slowly explode into exotic flowers.

Through a strange route, I felt I had come home to Philadelphia.

But it was another branch of nature that was the most fascinating and reassuring. The human beings who lived here were as comfortable and welcoming as the soil in which I planted things. Differences in occupation, modes of dress, and style of living were absorbed without comment. In a few months I had been invited to join the Home and School Association, the Arts Center, League of Women Voters, SNCC, the Urban League, and CORE. We had even received a pleasant letter from the local rabbi who had assumed that because we bought our house from a Jewish family, we must be Jewish, too. He and all the other groups I chose not to join seemed delightfully unconcerned. One could be active or lethargic in Mt. Airy. Along with acceptance of ethnic and religious differences came a tolerance of all the other quirks that make people individuals.

When I first learned Mt. Airy's history I believed it could be a blueprint for successful integration everywhere. Parts of it, I suppose, could be. The first Negro families moved into West Mt. Airy in 1951, buying the large houses along Lincoln Drive. White families, facing the postwar servant problem, had offered them for sale and moved to the expanding suburbs. Soon the smaller houses near Lincoln Drive were sold to a few Negro families. The luck of Mt. Airy was that, first, several alert white home owners realized the neighborhood could panic and took early countermeasures; second, that the director of Philadelphia's Human Relations Commission lived here and his expertise was available to his neighbors. Instead of trying to prevent more Negro families from moving in, West Mt. Airy Neighbors Association was formed, largely to encourage white families to stay. Rabbis, priests, and ministers were drawn into the early planning; the Arts Center was established so families could get to know each other across color lines and through common interests. Enthusiastic white home owners systematically visited their dubious white neighbors, encouraging them to stay calm.

Mt. Airy had always been a neighborhood of intellectuals. The tiny row houses were more likely to be occupied by school teachers and social workers than by the factory workers and clerks of my childhood neighborhood. The larger homes were owned by college professors, young lawyers; the truly large houses held many old Philadelphia Quaker families. I was told that the Henry School, traditionally excellent, was one of the magnets that brought families here who were more concerned about education than a fashionable suburban address. The beauty of the neighborhood was surely a magnet, too. Fairmount Park surrounds it on two sides; the enormous trees, typical of old established neighborhoods, make green tunnels of the streets in summer. Most of Mt. Airy's residents were not gullible enough to be panicked by myths, and the area was too attractive to flee without a lot of thought.

The biggest crisis, I understand, was when the school began to have more Negro pupils than the neighborhood had Negro families. When Henry School was known to have accepted some Negro students, others transferred from the inadequate schools nearby. The former principal panicked at his darkening and unfamiliar student body. Evangeline Peters was hand-picked for her belief in integrated education

— 141 —

and, I suspect, for her dynamic powers of persuasion. She literally sold integration to parents, district supervisors, and realtors. White parents were told the benefits of interracial experiences for their children; district supervisors were persuaded to send the best equipment and the best teachers; realtors were indoctrinated with the saleability of "our exciting school programs." Rumor had it that Vangie Peters even approached pregnant white women with her own five-year plan in mind. She would not discourage Negro families from coming in; therefore, she had to attract and keep white families to prevent re-segregation. Her phone call to me, my tour of the school, my choice of teachers was now explained. I was white and my three white children were valuable assets to her school.

While Vangie Peters promoted the school, West Mt. Airy Neighbors sent brochures to the personnel departments of large firms urging them to recommend the neighborhood to new employees coming in from out of town. At the same time, the lawyer members of West Mt. Airy Neighbors watchdogged zoning restrictions to prevent speculators from buying large houses and converting them into apartments. A few realtors did try the panic tactics of post cards and phone calls urging nervous white home owners to "sell while you can," but the neighbors association got injunctions against illegal soliciting. The word went out among unethical realtors that "Mt. Airy is not ripe for block-busting." The banks and mortgage companies got the message, too. White home buyers were not refused mortgages as they were in some "changing" areas.

And by sheer accident we moved into Mt. Airy knowing nothing about it except that a Negro family lived on our block. Barbara Hamilton's belief that "we can't buy west of Wayne Avenue" was only a rumor; one family already had. But I think we moved in when our block was teetering in balance. If the Schusters put an extraordinarily low price on the house to attract a white buyer, it was a generous, civic-minded gesture few families could afford to make. When we did buy, two houses on our block went off the market; two others were sold, both to white families.

Ironically, we never became friends with the Negro family across the street, without whose presence we would not have bought the house. Our gestures of friendship were met with icy-cold rejection. The husband is a successful show-business figure; he may consider us non-swingers and dull. But it didn't matter. Nearly everyone else combined warm friendliness with a respect for privacy. It was (and is) the most fascinating American neighborhood I can imagine.

This was what I wrote to Joan and Paul. They couldn't move to Philadelphia because Paul couldn't leave his practice. But oh, if they could. The hurt and humiliations of the Bensons' house hunt couldn't happen in Mt. Airy, the one place where they would have the choices and the welcome Ben and I had had.

My mistake was believing the solution was for neighborhoods like ours to spread, for the successful story of West Mt. Airy to change the country. I thought there would be time enough.

Chapter Twelve

The fall and winter of 1962 was, for me, a period of luxurious ignorance; everything—our house, new friends we made, Spike's school experience—had turned out so much better than we expected that it was possible to believe that Ben's job was secure, too—or that he would find another one before too long. Dar Lewis, head of the Philadelphia office, didn't act as if Ben had been sent to him to be used and then fired. In fact, he treated Ben with a kind of caution: Ben was from the home office, and Dar Lewis wanted Ben on his side. And perhaps, we thought, the corporation had only sent us into a community that was more accepting of our beliefs. It was easy to be optimistic while Ben tried to establish contacts for other jobs, just in case.

It was easy too to be optimistic about civil rights even though America had its first race riot of the 1960s. In September 1962 it took 10,000 soldiers and 400 U.S. marshals to establish law and order in Oxford, Mississippi, when white students and townspeople erupted in violence over James Meredith's enrollment as the first Negro student at the University of Mississippi. White people smashed windows, wrecked cars. A French reporter was shot and killed. John F. Kennedy made a national appeal on television for sanity in Mississippi and understanding around the country.

But it seemed healthier to me to have white violence out in the open rather than operating quietly as I had seen it in Omaha. When formerly indifferent Americans saw the twisted faces, the sneers, the undisguised violence and hate on white faces in Oxford, they would understand how dangerous white obsessions with superiority could become. Already, Northern newspaper columnists expressed shock over the unbridled virulence in Oxford. What I never considered was that black people were seeing it, too; Northern black people who might never have experienced raw screaming white hate.

In December, I sat in the auditorium of our school, waiting to see Spike's class perform in the Christmas program—and trying to understand what made Mississippi college students hysterical at the thought of one Negro student. This room, with its variegated browns and pinks, represented their nightmares. What exactly were they afraid of? Intermarriage? The incongruities in this question had never seemed worth discussing, but now, waiting for Spike's class to perform, I tried to understand the Mississippi students' alarm. Obviously no white girl had to marry James Meredith or any Negro man unless she wanted to. Or did white men believe the myths of sexual superiorities and feel threatened? Logic always had to be left behind at this point, and I was not equipped to analyze anyone's sexual fears. I could only try to deal with what we saw around us and what we felt about our own children.

Ben and I had talked about whether integrated schools—or neighborhoods—encouraged intermarriage. We had concluded that it might tend to do just the opposite. Growing up with Negro children would make our children see them as ordinary human beings. When they did meet Negro people in college or later there would be no novelty, no forbidden-fruit attraction. I expected that my children would date interracially, probably in our high school, and this too seemed an advantage. My own dating experience bore this out. As a young girl I alone among my six cousins had been allowed to date Catholic and Jewish boys. (No Negro boys ever applied.) In spite of the dire predictions of my aunts and uncles, I was one of the two grandchildren who married "one of my own kind." Only after I had fallen in love with Ben for his qualities as a person had I realized, with some amusement, that he was a Protestant. I had made my choice free of the distraction of parental do's and don'ts or from a need to rebel. Ben and I could at least give our children the same freedom.

We could also protect our children from the kind of interracial marriage we had observed recently. The young white husband had insisted on telling us, comparative strangers to him, how angry his "bigoted parents" were over his marriage. His eyes sparkled and I felt he had told the story often before —of the hysterics, the threats, the estrangement. His Negro wife sat quietly, pregnant with their second child.

But what if one of our children did fall in love with someone black? Ben and I could admit to each other—and to ourselves—that it would hurt watching the pressures society would put on the marriage. Ben pointed out, however, that we could not choose our children's mates any more than our parents had chosen for us. "If I could, though," he continued, "I have to admit that I'd rather have Sarah marry an honest, loving young man who was black than have her marry a white Protestant bigot!" I had never thought this kind of choice through before, but now I agreed with all my heart.

That day, as I sat in the Henry School auditorium, I knew that my children's choice of a mate was far in the future, but their education was not. I tried to understand the rioting white Mississippi students from this angle. Were they afraid that Negro students would lower academic standards in their school? Everything I had learned in the past four months denied the possibility. Spike's first report card contained mostly B's and C's; to me his average progress was reassuring. All A's might have meant he was ahead of his class and possibly being held back by dull children; failing grades would have shown something else was wrong.

On the first parents' visiting night Ben and I looked over Spike's papers as we waited to speak to his teacher, Mrs. Grant. Peeking at the papers of other children, I saw that Spike's report card was accurate. Some children did better work than Spike; some not as good. Then I overheard two Negro parents talking to Mrs. Grant. The mother wore an ill-fitting coat and carried a worn handbag; the father apologized for his work clothes, explaining he had taken a few hours off from his job.

The father said, "How can we help Robert do better?" Mrs. Grant reached past me for the folder of Robert's papers; one of the folders into which I had peeked. Robert did much better work than Spike. What were these parents concerned about?

After similar experiences at the parents' discussion groups in the next months, I finally understood. These Negro parents were treating their children's education as if it were a matter of life or death. I wanted a good education for my children; they had to have it for theirs. My mediocre high school grades got me the jobs and opportunities I wanted, but being able to put "white" and "Protestant" on application blanks made it enough. Negro parents knew top grades were the only passport out of a lifetime of second-rate jobs. Their children were made to study as if their lives depended on it—because they did.

Later, I would meet Negro parents whose own third-rate education made them unable to help their children. I was to talk with parents who were ashamed to visit the school in their shabby clothes; afraid to approach teachers, to reveal their poor grammar and limited vocabulary. Yet I would never meet a Negro parent who didn't try, in whatever way he knew, to fight for his child's education.

I would watch how the school system fought against them; how when Negro children came into schools that had no Vangie Peters to help them, classes were suddenly enlarged; white teachers transferred to "easier" schools; repairs were made more slowly, equipment never arrived; discipline, not learning, became paramount.

But first, I was to discover my own inadequate education in American history. Barbara Hamilton's husband Leland provided it. My friendship with Barbara had grown quickly. I had made other friends, but Barbara and I seemed synchronized in our attitudes and interests. Our conversations melted from topic to topic and we laughed at the same things. We stood one day, across from the school, waiting for our children. A display for sun-tan lotion was in the drugstore window. Without words we read the promise of "deep natural tan," looked at each other and burst out laughing.

Ben and I, however, had not yet met Leland. There was always some logical excuse. Leland was involved in a great many projects beside his job as chaplain at the penitentiary. Barbara told me of the center for Southern immigrants he was trying to organize, the consumer education program; he was also trying to help a bankrupt church recover, and he was writing articles for Philadelphia's largest Negro-owned newspaper.

Finally, after several canceled dates, Barbara arrived at our house with Leland. My first impression of this stocky, muscular man was his physical contrast with Barbara. While Barbara was soft-looking, rounded, Leland looked as if he had been soldered together out of blue-black iron. He had, I decided instantly, the perfect appearance for a prison chaplain; the toughest convict could see immediately that this man was firm as an ingot. They might pound at him with false stories, but in the end the convict would more likely change than the anvil that was their chaplain.

Later, I learned my guess was accurate, but for the first part of our evening together Leland sat quietly, observing Ben with eyes that paced back and forth across Ben's face. Now the iron ingot seemed to become an impatient black leopard as Leland sat, poised at the edge of the chair, staring mostly at my husband.

Leland had, however, dropped his hardness for a revealing moment when he met our children. Strangers usually respond to roguish roly-poly Noah or to Sarah's delicate femininity; Spike, lanky and overlooked, hangs shyly back. I was Leland's friend from the moment he reached past Noah and Sarah to draw Spike to him and say some quiet words that made Spike grin.

Leland then resumed his watchfulness of Ben. Long ago I had learned from Joan Benson that white men are disliked and distrusted far more than white women. The men are blamed for the closed employment doors, the real estate practices; white women at least brought baskets of food and manned the committees for the "underprivileged," patronizing as their attitudes might sometimes have been. I had been puzzled at first when black people asked often, "Does your husband feel the way you do?" I had always replied, "Yes." Their expressions of surprise annoyed me.

I had also learned from Joan that while all white men are distrusted, Southern white men occupy the very bottom of the scale of trust. Leland would eventually find that Ben had been born in South Carolina. As much as I wanted Leland and Ben to like each other, I had decided that prejudice against all Southerners was from the same reeking pot as other prejudices. If Leland couldn't see past geography, then Leland was a narrow man.

Abruptly, Leland joined the conversation. He asked Ben questions about his work. Ben has no Southern accent left except for a few inflections on certain words, but Leland's ears picked them up. Where was Ben born? Why, *he* was from South Carolina too. Born in a town nearby. Then Leland said, "Hey, maybe we're related."

Ben said, "Could be, Cousin."

Leland was silent. Then his laughter was suddenly warm. He went to Ben and held out his hand. "Well, I never expected to meet a decent white man from *South Carolina!*"

It happened so fast, it took time to understand what had gone on. Leland had made his test; Ben was supposed to recoil instinctively at the thought of being related to anyone as black as Leland. Beneath Leland's jocularity, there had been a land mine planted for Ben to trip on.

Now Leland became the articulate, outgoing man we know. When Barbara insisted we describe our belief that our suburb would welcome Joan and Paul Benson, Leland whooped with laughter. St. Paul's Epistle to the Romans, Leland said, stated that "the just shall live by faith," but even St. Paul couldn't have meant *that* much faith!

We had, however, passed Leland's test. The black leopard who sat silently, ready to pounce on any bigoted statement Ben or I made could now pace naturally. In the many years of our friendship, Leland has never occupied the same chair for more than a few minutes. When he talks in his half-growl, half-purr voice, he must apparently walk. During sermons he prowls the altar area in the same way, back and forth, sometimes down among the pews. That evening Leland began pacing as he told us of his work at the prison, of the convicts who were hopelessly damaged and those who could be rehabilitated. As a chaplain, Leland looked into men's personalities in the same way he examined the mechanical objects it was his hobby to repair.

The Hamiltons would become our closest but far from our only black friends in Philadelphia. And with each new black person we met there would be the tests; the initial test and continuing tests. Some we must have failed; black acquaintances did not always become friends. We learned only about the tests we passed; laughing confidences of "When you said (or did) *this*, then I knew you were all right."

I could never resent the tests as some white people have told me they do. One white man "active in civil rights since college" told me that a black friend of seven years standing "admitted he was still testing me." The white man was irate. "By now he should know me!" But to me, the longest tests have always indicated the deepest hurts. We whites would have to be naïve to expect that hundreds of years of humiliation can be forgotten the moment we wish it to be. At times, the most poignant part of the test is that black people have enough trust left to give it. Testing implies we might pass the test. It is safer and easier for a black person to turn his back on us. If he does not gamble on our sincerity, he cannot be hurt if we prove false. Testing shows an optimism I doubt I could duplicate if I were black.

In fact, Ben and I have come to suspect Negro people who accept us too readily. They could be Uncle Toms, people so anxious to be accepted by whites that they will say only what is reassuring and flattering. These would be shallow and false friendships. With all we know now, any black person liking us on sight would appear to have something wrong with them. If they are interested in us as people, they should want to know if we are sincere. If they are eager only for what they believe is the prestige of white friendships, then they are snobs, hypocrites—and Uncle Toms.

Some tests, however, given us by people who later become friends, were passed only through luck and misinterpretation. Barbara once told me as we walked along a downtown street, "See! This is another way I know you're all right. You *look* at black people. Most whites don't. They look through us as if we don't exist." Sure, but I reminded Barbara that I knew so many black people, I *had* to look. It might be someone I knew. White people with no black friends could afford to pass by without looking.

To Mrs. Jefferson, who cleaned for me each week, I was "different" because I taught my children to call her "Mrs. Jefferson—instead of Clara as the other white ladies let their kids do." It was, Mrs. Jefferson told me, the talk of the trolley stop when other cleaning women heard my children call "Good-bye, Mrs. Jefferson" when she boarded the trolley. My children are taught to call all adults by their formal titles, but it had taken Paul Benson to teach me why *I* should do the same with Mrs. Jefferson. Until Paul mentioned bitterly the Southern custom of never referring to Negro people as Mr. or Mrs., I would never have realized that Mrs. Jefferson appreciated this small dignity from me.

Another friend said she had judged me because I eagerly accepted for Sarah a coat her daughter had outgrown. "Taking hand-me-downs from black people," she laughed, "would be out of the question for most whites."

But there was always a bittersweet quality about passing those tests. They revealed, of course, the all-pervading distrust of my group, but they were also a negative, rather than positive, acceptance of me. I was not pronounced a good person; I was only pronounced not as bad as other whites they had known. For once in my life, I could understand the mixed emotions of minority group people who are told, "You may be (Jewish, Italian, Chinese, etc.) but you're different!" Often, I would try to convince my judge that there were millions of white people exactly like me—he had just never met them. Really? I knew I was not believed; I was a "good WASP," a curio.

These things were difficult to explain to the white neighbor who asked me earnestly why she had not been able to make black friends. She had said, "I just *love all of them,* but I have no Negro friends!"

I said, lightly, that I sure didn't *love* Negro people as a group; that some of our black neighbors bored, irritated, or angered me. One light-skinned family who forbade their children to play with Barbara's children "because Mommie says you're too black" were bigoted *black* snobs. Another neighbor was a dominating clubwoman who publicly demeaned her husband. In a burst of frankness, I finished with: "And your next-door neighbor is sweet and pleasant, but honestly, she seems kind of dull!"

My WASP neighbor's relief seemed both amusing and pathetic. "Oh, my gosh, I'm so glad to hear you say that. I thought I was prejudiced."

The experience of being distrusted because we were white was something my neighbors and I could work through only in a neighborhood like ours. And perhaps only during the relatively serene times of 1962. Then all we had to cope with was distrust and withdrawal; black anger and hostility was still hidden.

And so, our first six months in West Mt. Airy were full of wonder. What I had stubbornly believed in Omaha—that people could live together—was a fact here. Each week, each month, I found new white people who had come with their children for the same melting pot mixture we had sought.

I remember saying happily to Ben that Grace Christopher could surely raise her son in this portion of America. Then I went out into the world.

Leland Hamilton asked me to write an article on Negro history.

Barbara Hamilton and I went shopping together.

That was the end of the peaceful six months.

Chapter Thirteen

No one would have been happier to leave well enough alone than I was as 1962 turned into 1963. Once again, I had everything I wanted. This time, though, my American Dream involved people instead of possessions and it had come true in a community where Americans did blend and complement each other. National events, however, would push us off that plateau; Leland and Barbara Hamilton only hurried the process.

Leland proved to be the least other-worldly minister I had ever met. He was a *Servant* of God, he said; God saw to men's souls and Leland felt the more everyday problems were left to him. When Leland was hired at the prison, he was told they were giving him an opportunity as the first Negro chaplain. Eventually he learned he had been brought in to counteract the mounting Black Muslim conversions among the Negro prisoners. To Leland, however, job placement for convicts was more important than their conversion or reconversion.

Leland's search for jobs for parolees led him into a friendship with the publisher of the Philadelphia *Tribune,* one of the oldest Negro-owned newspapers in America. Suddenly, Leland announced he was in charge of a special edition of the *Tribune* honoring the one hundredth anniversary of the Emancipation Proclamation and that, because of my advertising-writing background, he was sure I could write an article on Negro history. Leland handed me an armload of library books, a deadline, and suggested I trust in the Lord. Amen.

It never occurred to me that Negro history was any different from the glimpses I had been given in high school. Now, reading, then plummeting, through the books Leland gave me was like taking a familiar walk and finding the landscape and people were unexpectedly different.

I have never before questioned or noticed that almost every historical hero I had been offered was white and presumably Protestant. Reading about black American heroes, I felt as cheated as if I had been taught about the Civil War without Robert E. Lee or Western expansion without Lewis and Clark. Why was I taught about Paul Revere and not about Crispus Attucks? Attucks was a Negro seaman who, during the Boston Massacre of 1770, stood at the head of a group of colonists when British soldiers advanced on them. A six-foot giant, Attucks cried to his companions, "Do not be afraid." He may well have altered history by standing firm during a British test of American determination. Attucks, an escaped slave, was shot and killed, the first man to die for American freedom.

It was apparent why Nat Turner and Denmark Vesey were ignored; these black militants of the 1820's were as unpopular in the America of their time as the insurrectionist, George Washington, was to the British. At first, I could not understand why Benjamin Banneker had been omitted from "standard" histories. His quiet intellectual fight to prove black men were equal to whites was conducted in a moving correspondence with Thomas Jefferson. Banneker, a self-taught mathematical genius, made the first wooden clock and probably the first clock of any kind wholly made in America. He published almanacs, became an astronomer and a well-known naturalist. George Washington appointed him to the committee planning the city of Washington, D.C. When a white committee member resigned and took the completed plans with him to France, Banneker's astounding mind reproduced them from memory. Banneker wrote challenging letters to Thomas Jefferson, trying to convince Jefferson that *men* were as equal as Jefferson's own words in the Constitution proclaimed they were. Banneker beseeched Jefferson to feel the same hatred of tyranny over his own slaves as he had felt over the tyranny of the British. But in spite of his admiration for Banneker Jefferson never recanted his "suspicion" published in his *Notes on Virginia* that "the blacks are inferior to the whites . . ." Banneker lived to see slavery expanded and his friend Jefferson waver over the "morality" of slavery.

Then I did understand why Benjamin Banneker was omitted. It would be embarrassing. Jefferson's "all men are created equal" had an unseen asterisk to it—white was what was meant; just as Patrick Henry's "Give me liberty or give me death" was not meant to apply to the slaves *he* owned.

So Harriet Beecher Stowe was offered me as a heroine instead of black heroine Harriet Tubman. Harriet Tubman, illiterate because of laws forbidding slaves to be taught to read, became nonetheless the leading "conductor" of the Underground Railway. An escaped slave herself, she went back South again and again to lead other men and women north and to freedom. She was hated by slave owners, and rewards for her capture mounted. Once on a train, she was almost cornered. She picked up a newspaper, pretending to read it. Her pursuers knew the woman they searched for was illiterate and so passed her by. She said later, "I prayed I was holding the paper right side up." Later, during the

Civil War itself, Harriet Tubman served as a spy and a nurse. She was buried with military honors, but buried also in our history.

It began to seem as if all these black heroes had been hidden out of embarrassment. Certainly it was awkward to admit that many of the men signing the Declaration of Independence were, at that moment, holding other men in slavery. But what if I—and now my children—had been taught that countries as well as people make mistakes; that the measure of character is whether we face and correct our errors—or hide the evidence. This history lesson would have been more reassuring and important to me as a child than the memorizing of dates. It would have been far more exciting and challenging than the myth that Abraham Lincoln ended all problems with the stroke of his pen.

If American history had been taught me as an exciting struggle to do right rather than as some fairy-tale myth of perfection, perhaps historians could have given me Sojourner Truth along with Susan B. Anthony as my women's suffrage heroine. Unlike Miss Anthony, the well-educated daughter of a wealthy man, Sojourner Truth was an ex-slave. Yet in 1843, before Susan B. Anthony spoke out, Sojourner Truth held audiences so spellbound with her oratory on women's rights that some doubted she could be "merely" a woman. A heckler accused her of being a man in disguise. Sojourner Truth ripped her blouse to the waist, exposing her breasts to the entire audience. It was to *his* shame, she told the heckler, not hers, that such proof was necessary. Abraham Lincoln honored her at the White House, but my history books (and those of my children) do not mention her name.

Nor do they mention the names of African civilizations that predated ours! Nubia, whose black king, Piankhi, organized complex military strategies to free his country from Egypt in 700 B.C.—before Rome was built; or Askia the

Great, who ruled the powerful and enlightened empire of Songhay before America was discovered. Songhay's universities were famous and its cities lauded for their safety and hospitality while America was a wilderness. Did we suppress the stories of these empires because we eventually captured and enslaved their citizens?

Why did white history books hide even contemporary black Americans? I was taught all about Henry Ford's invention of the automobile as an example of American inventiveness and enterprise. Why had no one told me about Garrett Morgan, the Negro inventor whose indomitable perseverance made Ford's expansion possible?

Morgan's first invention, the gas mask, got world attention in 1916 when a mine explosion in Ohio trapped over twenty-five men in a smoke-filled tunnel 200 feet down. Someone remembered that Morgan had tried to interest manufacturers in a mask that allowed men to walk through smoke. Morgan and his brother were rushed to the scene; they put on their masks and carried most of the unconscious miners to safety. Their heroism publicized the successful invention and, at first, orders poured in from fire departments all over the country—until Morgan's color became known. Orders stopped and he was forced to sell out to a white manufacturer. Morgan returned to his workshop and, in 1923, invented the electric stop-and-go signal. This time he sold the rights immediately, to General Electric, for $40,000. The irony, of course, was that Selma, Alabama, police wore Morgan's gas masks while tear-gassing black Americans and that Ford's cars would have created chaos without the invention of a Negro man.

The most appalling racial irony was the death of Dr. Charles Drew who had developed the storing of blood plasma which saved hundreds of thousand of lives during World War II. In 1950, Dr. Drew was badly injured in an automobile accident in North Carolina. He died because the blood plasma transfusion was available only at the white hospital and Dr. Drew could not be taken there.

The list of hidden black heroes continued, back and forth in our history: Elijah McCoy who invented the first self-oiling machine, so superior that buyers added a phrase to America's vocabulary by demanding "the real McCoy" machine; Dr. Daniel Hale Williams who performed the first successful open-heart surgery in 1893 (and still was not allowed to practice in white hospitals). There is also the disturbing story of Henry Blair of Maryland who took out a patent on two corn harvesting devices in 1834 only to have them declared invalid twenty-three years later. The attorney general ruled that since Blair was a slave at the time and not a citizen, the government would not honor the patents.

This was the rebuttal to what I had heard so often, "Why don't 'they' help themselves?" *They* had and no one spoke of it; *they* were censored out of American history. If I felt cheated, black children were cheated out of far more. The self-doubt in each human being was reinforced in black children who were taught, as I was, that America was built by white people—alone. The only heroes they were allowed were docile, accommodating Booker T. Washington who preached social segregation to delighted white audiences and George Washington Carver, the quiet Alabama genius who saved Southern agriculture in his laboratories, yet drank obediently from the "Colored Only" fountains.

Midway through the long list of black men and women casually forgotten by American historians, I went to our school to see if, perhaps, they had been added since my schooldays. In a third-grade classroom, where 70 per cent of the children were black, I paged through their history textbook. "George Washington was a good man who treated his slaves well," it said. In the fourth grade the class studied "Famous Pennsylvanians" under a Negro teacher. The textbooks spoke of Benjamin Franklin, William Penn. Even the teacher confessed she didn't know about Richard Allen, the famous Pennsylvanian who had founded one of America's largest church denominations, the African Methodist Episcopal Church, and had been decorated by George Washington for heroism during the Revolution and Philadelphia's yellow fever epidemic.

I remember vividly the last book from Leland's stack that I read before writing the article. It was *The Black Muslims in America* (Beacon Press, 1961), a detailed and dispassionate book by C. Eric Lincoln. My white newspapers and magazines had painted the Muslims as wild-eyed insurrectionists; now I read about their deep dedication to self-improvement, the taboos against drinking, smoking, gambling, promiscuity, their astounding record in reclaiming former dope addicts and alcoholics, their protectiveness toward women and children, the religious edicts against installment buying and ostentation.

Yes, the rage against "blue-eyed devils" was there. It looked different to me now. After all I had seen and read, the rage seemed both normal and healthy. The Muslim leaders were saying, "*You* are not inferior because you are black; the blue-eyed devils have kept you down. It is *their* injustice; not your inferiority."

Suddenly, it seemed important that every black child bending over those degrading history textbooks hear what the Muslims were saying. And that people like Mrs. Jefferson who cleaned for me read the hidden history of her people. She had looked at me incredulously when I told her about Crispus Attucks and Garrett Morgan and Charles Drew. "Was that really true? *My* people did those things?" I knew she only half believed me; white folks books didn't say so.

I began to write Leland's article now, my anger overcoming my inexperience. The last part of the article now reads like a recruitment brochure for the Black Muslims. Their outrage matched mine, but I was forever ineligible to join.

Leland paid me the compliment of saying "You write like a Negro!" If I had dug deeper into the compliment I might have been more prepared for what I was to feel at the Emancipation Celebration he invited us to attend a few weeks later.

Meanwhile, my trip to downtown Philadelphia with Barbara Hamilton was a gesture of celebration that the article was finished. It was to be relaxing, fun, uninvolved with the outrage I had felt over suppressed black history. Instead, our shopping trip brought history painfully up to date.

The irritable glare of the tight-lipped trolley conductor began our day. Grouchy conductors were part of life to me. But when a Negro woman with her child got up to leave, bending down to brush cookie crumbs off the seat, the conductor stopped the trolley so quickly that the woman nearly fell. "Hurry up," he yelled. He opened the door briefly, then slammed it, nearly catching the woman and her child. "Pigs," he called after her. "All of you—pigs!"

I stiffened; Barbara put her hand on my arm. "Don't get excited," she said. "It happens all the time. In fact," she said with a tight smile, "watch what happens at the corner."

Up ahead, I could see four Negro women at the trolley stop. The conductor sped past. "He will only stop," Barbara said, "if there are *white* people standing there." At the next corner he did stop—near two white women hurrying toward the stop. The Negro man at the stop had to walk back to board the trolley.

Something had to be done. No, Barbara said, if I spoke to this conductor he'd become vulgar and obscene. Write to the company? Sure, if it would make me feel better. She had written letters and gotten form apologies. But even conductors like this were better than the transportation in her old neighborhood. As soon as a neighborhood becomes all black, Barbara explained, bus and trolley service is cut to the bone. As we got off the trolley, I glared at the conductor whose eyes were red and watery. He glared back. I took out a pencil and paper to copy down the trolley number. He opened the door while we stood on the curb and spat.

In Wanamaker's, Barbara and I tried on dresses. At first the pleasant saleswoman made me forget the trolleyman. I remembered Joan Benson telling me that in Texas she was never allowed to try on anything in the stores or return garments that didn't fit since no Negroes had these privileges. Then, as I took another dress from the rack, the saleswoman whispered to me, "No, not that one, dearie. Your maid is buying that."

I gasped "She's my *friend*—not my maid!"

The saleswoman looked at me closely, shrugged and walked away. I stood leaning bleakly against a counter while Barbara chose a dress. I resented each bill she placed in the hand of the saleswoman. But I couldn't bring myself to tell Barbara about the woman's humiliating assumption. As we walked out of the dress department, headed for the restaurant, Barbara said cheerfully, "She thought I was your maid, didn't she?"

I must have looked doleful to Barbara. She was, I know, trying to cheer me. "Don't let it shake you," she said. Barbara then started to tell me how much better her life was than that of her parents. She ended by giving me my first glimpse of Northern big-city ghetto life.

Until now, all our black friends were Southern born. I could feel a certain Northern disassociation when they described their experiences, but when Barbara talked about her childhood in New York my insulation was gone. What happened to her could have happened to any black family in Milwaukee while I was growing up, indifferent and unaware, on the other side of town.

At the restaurant table, as we waited for our order to be

taken, Barbara began by saying that she never expected to live in a neighborhood like Mt. Airy or to send her children to a school as pleasant as ours. She had been born in Harlem. Her father was a tailor and rich by comparison with most of the people around them. But the neighborhood was crowded and the rents high; her father used to tell her that soon—someday—they would move.

It was when she started school, she said, that her parents became determined to get out of Harlem. Her first grade teacher, a young white woman, screamed at the class one day, "I don't know why I bother! None of you is going to do anything but scrub toilets anyway!" Barbara said she could still remember the woman's red face and she could remember looking around at her friends. One girl burst into tears; several children slumped down in their seats; a little boy stared with undisguised hatred.

"I think the woman was frightened by the stunned silence in the room. She told us she'd 'get us' if we told our parents. But I told my mother. She said not to worry. I'd go to a new school sooner than I thought."

Barbara had gotten the details later from her grandmother. Her parents decided it was futile to rent in a "better section." The "better sections" that neighbors had moved to soon became just as overcrowded. Landlords cut up apartments into ever-smaller units as whites moved out. Barbara's parents felt the only hope was to save for a down payment on a house. All Barbara understood at the time was that suddenly her mother went out early each morning and returned late at night. She had gotten a job as cleaning woman in Scarsdale. Until then it was a matter of pride to her father that his wife not be allowed to work.

"My mother was a secretarial school graduate but she couldn't get a job in an office. I think I can remember the late-night arguments and somehow I knew finally that my mother was scrubbing toilets and I pushed the teacher's words out of my mind."

Barbara was quiet for a moment as we sat in the restaurant. Her soft, round face looked vulnerable and defenseless. She said she hadn't thought about any of this for years. At that moment the waitress, her blonde hair swinging in ill temper, flung a handful of silverware in front of us and flounced away. Barbara looked after her and then continued tightly.

"My mother took the long train ride to Scarsdale every day because they paid more out there; she worked for several families as their maid's helper for heavy cleaning because that paid more too. At home she and Dad never seemed to eat. I learned later they lived on canned tomatoes to save every cent.

"When Mother became ill, everything they had saved went for hospital bills. And when she died my grandmother paid for the funeral. The funeral was the last time I saw my father. For a long time I didn't understand why he left. But he was forty-five when Mother died. I think he just gave up. Every once in a while my grandmother would get an envelope with a few bills in it. She said he told her he was going to pay for my mother's funeral."

Barbara shook her head as if to chase unwelcome memories. This was not what she had meant to tell me, she said. She had gone to live with her grandmother in Larchmont in a tiny, neat house in the Negro section there. She had been treated pleasantly in the all-white high school as one of the few Negro students; gone on to college in Philadelphia, met Leland, and she had her happy ending.

"I go back to Harlem and I know how lucky I am. Mother and Dad gave me something, even if they never saw me get out of the neighborhood. A lot of my friends didn't make it. My best friend now has ten children; she tells me she just doesn't care anymore, one way or another. And I went back to my old school. I put on my best clothes. That first grade teacher is still there. I could hardly believe it."

Barbara's face looked soft and wistful. While she talked I had been comparing everything in my life that had been so different. My mother, self-taught, had been a secretary; my teachers had treated me as a child with a precious potential; my father had left me too, but in anger, not in defeat. I didn't know what to say to Barbara. Just then the blonde waitress crashed down two cups of coffee, leaned over Barbara's shoulder and put the check in front of me.

Barbara reached over, grabbed it and said loudly, "My treat, Lois." Then in a quiet hiss, she said to me, "That's it. I can take the bad service and the stares, but I can also take the check."

I looked around. Yes, there were some white women looking at us; the service had been bad, but no worse than I had experienced before. I turned back to Barbara, ready to tell her she was imagining things. But all of a sudden I realized that for Barbara the strain was never to be sure. I could dismiss rude waitresses and trolley conductors as unpleasant people; I never had to wonder if they were expressing their contempt for my color.

We left Wanamaker's and walked to the local train station. I did not want to take the trolley home. We would take the Chestnut Hill Local instead. As we walked through the courtyard of City Hall and emerged at the street, Barbara pointed to a well-dressed Negro man carrying a brief case in one hand while raising the other to signal a taxi.

"Watch what happens," she said. Cab after cab passed him by. I saw one taxi turn his signal light off a few yards from the young black man. Two white men approached the curb near us. A taxi passed the black man, stopped for the white man. The Negro man put his brief case down. He stood as still as a figure in brown marble, not moving for minutes. Then we saw him pick up his brief case and cross the street

— 165 —

to a bus stop. He stood with his head down, the highly polished new brief case dangling from a listless hand.

We took the Chestnut Hill Local home instead of the trolley. A group of white college-age girls sat giggling a few seats behind us. As we hurried to get off at our stop, I saw one of the girls put her foot out as I passed. I caught myself as I tripped. The girl, I am sure, was no more surprised than I was when I stopped, took a step back, and kicked her ankle. I got off the train feeling childish, petty—and deeply satisfied.

That day ended my fantasy that racist problems had been left behind in Omaha. I had only begun to see them there in their mildest forms. Now I knew that the eroding drip-drop of daily humiliations had no geographic limits; if they happened in Nebraska and Pennsylvania, they happened all over my country.

This was, I think, the end of my voluntary learning. From then on, experiences came to us. I was like Bluebeard's wife; I had opened a door and it was impossible to close my eyes to the sight and meaning of everything inside, no matter how much I would wish it.

The Emancipation Celebration a week later showed me how far I had gone inside that room. The celebration was held in an immense downtown Negro-owned church, crowded beyond capacity with Negro people. From their clothes and demeanor I took them for middle-class people, much like myself.

Each speaker seemed to increase in emotional intensity. First, an elderly dark-brown-skinned gentleman, a prominent doctor spoke glowingly of the important achievement of Emancipation one hundred years ago that day. I wondered if this portly, well-satisfied gentleman had read any textbooks lately. Then, a light-skinned, red-haired young man reminded the audience that "Lincoln freed only our ancestors in the South—only Southern slaves. His Emanci-

pation Proclamation did *not* apply to slaves in the North."
He was not angry, only wryly cynical, pointing out that the
proclamation was not as much a humanitarian gesture as it
was a military gesture, designed to create chaos in the Con-
federacy.

Then a tall, dark-skinned man, a dentist from Georgia,
mounted the rostrum. His voice was resonant with emotion,
but he spoke slowly at first. Independent nations were
emerging in Africa, he said. "We have our history now—we
have our heritage. . . . White domination is crumbling." He
began to name the countries where "black men have risen
up to take their homelands back from white oppressors."

The huge room, filled with at least 2,000 people, was absolutely still now. At the mention of "white domination,"
"white oppressors" a few heads turned toward us. I returned
a quick, bland smile, hoping to show I took it impersonally.

"These black men in Africa waited—and they prayed—
and they petitioned—and finally they didn't wait any more,"
he said. "We have waited; we have prayed; we have petitioned. *And one hundred years is long enough to wait.*"

Somewhere in that large room one voice said, "Amen."
The speaker continued now. "Kenyatta didn't wait." A soft
chorus of "Amen" came now. "Tshombe didn't wait."
People began to applaud. "Kasavubu didn't wait."

With each name of an African leader the cheers and applause increased until I could feel an immense force gathering and rolling in plangent cadence. And I found I was
cheering and applauding too. All the anger I had had to put
aside—the anger at the powerful white people in Omaha who
wouldn't lift a hand for the Bensons, the corporation that
sped us out of town, the Philadelphia trolleyman, the saleswoman, the waitress, the all-white textbooks—all this anger
combined with the fury I could now feel around me.

The speaker continued to call the names of black heroes.

People rose, applauding louder and faster. "We too will have our freedom now," the speaker cried, ringingly.

The elderly woman standing next to me had tears rolling down her cheeks. I was standing, cheering and applauding. The speaker bolted from the rostrum and I turned to Barbara, ready to say, "Yes, we'll have our freedom *now*."

Only then did I realize I was shouting for a freedom I'd always had. I had heard and felt black anger for the first time; I had been in the middle of it and joined it. But incredible and illogical as it sounded, I felt comfortable and relieved when we left the church.

Chapter Fourteen

The black anger evident at the Emancipation Celebration remained suppressed during the rest of 1963. At times I couldn't understand why. On April 25, Attorney General Robert F. Kennedy visited Governor George Wallace in Alabama to ask him to obey school desegregation laws. On June 11, Governor Wallace personally attempted to bar two young black students from the University of Alabama. That evening on nationwide TV, President John F. Kennedy appealed to the South to reject prejudice and violence and to the entire nation to examine its conscience. The next day, civil rights leader Medgar Evers was murdered on his doorstep in Mississippi. Through all this, black people in the South patiently continued their nonviolent demonstrations.

White violence would come North that summer. But in early spring I still believed that experienced Northern liberals were effectively fighting problems I now knew existed even in Philadelphia; people like Harper Thorpe, for example, the insurance man whose sister had sold us our house. Harp's enthusiastic welcome to Ben—"We need more liberals here like you"—suggested he was working diligently on

Northern discrimination. Harp was active in a number of civil rights groups and often pictures of Harp would gaze out at me from the newspaper, his freckled face the only pink face among brown ones.

In March, Harper Thorpe had phoned to invite us to a cocktail party to raise funds for SNCC's Southern voter drive. It seemed odd that he would ask me for names of Negro couples to invite. Surely he must know more black people than we did. But I gave him five or six names, including Leland and Barbara.

On the afternoon of the party, only one Negro couple was there. They were Jack and Gloria Clinton, the couple who lived near Barbara and who had forbidden their children to play with Jimmy Hamilton "because Mommie says you're too black." Even though I disliked Gloria Clinton because of this episode, I could never share black friends' anger at people like the Clintons whom they labeled callous "Toms." It seemed to me that black people should have the same privilege of indifference as whites. Jack Clinton had worked hard, became a doctor, and if he chose to ignore the problems of other black people, it was no worse than whites ignoring the problems of the white poor in Appalachia.

But when Harper Thorpe, fuzzy tongued from several of his own cocktails, asked Jack Clinton later, "What do your people really want?" it was hard to know which was more appalling—Harp's naïve questioning of one black man or Jack Clinton's answer. Jack had turned red beneath his light-beige skin. His smile looked forced as he said that he thought things were fine, but that, you know, some people want everything right now. Chronic complainers, he said. Harp nodded his freckled face. "You're a smart boy," Harp said. "Have another drink."

The next day Barbara Hamilton and I sat on her patio watching our children experiment in the first spring mud. I told her about the party. Barbara sighed and said she thought it was time for me to learn about "white liberals." She would sound bitter, she admitted, but it was important that I know. "I believe you're sincere, Lois," she said, "but you're much too gullible." Then shyly, "You know, I pray for you on that score."

"Jack Clinton," Barbara began, "is a Tom and he did not tell unpleasant truths to Harper Thorpe because he knew Harper did not want to hear them." Jack wanted white friends and he was smart enough to tell them only what they wanted to hear. She had wasted many years believing in white liberals and she had gradually noticed their abrupt withdrawal if she talked of things that were too true or too close to their own lives.

"I finally gave up on all whites," Barbara said, "because I was just plain tired of being disappointed." She grinned suddenly, realizing what she had said to me, touched my arm, and explained that my friendship with Joan Benson told her I might be different.

"But with people like Harper Thorpe," she said, "I've developed the technique of turning off the sound and just looking at the picture. It was hard at first; you want to believe people care; their sympathetic words sound good. Eventually, you find they are only words.

"Take Harper Thorpe's speeches at Brotherhood banquets, and then take a look at his all-white neighborhood, the private schools where he sends his children. Remember the clubs he belongs to, clubs that allow no Jews, let alone Negroes. If socially prestigious Harper Thorpe had tried to change the WASP-only policies of these famous clubs, it would have made the newspapers. Obviously, he hasn't tried and he hasn't resigned from them. This would be an action too close to home."

Leland had gone to Harper Thorpe's office one day; Harper Thorpe employed no Negroes. Harper Thorpe, Barbara said, and her round soft eyes showed no pleasure in the statement, makes his speeches and carefully avoids any step in his own life where he could conceivably make a difference. "And," she added, "Harper Thorpe knows what happened to Ben. Has he made any attempt to help Ben make contacts for another job?"

We had told Harper the story of the Bensons' house-hunt and Ben's sudden transfer here. Harper had expressed long, loud anger at "that racist company." But, no, I told Barbara, he hadn't offered Ben any help. In fact, now that I thought about it, Harp's initial enthusiasm about introducing us to "friends of ours you'll love" had mysteriously stopped at that point. "But then, why is he involved in civil rights at all?" I asked Barbara.

In his case, Barbara said, it was probably his political interests. A lot of black people were impressed with his words and some whites were impressed too, especially since he actually said little.

Look, Barbara continued, she was not going to stereotype whites as they stereotyped blacks, but white people did break down into certain categories; politicians represented only one type. There were others who actually profited financially from keeping black people down—the ghetto landlords, big corporations who needed cheap labor pools, merchants who needed gullible undereducated people for their rackets, real estate block-busters. These white people literally couldn't *afford* to have consciences. Forget them. They couldn't change. Forget, too, the whites who desperately needed someone to look down on. Color was handy; the white cab driver could use it to feel superior to the black chemist.

But it was the white liberals who, she had come to believe, were more destructive than the greedy or the damaged-ego whites. These were the people who made the brotherhood speeches, who cultivated people like Jack Clinton. They knew racial discrimination was wrong and they wanted to do something about it, but not too much—only enough to make themselves feel better. And they could make themselves feel better by marching in the *South,* by working for laws that were never enforced, and by belonging to an organization. Bitterly, Barbara said, "There is nothing better for avoiding individual responsibility than joining—or organizing—a large useless group to hold meetings and *do* nothing."

The end result, Barbara said, was that blacks had wasted time for years listening to meaningless promises. Martin Luther King's bus boycott, the sit-ins by black college students in restaurants in the South—these actions by black people caused the changes.

"And then, of course, we get the kind of whites who are outcasts in their own groups. They try to get both revenge and status by joining us. They get the revenge by screaming 'Bigot' at others and status by reaching down to help the black people they're convinced are inferior."

I thought of Ruth McPhetridge, the white president of the Urban League Guild in Omaha, with her sad, angry eyes and deep lines in her pink face. I couldn't believe she fitted in with any of Barbara's descriptions. Then I remembered what Janet Adams said the same night she told me about her classmate's lynching. Janet had said that black people couldn't afford to become bitter; that Ruth, a white, had made herself ineffective through her bitterness.

When I told Barbara about Ruth McPhetridge, Barbara said she'd known of a few whites like that. Older whites, she said, had often fought for so many years with so little progress that they simply gave up. "Black people can't give up even if they want to. Perhaps God planned it that way—to give us a way to our strength."

I had to ask Barbara, "What group do I fit in?" I thought she would give me an honest answer. She did.

A frown made darker lines on her sable-brown forehead

and she put her hand on my arm. "I don't know," she said, "and I don't think you know yet yourself."

The next events didn't clarify my feelings. On August 29, 1963, the day after the massive, peaceful march on Washington, violence came north. A medical technician and his wife and daughter moved into Folcroft, a neighborhood not ten miles from us. Mobs attacked the house with bricks, garbage, paint; they broke windows, ripped out utility wires. The mob was white; the family was black. As I listened to the newscasts I didn't feel anger; just a strange desperation. On TV we watched state troopers trying to hold back the white crowds. This time those jeering white faces were not in Birmingham, Alabama, or Oxford, Mississippi; they were in Philadelphia.

Spike, now seven years old, was terrified. Would "they" do that to his friend Michael's house? He had seen the TV newscast before I realized it was on. He had seen the interview with the Negro family and seen the white faces, distorted by hate. I tried to comfort Spike. No, they wouldn't hurt Michael. Yes, he could go to Michael's house to make sure. Why did those people act like that, Spike wanted to know. They were sick people, I said, and they lived far away. People in our neighborhood were different.

I called Dolph Priest, a reporter with the Negro-owned newspaper who had become our friend. Could he get me into Folcroft with a press pass? Dolph, usually calm and cynical, sounded alarmed at my request. My God, he wouldn't help me get anywhere near Folcroft! The people there were way out of control; I could get hurt. My going out to talk to these people would have been ridiculous, I know, but that summer Sunday it would have been easier than sitting at home, quiet and helpless.

Two weeks later, on September 15, 1963, four little Negro girls were killed by a bomb in a Birmingham, Alabama, church. Whatever I had felt over Folcroft was deepened and expanded now. I took Ben to the airport that Sunday and I remember walking along the long hallways, wanting to stop the Negro people I saw and tell them I was sorry, to apologize in some way for the white violence during those two dreadful weeks. There were no smiling Negro faces that day. All the families walking along those glass-enclosed corridors were subdued and silent. Heads were bowed and even the little Negro children seemed quiet and aware of something awful that had happened. No one looked at me and as I passed small groups of Negro people the airport corridors seemed very wide indeed.

If a Negro mob had attacked a white family, if a Negro bomber killed four white children, I could imagine how "my" people would respond: Not with their heads bowed in acceptance of a tragedy. Indeed, when black ghettos exploded later, I found how we did respond. But on Monday, at our school, I remember my surprise that Negro children could still call "Hi" at me and smile.

Leland Hamilton's request came then, when my feeling of guilt was high. He told us that one of the convicts he worked with at the prison, a young man named Digger Pierce, was up for parole. If we could give him a job—fixing the basement or something—he could get his parole. Digger had been in prison twice, both times for burglary, but Leland felt he was ready to stay straight *if* he could get a temporary job with us while Leland found him a permanent one.

It wasn't an easy decision. We had been saving every penny in case Ben's job ended before he found another; the thought of a criminal in my house was hardly reassuring. But, I told Ben, if it meant a man's freedom . . . And I felt it was at least one small, but tangible, something we could do.

Still, I pictured a tough-faced, hard-eyed man, and when Leland brought Digger Pierce to our house Digger's shyness was the most outstanding thing about him. How could a burglar be shy? He was, though. This tall young man with skin the color of rain-drenched earth limped bleakly behind Leland as they came up our driveway, like a child being taken back to school after a misdemeanor. Digger's limp, we learned later, came from a broken ankle hastily repaired by a reform school doctor. But that day we knew little about Digger except that he was trying futilely to hide his six-foot-plus frame behind Leland's stocky five-foot-seven.

Digger's clothes reflected the taste of many relatives—or more accurately, the employers of many relatives. His jacket was too short, his shirt too large; his trousers, gathered at the waist, ended well above his stiffened ankle. His clothes, like the lines of his glossy brown face, mostly drooped down. Even the tight jacket managed to droop as limply as Digger's mouth, both, I suspected later, from having been buttoned up too often.

Digger was not sullen, merely bashful. When Ben spoke to him Digger jumped in panic, but then answered with a direct, level gaze before looking down again at his shoes. The first few days he spoke so quietly I could hardly hear him. He worked diligently in the basement, limping agilely as he put some waterproofing gook on the walls. When I talked to him he flinched. It was a strange feeling to have this tall man terrified of me. Then I realized that the parole officer would be coming to visit me; I had Digger's freedom in my hands. From then on I tried to say something complimentary about whatever it was he was plastering on the basement walls.

My children cracked Digger's shyness first. They loved this nice giant in our basement and he insisted they were not underfoot. Sarah, now four, sat happily on his ladder; Noah and Spike, who were now five and seven, rushed down right after school to see "Mr. Pierce." Digger's first direct statement to me was that this was the first time in his life *anyone* had called him Mister Pierce.

Shortly afterward, Digger began to talk. First, he told me he had a son—Kevin—the same age as Noah. Then, several days later, he volunteered the information that he was getting married. He looked up at me from his seat on the basement stairs, perhaps to see if I showed shock at the unconventional reversal of parenthood and marriage. I guess I didn't or else Digger simply wanted to talk about it. He had gotten "a wonderful girl in trouble" just before he was arrested and had promised to marry her if she would wait. She had—for five years, apparently—and they were to get married the next week end.

I didn't hear the rest of Digger's story until after I had come home one afternoon, fuming and frustrated by some police action I had seen. I had been in a traffic tie-up on Germantown Avenue, stalled in front of the YWCA and watching a group of black teen-agers laughing and talking together on the sidewalk. Just as the traffic began to move a police car pulled up and two policemen leaped out, their clubs held high, and charged at the group of youngsters, scattering them. I was astonished, then angry at the absolutely unreasonable attack. I drove around the block, planning to ask the policemen why they had attacked the youngsters. The second time around I saw the policemen sitting laughing and eating ice cream cones in their car. But on the crowded street there was no place at all I could park my car to talk with them. I came home filled with anger and frustration. I told Digger what had happened.

When Digger said, "Don't worry about it, Mrs. S.," I wanted to choke him. Cops "were like that," he said. All he hoped was that he'd never have to see another one. He was staying "stone clean" from now on.

If Digger had told me all this before the parole officer's visit, I might have suspected his motives. But the parole officer had already called on me. There was no reason for Digger to talk now except that he wanted to. And I wanted to listen. I had become more and more curious about how this gentle young man had become a burglar.

"The Rev" (Leland) had convinced Digger it made sense to "stay clean," but Digger had also noticed that most of the men in Death Row were there for "jobs where they made less than fifty dollars." Digger was deeply impressed. He repeated over and over, "Fifty dollars—a lousy fifty dollars." He couldn't say it, but I sensed he was afraid of whatever had made these men panic and hit or shoot or stab someone during a robbery. Maybe he was lucky he got picked up the last time, he said. Five years was a good long time to think things over.

The first time he got arrested was bad, he said, and his brown forehead creased over the memory. It was a mistake, and it had upset his mother. Two cops and a white man came to his house and said he had held up a gas station. "They *pushed* my mother aside." Digger's hands clenched momentarily in anger. Then, calm again, he explained that he had never seen his accuser before. "I didn't even know where his gas station was!"

Digger accepted his false arrest philosophically. "Well, you know, this white man—well, a lot of people think we all look alike." Digger said this as if it were somehow his fault. The cops had taken him to Youth Study Center; he was fifteen.

I asked all my middle-class questions in horror; couldn't his mother get a lawyer? Couldn't he prove he didn't do it?

Yeah, well, he was playing football in a lot when the robbery took place but "nobody's gonna take what my friends said over what the man said." The lawyer told Digger to plead guilty. "He said it would be cheaper that way for my Ma."

So Digger had docilely gone to a reform school.

I asked, "What about your father?"

Oh, well, that was another story. His father was a good man; he worked every job he could get, but he got sick. Then he couldn't find any job at all. He left so his family "could get on the welfare." Digger's eyes were intense, convincing me his father had done the right thing. "He got money to us through my aunt. Then we didn't hear no more. His last letter came from Texas . . . Sent me money because he said I'd be nearly a young man." Then Digger looked through me. "Wish I knew if he died or what."

This was the second time black people had told me of absent fathers who nevertheless sent money. My quick twinge of envy was ridiculous, I told myself. My own father had sent none. Still how could I envy an ex-convict with a poor education and not much hope for a future?

Digger went on with his story of reform school. He made friends who taught him how to stay away from the worst guards. "I'm not gonna tell you about what those guards did to kids. But if one of your kids . . . well, they won't." I hoped so.

The broken ankle, Digger said, was his own fault. He liked fooling with machinery. A motor fell on him. The doctor at the reform school thought it wasn't hurt bad, but it never healed right. Digger looked at his stiff ankle as if it had betrayed the doctor.

Digger got out of reform school when he was eighteen. They taught him to type but there were no jobs for a young, disabled ex-convict. "None of my buddies found jobs either —so we were *real* smart," Digger said sardonically. "We broke into a TV store. Man, didn't get three blocks before we got caught. We musta been nuts—scared kids runnin' through the street carryin' them little TV sets." Digger was able to laugh at his lack of aptitude for burglary.

"Then I met the 'Rev.' First man I could ever talk to. You know, he ain't like no minister. And anyway, the other chaplains—well, excuse me for saying it, but I couldn't talk to no white man anyway, you know. The 'Rev' came up like I did."

Digger now sat straight, proudly telling about his happy

ending. The "Rev" had some other jobs lined up for him; in the summer he was going to try to get into maybe construction. He could move fast even with his bad foot. And he was marrying Louise.

Where Digger was born and raised, Leland explained a few days later, his ending *was* happy. Digger wasn't the first, nor would he be the last kid falsely arrested. Digger had not become bitter. Okay, so he was not the brightest guy, but maybe that was part of his luck. The bitter guys were the ones who ended up in Death Row; they were smart enough to know why they were bitter. In Digger's neighborhood he was lucky to merely stay alive, Leland went on. Half the kids Leland himself had gone to school with were either dead or in prison.

Look at what they see, Leland said, pacing the room as if it were a cage. The only "successful" black people in the ghetto are the numbers writers, the prostitutes, the pimps; these are the people with money to spend. The other black men, the "honest" men, work all their lives for low wages at dead-end jobs. "Most of those kids never—never—see a black man who got ahead by honesty and hard work. The smart kids figure this out early." And the Negro mothers? What do they say to their kids? Leland smiled bitterly. "Here's the dialogue: 'Son, you behave yourself and study hard and you'll have a good life.' 'Like who, Ma?' 'Never you mind; just listen to me, child.' "

Yes, I could understand. The child would listen; he would also look around him.

"And the worst part," Leland said ruefully, "is that black crime is always such petty crime. May God forgive me, but our people never get a chance at the big profitable crime! We can't embezzle or take bribes or evade income tax. We don't get jobs where we *can* embezzle, we're never important enough to bribe, and the Lord knows we don't have enough income to make evading the tax worth while. Those are all white people's crimes."

"Black people," Leland said, "get arrested for the nickel-and-dime crime—*if* they're lucky. Watch the newspapers and see how often black 'suspects' are shot by cops while they're 'escaping.' Then notice how seldom this happens to white suspects!"

But the worst job for black men, Leland said, was working for white racketeers, the white vice lords in dope or numbers. They used up black men like Kleenex—for taking the risks and taking the raps. No, Digger was lucky that he had no real aptitude for crime; he'd live longer. On welfare maybe, but he'd live.

Not necessarily, I found out about a week later.

Digger sat on our front steps for a moment after carrying out some debris from the basement. I was pruning a shrub near him, but out of sight of the police car that pulled up in front of Digger. I heard a man's voice say, "Move on, you black bastard." I stood up and stepped out onto the front walk. The young policeman saw me. His pink face turned red, but he had his hand on his gun and Digger was half up, ready to run.

The policeman's eyes quickly assessed me and my pruning shears and probably the indignant expression on my face. Before I could say a word, he jumped back into the car and literally zoomed away. Digger was shaking. "Don't never stand between a black man and a cop. Don't you never do that!" he said. He did not have to tell me what might have happened. If the policeman had been nervous enough to fire; if I had stepped out at the wrong moment; if there were no witnesses, Digger might have made Death Row for a lot less than $50.

But the last experience we were to have with Digger before he left our house was, somehow, the most distressing. I was slowly shedding my own prejudices about convicts, unwed fathers, crime in the streets. I thought I had no anger left over what had happened to Digger and the resignation with which he accepted it. Then, during his last week with us, Digger asked if we would do him a favor. Would we let him bring his son, five-year-old Kevin, to visit on Sunday?

"You know, Mrs. S.," Digger said, "I've been walking through my neighborhood and thinking about the fact that Kevin don't see no white faces except the old people who run some of the stores. And Kevin's never talked to a white kid ever!"

"Sure, we'd like to meet Kevin," I said. I was glad that Kevin would be no novelty to my children after their predominantly black school.

For the next few days all Digger talked about was Kevin; Kevin was learning to like him; Kevin ate too much; Kevin was taller than Noah. I had told Digger about the black heroes I had read about—Charles Drew who developed blood plasma, Garrett Morgan who invented the gas mask and stop light.

"Gee, Mrs. S., really? These guys were colored?" Yes, and Kevin could grow up to do things like that, I said. Then Digger shook his head. No, Kevin was retarded. Oh. There was nothing I could say to that.

When Digger limped up our driveway, holding the hand of a little boy, the drooping lines of Digger's face were gently turned up at his mouth and eyes. He led Kevin as if quick movement would break him. In contrast to Digger's hand-me-downs, Kevin was buttoned into a heavy coat with the shape of brand-newness and the fit of quality to it. Digger limped in front of him, smiling, reaching back for the little boy's hand. The child looked up at Digger as if this large new father was still a toy he must treat carefully.

When Digger brought Kevin inside, I looked for some dull-eyed sign of retardation. When my children swooped down on Kevin and pulled him away to the playroom, I could see nothing but bright eagerness and the quick, sure movements of a normal child. Digger sat down with Ben and me to drink coffee. I asked, "Who diagnosed Kevin as retarded? A doctor? At what age was he tested?"

Digger replied, "Oh, the kindergarten teacher she said Kevin was retarded."

Had she tested him?

"Yes," Digger nodded. "He couldn't write his name and he couldn't button his coat. That teacher said he had to do those things. He's retarded, she said. He was put in with the other slow kids." Digger smiled, bravely but bleakly.

But Noah couldn't write his name! What kind of kindergarten teacher would expect this of a five-year-old? Just then the children came into the room to get Kevin's coat. I inspected it. Look, I said to Digger, *I* can't button this coat without difficulty! It was a heavy, expensive coat of thick material that made buttoning genuinely difficult, even for me.

At that time I didn't know about the sick or incompetent or simply sadistic teachers who sift down, too often, into the slum schools. But I did know that Kevin had been labeled retarded on capricious evidence. I never found out what had happened; I suspect now that some overworked, overtired woman learned that Kevin was an illegitimate child of a convict, or perhaps Kevin had irritated her in some way. Since then, I have met many bright, unconforming children whom teachers cannot "reach," and I've met the teachers who handily label their own failures "retarded."

That day when I compared Kevin with Noah the drooping lines of Digger's face straightened just a little. Noah couldn't write his name? But Kevin did other things. "He can't make up his mind. He cries a lot. Loves people one minute—then says he hates us." My copy of Gesell's *Child Behavior* was in the next room. I grabbed it and flipped to the chapter I had been reading about Noah's out-of-bounds five-year-old behavior. Look. All *normal* five-year-olds act like that!

For the next hour Digger and Ben and I talked about children; each time we compared experiences Digger became more jubilant. Normal kids—*white* kids—did these things too? We gave Digger books to take home. Prison libraries had not included Dorothy Baruch or Selma Freiberg's works.

Digger never shared my anger at the teacher who had labeled Kevin retarded. He would see the principal and get Kevin tested the right way. But the test didn't matter to Digger anymore. He had made his own test. Our children had sucked their thumbs, wet beds, had tantrums, too. Kevin was okay. "My God," Digger repeated over and over while we talked, "My God, you just don't know what you folks are doin' for me!"

When Digger left with Kevin I watched them go down our driveway. This time Digger limped a dance as he boxed and tussled with his son. Digger, in his rag-bag clothes, lifted Kevin, tossed him in the air, and Kevin laughed.

Before he left, Digger had said with all the lines of his face turning up now, "How much does it cost to go to college?" For Kevin, Digger would fight.

Chapter Fifteen

During the twenty-four months we had lived in Philadelphia, our worry about Ben's job gradually diminished. Perhaps we were so busy living that our initial concern faded into the background. And, of course, it was still possible that Ben's job with the corporation would continue.

As it turned out, it was lucky Ben did not grab at some of the advertising-merchandising jobs offered him. He rejected an offer from one company when he found out that they had a reputation for unethical practices and from another when the president of the firm talked balefully of their "Jew-boy competitors." Ben also turned down out-of-town offers. Our children were blossoming in their happily mixed school. Sarah was in kindergarten now, Noah in first grade and Spike in third. Their unself-conscious, open friendliness with the potpourri of children was delightful and, we felt, important. We loved our neighborhood and hoped to stay.

Early in June 1964 Ben showed me a clipping from the *Wall Street Journal* that moved us back toward reality. Two executives, one in Dallas and one in Bethlehem, Pennsylvania, had "lost their jobs recently . . . because [of] controversial community activities during their spare time." The marketing vice-president in Dallas had written an article after President Kennedy's assassination on "the climate of hate" in Dallas, but the man in Bethlehem was fired when a volunteer race-relations group he had been active in published a study of limited job opportunities for Negroes in Bethlehem. If this man's employers felt the study was an indirect criticism of their company hiring policies, Ben pointed out, firing the man only publicized the whole issue.

I agreed, but there were times when I almost wished Ben had been clearly fired. It might have been better than a false security. I was critical of Ben for what I felt was his unrequited loyalty to a corporation that had demoted and transferred him; he would not take as much time as other men would take from their work to hunt a new job. Ben stubbornly insisted that he had to do his best, both for his own conscience and because the job might be permanent after all.

Meanwhile Ben tried to use some of what we had learned about the black community in his job with the corporation. Dolph Priest, our cynical black friend and journalist, pointed out, "There's more of us than people like to think." Dolph's attitudes toward discrimination were as hard as the finish on his Brooks Brothers' suits. To him, "racism is too profitable to white business for them to end it." But, Dolph said, wryly, "Someday they're going to find out that in Philadelphia alone black purchasing power is nearly three-quarter of a billion dollars!" Dolph brushed an imaginary speck from his well-cut jacket and said blandly, "Maybe then white business will learn to love us!"

Soon after Dolph's remarks, Ben checked the corporation's milk and ice cream sales in Negro neighborhoods and found they were meager. A Negro market study, Ben felt, could show the sales potential and stir the corporation's interest in ghetto problems.

Dar Lewis, the cautiously neutral manager of the Philadelphia branch, okayed the study after Ben mentioned the purchasing power of the black community. Ben helped the company's advertising agency organize the research. He suggested integrated ads be evaluated. Pepsi-Cola had used them successfully.

When the study was completed in January 1964, Dar Lewis called Ben into his office. Forget the whole thing, he said. The survey showed that 10 per cent of the white customers objected to integrated ads. Ben told me he had argued that this meant 90 per cent of the white customers didn't object.

"Drop the subject," Dar Lewis said. "The decision is final."

Four weeks after the Negro market study, Ben was moved to a smaller office. A month later, the desks of two office girls were crowded in with him. On June 29, 1964, he was told that his department was being dissolved and his job was over. Although Ben had been given this news in the afternoon, he didn't tell me about it until after I finished making a report at our school's parents' meeting that night. He didn't want me to be upset. I can remember Ben's face drained of color and his words, "They told me today my job's over." We had previously invited the committee chairman to come with us after the meeting for coffee. Both Ben and I were too befuddled to cancel the date. We sat in our living room, making conversation with the man, my mind hardly on what he was saying, my stomach feeling hollow with wanting to be alone with Ben.

But when we were alone all I could do was remind Ben we had been thrifty and that I would go to work myself if necessary. I could not feel as sorry for us as I might have two weeks before. Just as Warren Platt's death minimized Ben's demotion, another family we had just met made Ben's unemployment minor by comparison.

We met the Buchanans because of another Panel of American Women. I had formed a Philadelphia Panel shortly after my disillusioning trip downtown with Barbara Hamilton.

This time, it was easy to find a Catholic, Jewish, and white Protestant panelist right in our neighborhod. Barbara was the Negro panelist and, again, I moderated.

At a Panel appearance before an Episcopalian congregation in the suburbs, I was introduced to a small, quiet, brown-skinned woman with wistful eyes whose name I recognized immediately. I will call her Betty Buchanan to preserve the privacy she has sought for so long. She and her husband were the couple who had moved into the Folcroft section of Phila-delphia a year ago and who had been attacked by white mobs. After the three days of rioting by whites who threw firebombs into the house, wrecked utility lines, and tried to enter the Buchanan home, state troopers had restored order and the story disappeared from the newspapers. I assumed that the people of Folcroft had calmed down and that the Buchanans had finally been accepted by at least some neighbors who had gotten to know them.

I was surprised at meeting Betty Buchanan to find she was unlike what I had expected. The newspaper pictures made her seem taller than she was. The television scenes I had watched had shown the mob rather than this small woman with the terra-cotta complexion and wistful gaze. I had be-lieved anyone willing to be the first Negro family in an area would be poised, confident, and aggressive. Betty Buchanan was subdued, spoke with a slight stammer, and smiled tim-idly.

Yes, she said, they were still living in Folcroft. I asked how things were going. Well, she answered, she would certainly like more visitors. Her house was all fixed up now and it would be nice to have company. During the riots, ministers, rabbis, and heads of civil rights organizations had kept the beleaguered couple company. Apparently, now that the crisis was over, they had gone on to other things. I remembered how desperately I had wanted to go out to Folcroft, to do something to help. Well, loneliness could be as devastating as bricks and jeers. If the Buchanans wanted visitors, this was something Ben and I could do to help, late as it was. Betty Buchanan accepted my offer to visit them with eagerness. We set a date for the following Sunday.

When Ben and I drove through the streets of Folcroft hunting the Buchanans' address, I tried to picture the rioting we had seen on TV newscasts. The cameras hadn't shown how bleak the area was. It looked like an army post, straight streets of identical brick row houses built on flat, treeless land. Each house had a rug-sized area in front of it and the only variation was that some families planted lawn; some had cemented patios with a cardtable or a lawn chair on them.

Except for the hair rollers on the women and the sleeveless undershirts on the men, these serene-looking people sitting outside their homes resembled those I had been raised with. I simply could not imagine them putting down their beer cans, Sunday papers, and bowls of potato chips to throw bricks and garbage at anyone. The rumors of "outside agitators" were undoubtedly true. People from other areas must certainly have come here to create the disturbance. These pleasant, placid people couldn't riot.

When Ben and I had trouble finding the street on which Betty Buchanan and her husband, Chet, lived, I wanted to stop and ask directions. Ben said, "No." I felt he was being silly and overcautious. I had also wanted to bring our children along to play with the Buchanans' four-year-old daughter; Ben said, "Maybe next time."

The Buchanans' house, when we found it, looked exactly like the others except for slight traces of paint on the brick where the word "Nigger House" had once been written. As we walked up the cement stairs to the door, I saw a woman watching us from a screen door two houses down. She didn't return my smile.

Betty Buchanan opened her door before we had time to ring the bell. We entered an attractively decorated living room, small but done in tasteful colors. Large, healthy plants were everywhere, on the window sills and the glossy tables. I could see into the kitchen with its gleaming copper kettles hung on the wall. More plants were on the kitchen counters.

Just then, Chet Buchanan came down the stairway from the second floor. He was an appallingly thin man with a gentle face, and I noticed that his hands clenched and unclenched constantly. His large clear eyes had traces of laugh-lines at the corners, but his high forehead was creased with lines that looked new.

Betty served coffee. Chet drained his cup in one gulp, then sat silently while Ben, Betty, and I talked about our children and the weather. Betty spoke wistfully of gardening. I thought her wistfulness was because her yard was so small. Ben had cautioned me, unnecessarily, against talking about the riots.

When Chet Buchanan finally entered the conversation, it developed that he *did* want to talk about the rioting. He plunged into the topic with an apparent compulsion, as if by describing it over and over again he could make it more —or less—real, or understand somehow why it had happened.

"This whole neighborhood saw us looking at the house," Chet said. "No one said or did anything nasty until the moving van tried to unload our furniture." Chet shook his head and looked at us as if we could explain. I could not. The attack on this quiet attractive couple made even less sense now that we had met them.

Betty put her hand on Chet's arm. She smiled apologetically. "You see," she said, "We just didn't know. I came from a small Vermont town where we were the only Negro family. Everyone was nice to us. Chet is from Mississippi. He thought things were different up North."

Just then, Lucy pulled her mother's skirt. Could she please go outside? "I'm sorry, honey. No," Betty told her. As if the conversation were routine, Lucy went quietly back to her bedroom. "I'm afraid," Betty told us. "Someone drained the brake fluid of our car last week and smeared the windows with tar."

But the Buchanans had been in Folcroft for over a year! It seemed impossible that the harassment was still going on.

Well, Betty told us, some things were better. During the first few months, people had gone into the vacant house adjoining theirs and played radios at full volume all night. This had stopped. "But they still call out names when I try to work in my garden," she said, glancing at the bushy patience plant still imprisoned in its indoor pot. "Yet I can't help feeling that they were all basically unhappy people even before we came," she said. "A woman who used to live here telephoned me. She said she'd moved out because the people here were forever suing each other over boundaries and where cars were parked and silly things." Betty Buchanan shook her head. "But we didn't know."

While Betty talked, Chet had remained silent, staring down at his hands. Suddenly he looked up at us and said, "I am not running from those people. I am a *man*. I can defend my wife and child."

Then Chet's belligerence dissolved into a pathetic questioning. "If I ran," he said softly now as if accepting a prison sentence, "no other family like mine could ever move in here, could they?"

We did not have a chance to answer Chet. He shook his head again and went upstairs. Betty explained he had to get dressed; he was going to work. The hospital at which he was employed as an inhalation therapist had been very helpful, very understanding. He was working this Sunday, but usually he could stay home on week ends with her and their daughter Lucy.

With a glance at the direction in which Chet had disappeared, Betty said to us, "We can't leave here. All our money is tied up in this house, and anyway, Chet can't leave."

Chet called down to us that if we followed him when he left, he would lead us over a short cut away from Sunday traffic. We said good-bye to Betty and little Lucy and then Chet opened their front door. When I first saw the crowd of people gathered across the street, I looked to see if there had been an accident. Then they began to yell, "Nigger-lovers," and I discovered we were the accident.

As I looked down from the Buchanans' steps, I saw about forty people standing on the sidewalks and lawns across the street; the same men in undershirts and women in hair rollers we had seen sitting peacefully in front of their homes. Now their faces were twisted into expressions of contempt and hatred as they yelled names at us. Among the harsh adult shouts the piping little voices of children repeated the same ugly words. And I could see empty bottles in the hands of some people and, in others, objects held inside clenched fists.

Ben tried to pull me down the stairs to the car, but I resisted. He went ahead and stood at our car door yelling, "Come on." I felt hypnotized. In the June sunshine with rosebushes blooming, these hostile people seemed incongruous and unreal. I remember thinking that I should be afraid, but nothing in my entire life had prepared me to fear a crowd of people.

Chet Buchanan stood next to me at the top of the stairs. "See how they are!" he said loudly.

Yes, I did, and to me it had a compelling fascination. I was going to go over there and talk to them. I called out, "Hi. I'll be right over." I remember smiling to let them know I was interested in whatever was upsetting them.

The yelling ceased abruptly, leaving an unfinished silence as if a clock had suddenly stopped ticking. I started down the stairs with my smile. Ben grabbed me at the sidewalk and pulled me to the car.

"My God, Lois, get in!" he said with an urgency that scared me.

I stood unwillingly at the door. A little child on a tricycle called "Nigger-lover" in a cheerful, parrotlike voice. Chet was at his car. He called over to us, "See. See. But they'll have to kill me to get me out of here." Chet's eyes didn't match his words; his eyes were soft and hurt, while his mouth was a tight, hard brown knot. Ben literally pushed me into the car as Chet jumped into his. When we pulled away something went *clunk* on the roof.

As we drove away from Folcroft, I argued with Ben. Those people would not have hurt me. This was America; not Nazi Germany. They had stopped yelling when I smiled at them. We could have talked. Unlike the silent people in Omaha, they would have told me how they felt. I could have tried to tell them about my neighborhood.

"Somebody has to do something," I told Ben. "The Buchanans can't live like that! If Chet reacts that strongly every time he leaves the house, I'm afraid for him."

Ben said, "Okay, I'm afraid for him, too, but you're not the person to talk to that mob. The only reason they stopped yelling was because you confused them with that crazy smile of yours. You confused me, too. I was ready to carry you down those damn stairs. Honey, couldn't you see that those people had rocks in their hands?"

It was only five days after our visit to Folcroft that Ben lost his job. The news of Ben's unemployment created a warming wave of compassion from black friends, more far-reaching than I would have believed possible. It began with Dolph Priest wanting to give us his savings which must have taken years to accrue from his reporter's salary. Barbara and Leland made us the same quick offer. Then one evening Ben got a telephone call from a man who said he had heard about Ben from Leland. Could he come over and talk with him?

When the man arrived, his great shyness was painfully obvious. He was tall, very dark-skinned, and sat in our living room with his head down. He told us he was the first Negro chemist with a large company. He wanted to know something about Ben's background so that he could talk to the personnel manager of his firm about a job for Ben. The chemist never raised his eyes. He listened and made notes on a small pad. Just before he left, he stared down at the bottom of our front door, shook his head and said, "Lord, man, we've got to help you."

The job never materialized, but that evening it didn't matter. This incredibly shy scientist had wanted to help us so much that he made himself approach two strangers. For him, it was the most difficult gift he could give.

There were other unexpected reactions. Leland paced the floor of his own living room in his caged-leopard custom, talking of the frustrating collapse of some of the contacts he had tried to make for Ben. He stopped suddenly in the center of the room, whirled toward Ben, and asked, "How do you really feel? How much bitterness do you really feel toward black people for getting you into all this?"

Ben looked astonished. "Black people? Lee, it was white people who fired me! Why would I feel bitter toward black people? Listen, if those nuts on Lindley Road in Omaha really did manage to get me fired, they're the people I should be bitter about."

For once, Leland stood still as Ben spoke. I added that if Ben felt bitter toward anyone, it should be toward me. I had started everything by rushing to Mrs. Kozarik without thinking about neighborhood reaction.

Ben laughed and reached across the sofa to give me a quick hug. He had reassured me repeatedly that he was glad I had approached Mrs. Kozarik. I tried to explain to Leland and Barbara that, financially insecure as we were at the moment, we had gained so much. Never before had I felt so alive and involved with people and with my country. Ben and I had become even closer; our children were growing up in a stimulating community.

"Rather than bitterness toward black people," I told Leland, "I think it would be closer to gratitude."

All right, Leland said. He hoped we felt the same way after more than a month of unemployment. Leland went on with his pacing and his dialogue with Barbara concerning who might be helpful.

Ben hadn't told Leland about a recent ironic job interview. I didn't bring it up either. Ben had been receiving the indefatigable help of Judge Raymond Pace Alexander, the prominent Negro jurist who was one of our neighbors. We had gradually become friends with this charming, gregarious man who had fought for Negro rights before most of today's militant leaders were born. Judge Alexander and his brilliant wife, Sadie T. M. Alexander, also an attorney, had brought suits to end segregation in theaters and restaurants during the days when these actions were dangerous and totally unsupported by public conscience. During Ben's unemployment Judge Alexander had arranged interviews with every important personage he knew.

Many of the people Judge Alexander arranged for Ben to see were startled when they saw Ben was white. Ben had told me recently that in one job interview conducted by a Negro man, the man looked terribly uncomfortable. He had wrinkled his brown forehead and said, "I hope you believe I don't enjoy telling you this. But the company believes we should hire a Negro for this job."

Ben told me he just couldn't help laughing. "I figured something like this just had to happen eventually. I told the man I didn't feel qualified for this job anyway and that if I were in his place I'd certainly enjoy the switch!"

The black man had looked relieved and grinned, "Fella, it was hard not to!"

In the weeks after Leland's question about "bitterness toward black people," it was hard to resist feeling bitterness toward whites like Harper Thorpe. Harp had worked his freckled face into a grimace of sympathy when Ben told him he was no longer with the corporation. He denounced "that bunch of bigots" and then glanced at his watch. He would call Ben for lunch soon. It was humiliating that Ben had to call him but, Ben told me, it was necessary. Harp was never free for lunch.

People like Harper Thorpe were balanced by others such as the head of a Jewish community group. This man was working to open executive suite jobs in certain industries formerly closed to Jews. For Ben, he arranged interviews at Jewish companies. Another Jewish friend, a professor at a university, went over the head of his superior to hurry an answer for Ben. As hard as I tried to avoid the comparisons, it was steadily more and more apparent that our friends who were black or Jewish were more actively trying to help than were the white Protestants we knew. Perhaps minority group people knew best what Ben was experiencing.

Sadie Alexander did, and I will never forget the special warmth her help gave me during what turned out to be nine months of unemployment for Ben. I had called her apologetically one night, knowing that she was leaving for Europe the next morning, but I needed the correct spelling of the name of a man to whom Ben was sending an application. It would just take a minute, I said. Sadie Alexander's crisp voice said, "Hang up. I'll call him—and I'll call all the other people I know on the board of directors."

I was embarrassed. No, I didn't expect that. Just the right spelling. She had just told me she was exhausted from packing.

Sadie Alexander has an abrupt manner that cuts quickly to a problem's core. As the first Negro woman in America to earn a Ph.D. or to graduate from the University of Pennsylvania Law School, she perhaps had to put time-wasting aside long ago. Her words to me now were clipped and firm as a motion in court.

"Lois," she said almost angrily, "when Raymond and I were young, no one helped us. Colored lawyers couldn't, white lawyers wouldn't. I made up my mind that I would never let anyone feel as helpless and friendless as we felt. Now will you please get off the phone," she said, "and let me call those people."

It would be a lie to say that all the generous compassionate people who gave us so much support made Ben's joblessness pleasant. Parents with three children and no paycheck would have to be insane to be cheerful. And it was taking time, much more time than we had anticipated, for Ben to find a job. Almost three months had passed without success.

Still, there was always the comparison with people worse off than we were—the Buchanans trying to live surrounded by unsuppressed hatred and other black friends whose achievements and money could *never* buy them the dignities Ben and I took for granted. It was only a few weeks after Sadie Alexander stopped her packing to telephone in Ben's behalf that her grandson was coldly rejected by a white barber. It was a month later when she returned from Europe that a cab driver, apparently glancing only briefly at his light-skinned, regal-postured fare, told her as he drove her home, "Too bad all those niggers moved into your neighborhood." During the next months of Ben's job hunt, Leland was stopped and frisked because "some nigger held up a gas station"; Dolph Priest waited, impeccable and impassive amid his brand-new luggage at a newspaper convention headquarters hotel in Chicago, as a genial room clerk served every white person in sight and only in exasperation finally turned to Dolph with "Okay, boy, come here."

Once I had not been able to understand white antagonisms. Now I could not understand black patience.

Chapter Sixteen

The long hot summer of 1964 was one of job-hunting for Ben and turbulent new insights for me. It would also be the first summer of Negro violence. Black patience had finally exploded.

Until now, the riots severe enough to require National Guardsmen or state troopers—in Little Rock, Oxford (Mississippi), Folcroft (Pennsylvania)—had all been white riots. I knew that tear gas and bayonets had not been used in Folcroft, but on May 11, 1964, I read that tear gas and bayonets had been wielded by guardsmen to break up a demonstration by black people in Cambridge, Maryland.

Even so, the first acts of violence that summer were still acts of white violence—until the middle of July. On June 9 police used tear gas, hoses, and clubs on Negro demonstrators in Tuscaloosa. On June 23 the burned stationwagon of three missing civil rights workers was found in a swamp near Philadelphia, Mississippi. Two days later, white newspapers reported that "300 white terrorists attacked Negro marchers in St. Augustine, Florida. Eighteen Negroes were hospitalized." In the beginning of July Lemuel Penn, a Negro educator from Washington, D.C., was shot and killed driving home through Georgia after having fulfilled his Army Reserve obligations. Four days later, three Negro men were shot trying to integrate a Texas beach.

All these events were telecast. Black people saw them just as I did. It seemed inevitable that they, too, would riot soon. On July 18, 1964, police killed a fifteen-year-old Negro youth in Harlem, and the first big-city black riots began. I read the newspaper accounts with confusion. Anger over the shooting of a child-was understandable, but I was distressed at the reports of looting. Protest was one thing, stealing was something else. The newspaper offered speculation, but nothing seemed clear. Philadelphia's black community would explode in August. By then I would understand more about white newspapers and much more about looting.

Ben was going out each day following up leads for jobs. He was also trying to sell—to supermarkets, banks, manufacturers, anyone who would listen—a program of profitable involvement in black problems. Ben explained to businessmen that black executive-recruiting, job training, and even recreation centers for ghetto youth would create loyalty and sales in Negro communities as well as work toward eventual lowering of taxes for welfare. Ben, quiet and reserved, is no salesman, yet he went to company after company. His stubborn belief in the obvious self-interest of business involvement carried him through dozens of rejections. In 1964, before black riots began, no business firms were interested in ghetto problems.

During the early summer months, Barbara and I were busy organizing a tour of our neighborhoods to be taken by the national delegates to the Summer Workshop of the National Conference of Christians and Jews. The Philadelphia director had asked for my ideas for their conference on "Rearing Children of Good Will." I replied that living in our neighborhood was the best way I knew to achieve this. He asked if I would organize a tour. Barbara and I began to recruit friends who would open their homes for small discussion groups after a bus ride through the neighborhood. On the day of the tour I directed the bus driver and talked with a blond, thirtyish, and pleasantly gregarious reporter from the *Bulletin* who rode with us.

When the bus passed a group of children playing hopscotch, a woman delegate leaned across the bus aisle, pointed to the children, and asked me, "Was this planned?" It took me minutes to understand what she meant. This interracial group of children seemed so unusual to her that she felt it must have been arranged as some special demonstration for the tour.

The reporter raised a sophisticated eyebrow. White bigotry, he inferred, was everywhere. He began to tell me his experiences covering the white riot in Folcroft. He had been punched and spat on by the Folcroft residents while reporting the disorder. Then he said, "That Negro couple had a lot of guts—no matter how much they were paid to move in there."

Paid! As we had learned only too thoroughly through Paul and Joan Benson's house hunt, Negro families with the means and the need could seldom get a house. No organization (NAACP was the rumored group) would have to pay a family to take a house, and, if civil rights organizations had the funds for this kind of useless nonsense, I wondered how much money it would take to pay the Buchanans for submitting to their ordeal.

The reporter, whose blond eyebrows were the most expressive part of his face, put them up, then down when I said these things. Yes, he supposed the rumor was illogical. He had not used it in his report anyway.

When the bus stopped at Barbara's house, the reporter headed confidently toward a small home next door to hers. No, this one, I told him, and we walked up the path to the Hamilton's big stone house. Inside, the delegates gathered in the sun room for their discussion. I waited there for the reporter who had stopped in Barbara's spacious living room to examine the ceiling-high bookcases. I could see that his pink forehead was wrinkling. Then he turned and inspected the entire room. Finally, he joined me and whispered, "You know, it's hard to believe this is a Negro house."

I hissed back, "What did you expect—watermelon rinds in the corner?"

He laughed goodnaturedly. "Well, you just didn't expect them to have houses like this."

About two weeks later I met a second reporter. His editor had asked him to follow up a remark I had made during the NCCJ tour—that one of the homes we had visited had been bought by a white family from a Negro family. This reporter was elderly, portly, and unsmiling. He sat resignedly in a chair in our living room and pulled out a folded sheet of paper.

"What's the name of the family who bought from colored?" he said wearily.

"Oh, there's more than one!" I told him. "At least five white families have moved here recently and bought from Negro families."

The man put his pencil aside and looked at me in cynical disbelief. I named the families. Then he brightened suddenly. "I guess," he said, "those colored sold because they couldn't keep up the payments."

Not so. One Negro friend of mine bought a Revolutionary period house to restore and had sold her smaller house to a white teacher; another black friend bought from a white family, redecorated extensively, and then sold the house at a nice profit to a white family. Mt. Airy attracted the kind of white families who felt perfectly comfortable about buying houses from Negro owners.

The reporter was not taking notes as I talked. Instead, he put his folded paper on the arm of the chair, leaned forward and said, "But off the record, isn't it true that most of them have trouble keeping their homes up?" Before I could answer, he continued, "And none of them could afford to live on a street like this?" His broad gesture toward our street ended as his hand pointed straight at the home of the Negro family across the street.

The reporter did not like any of my answers. An interview had turned into a silly debate. The story on Mt. Airy's unusual open-housing market never ran.

Until then it had seemed unimportant that articles written about the Panel of American Women were frequently inaccurate. The suburban weeklies that reported Panel appearances in their areas often printed statements we never made. One article quoted Barbara as saying that conditions were "fine" for most Negroes. Barbara and I laughed over the reporter writing what he wanted to hear.

Immediately after meeting the two white Philadelphia reporters from the *Bulletin,* considered our most liberal paper, I began to notice that in all newspaper reports "students," "parents," "demonstrators" were invariably white. "Negroes" were seldom identified as parents or students or even men or women. They were, too often, just "Negroes" with no identity at all beyond their color.

Ben pointed out that editors seemed to have their special viewpoints, too. He showed me the evening paper where, on page 3, a six-inch-long article was headlined: "Man Beats and Rapes Girl." Then he turned to page 22. A two-inch article was tucked away there reporting another rape. "Read them both," Ben said. The only difference between the two incidents was that in the prominent article, the girl raped was white and identified her assailant as Negro. In the tiny back-page report, the color of neither victim nor assailant was given but the location was in an all-Negro area.

On August 4 newspapers reported that the bodies of three missing civil rights leaders, Andrew Goodman, James Chaney, and Mickey Schwerner, had been found burned and buried near Philadelphia, Mississippi. The ghetto in Philadelphia, Pennsylvania, exploded on August 28.

I saw the by-lines of the two reporters I had met on several accounts of Philadelphia's disorder. By now I expected the same objectivity from white papers as from British papers when reporting the American Revolution. Stores, they stated, had been looted, windows smashed. But our then Police Commissioner, Howard Leary, had evidently calmed the area with no loss of life. I felt I would find out what had really happened when Dolph Priest's paper came out in a few days. Somewhere between the account in his black-owned newspaper and the white newspapers would be the truth.

I did not expect an eyewitness acount of Philadelphia's riot any more than I expected, three years later, to hear about Newark and Detroit's bloody events from a friend who had been in the midst of them. I didn't know Barbara's children were staying with relatives in the section of Philadelphia where the riots took place or that Leland and Barbara had gone to get them the minute police allowed them into the area. It was not until the next day that Barbara, still shaken, came over to talk about her terrifying weekend.

Barbara had come for her children early Sunday morning, before the broken glass was swept away. Policemen and park guards still roamed the area. "At each corner I could tell Leland which stores would have been looted," she said, "and I was one-hundred-percent accurate." Then devoutly religious, ethical, compassionate Barbara made a statement I simply could not understand. "I could feel only satisfaction that these store owners finally got what they deserved," she had said.

Surely thousands of white people who make black friends go through the same cultural shocks I was to go through when Barbara explained her statement. She introduced me to ghetto business practices she assumed "everyone" knew about. Barbara began by explaining that ghetto prices were higher. "Merchants know they can charge more. Women who work don't have spare time to shop around and can't afford the fifty cents car fare to go out of the neighborhood." And could I imagine, she asked, how it might feel to be poorly dressed and followed around a middle-class supermarket by a glaring manager who believed I was trying to steal something? Barbara said that she herself had been made to feel unwelcome when she stopped one day at a suburban market.

I had never considered these problems. All my married life I had driven my car to the supermarket I preferred, bought specials for my freezer, wrote out my check, and, when necessary, complained to a concerned manager if the produce wasn't fresh. I shopped with dignity and sufficient money.

I didn't know about the merchants who cashed welfare checks, deducting what they *said* was owed. But I could understand how timidity, illiteracy, and a fear of humiliation might make me accept arithmetic I knew must be wrong.

These were the stores, Barbara said, that had been smashed and looted. The merchants who intimidated their customers, who cheated them without bothering to make the dishonesty plausible, who sold wormy meat and rotting produce to people who couldn't go elsewhere and at prices the traffic *had* to bear. The honest merchants, the good people, weren't touched.

But the food stores were not the real tragedy, Barbara continued. Somehow people survived paying the extra dime on the bottle of milk or the high prices for limp vegetables and stale meat. Leland's consumer-education project was aimed at combatting the more vicious businessmen in the ghetto.

These "human vultures," Barbara said, her soft face hardening into rigid lines, practiced their rackets with home improvements, used cars, appliances. They depended on the trust and gullibility of honest poor people. Right now, Leland was trying to free a member of his congregation from having to pay $4,500 for a furnace in his $6,000 home. He was also attempting to get a woman out of a contract she had signed for carpeting and to which an exorbitant "delivery and installment charge" had been typed in above her signature. This woman was desperate, Barbara said, and had gone to a finance company to borrow money for the carpet payments. The finance company gave her a loan at 39 per cent interest. Barbara said she could sit all afternoon telling me of what innocent, trusting people had gotten into. "The young man who paid $17.50 a month for two years for his girl's engagement ring—he was so proud of it. He had never stopped to figure out that he'd paid a total of $420 for a ring that could be bought anywhere for $125."

As Barbara talked I remembered some inexplicable experiences I had had with home-improvement firms. A relative by marriage told Ben and me laughingly, "Oh, you don't want to buy storm windows from my company!" A salesman I had picked from the Yellow Pages to estimate on carpeting looked around our living room and said cheerfully, "No, dearie, we don't work for people like you. We work the colored sections." Barbara explained that these salesmen didn't want experienced, middle-class customers. Their profits came from the gullible.

The young man who overpaid for the engagement ring, Barbara continued, was really extraordinarily lucky. These merchants don't want people to keep up their payments. Their profit is in repossessing. Leland had followed one $95 television set through ten families as it was sold, repossessed, and sold again. This scheme involves enforcing the installment contract to the very letter. If the payment is late by one day, the judgment clause—a passage of 200 complicated words —can be exercised. A constable can move in and seize all the family's possessions for a sheriff's sale. The sale is held hastily with the merchant and the bewildered debtor the only bidder.

"It is legal in Pennsylvania," Barbara said, "for the merchant to bid a minimum amount, get all the family possessions, and then sell them for a tidy profit. They can even dispossess a family from its home."

While Barbara talked a memory forced its way into my mind. I could see my father's face and hear his voice. "See that car there?" I could hear him say. "Sold it to niggers a dozen times already." This memory returned with the same strength that I must have used to suppress it. I gasped at the physical nausea it produced. When Barbara asked what was the matter, I told her. Her face softened with compassion for me, but now I understood thoroughly what she had been telling me.

I could understand how it might feel to be poor and trusting and hungry for a luxury that reason told me I might never have. My need to believe the smiling salesman and his "easy" payments would be compelling. When I found he had lied and misled me, I could imagine the hurt and then the rage when I found my money, my luxury, and my hope were all gone.

Finally, some of the strange unrelated facts reported, but never analyzed, by white newspapers made sense. In Philadelphia's riot and in the ghetto explosions to come in other cities, white neighborhoods were never invaded, few policemen were killed, and the large majority of looters arrested were men and women with jobs. (In the 75 disorders later investigated by the Kerner Commission, fewer than 10 of the 83 riot deaths were of policemen, firemen, or National Guardsmen. The rest were Negro civilians.) Some experts said the riots were caused by anger over discrimination, the frustrations of poverty, or hatred of the police. But the anger and destruction flowed solely toward ghetto merchants. Action, someone said, follows the strongest motive.

Weeks later, the mother of another black friend confirmed what I had begun to suspect. She had been able to watch the rioters from her window. "They looked so happy," she told me. "Not angry. They reached in those store windows and walked away with such big smiles. Some were church-going people. I recognized them. But they walked proudly. As if they'd finally—at long, long last—beaten the system."

With my lifelong reverence for property rights and order, it was astonishing to find I understood. If I had been cheated and had no recourse, yes, I would pick up a brick. I would throw it in anger and I would reach in a window and take something in revenge. And I would feel satisfaction and no guilt.

Later, I explained my theory to Ben. He pointed out that if this were true—if dishonest businessmen created the anger that exploded in the ghetto—then our taxes paid for their protection. Our taxes paid for the guardsmen and the police and for the damage claims filed by merchants who had already made high profits off the poor. "These racketeers get fat off the gullibility and the helplessness of poor people," he said, "but in the end they victimize us, too."

In the weeks that followed Philadelphia's riot, few white people seemed to have dug deeply into possible causes. White people we overheard in restaurants and on trolleys took the riot as confirmation of what "we" had always expected "they" would do. They forgot "we" showed them how in Little Rock and Oxford, Mississippi.

When Ben went downtown for a job interview the Monday morning after Philadelphia's 1964 riot, he saw white people glaring meaningfully at black people, most of whom walked with eyes down. On a train platform, Ben said, a motherly looking white woman, well dressed and with an ordinarily sweet face, turned to a Negro man and snapped, "Why don't you people behave yourselves?" The man stood silently looking at the floor. Ben knew who he was; a dentist who lived in our neighborhood, as far from the riot area as we were from the white mobs in Folcroft.

I had expected hostility from black people when white bombers killed the four little girls in a Birmingham church. That hostility had never come. Anger was loose now though. It was directed by whites toward blacks.

Chapter Seventeen

In September 1964, the white men accused of killing Lemuel Penn in Georgia were acquitted by an all-white Georgia jury. In October, the Reverend Martin Luther King, then thirty-five years old, was awarded the Nobel Peace Prize. The following month, FBI Director J. Edgar Hoover publicly called Dr. King "a notorious liar" for saying that FBI agents in Georgia failed to act on civil rights cases because they were Southerners. On February 21, 1965, Malcolm X, the honestly angry man who had impressed me so profoundly on television, was shot and killed as he spoke to a group of followers in New York. Three Black Muslims were accused of his slaying.

I overheard a Negro woman mentioning the murder casually as I prepared food in a church kitchen. Spike's Cub Scout troop was having its annual Blue and Gold dinner that night. Spike had chosen this troop. He wanted to be with his friend, Michael. Spike was one of the few (perhaps three) white children in the troop, and I was the only white person in the kitchen when I heard of the assassination.

"Good," said a light-skinned Negro woman standing next to me.

A doctor's wife, also light-skinned, whose mink coat was hung carefully in a corner under her eye but away from the coleslaw, ham, and ice cream, said, "He asked for it."

I had already learned that a sense of social justice does not necessarily come with brown pigmentation, and I knew most of the Negro parents in this group were well-to-do and materially content. But couldn't anyone express bereavement? No one did.

Since the evening in Omaha, when Paul Benson told me something of the tall, slim man who said black men would have to fight in the streets to become men, I had followed the career of Malcolm X. I had never forgotten this man, the ex-pimp, ex-convict, ex-dope addict, who had raised himself to brilliance in a few short years. I had come to believe that if he had grown so prodigiously and had now begun to admit that white and black might work together, then his potential for good was great. Now he was dead at thirty-nine.

At first it felt strange to me that not one black person in that church basement shared my feeling of loss. Then I realized that my mourning was not for his loss to Negro people, but to America. I had an awful premonition we would miss him more than we knew.

The assassination of Malcolm X made Ben's eight months of unemployment seem relatively minor, but by February 1965 our financial problems were becoming acute. Although we had lived frugally ever since leaving Omaha, our savings were nearly gone. I was writing radio-television commercials at home and it was painful to think of leaving my children, but I knew that March 31 was the deadline for my taking a full-time job.

In the middle of March my brother telephoned. His next-door neighbor in Washington, D.C., was organizing a new department in the federal Office of Education and wanted men "with a personal belief in integration." My brother had suggested Ben. When Ben went to Washington for the interview, I was not optimistic. Although he had talked of trying to find something "outside the business world," I thought it impossible for a forty-year-old man to change fields; Ben had no experience in anything but advertising and merchandising. When Ben returned from his interview I was writing a television commercial at the kitchen table. He sat across from me and smiled jubilantly. I knew he had gotten the job. "I start next week," he said—four beautiful words after all those months of unemployment. Ben's job had come one day before my own deadline for job hunting.

"I'll be working on school desegregation," Ben continued, grinning. "And this Mac Puccelli—the head of the department—acts as if he really means to enforce it. I'll be working out desegregation plans with the school superintendents in Florida, Alabama, and Georgia."

As Ben began to describe the details of his new job, his enthusiasm was phenomenal. Never before had my quiet, reserved husband shown this much excitement. When working for the corporation he had displayed satisfaction over advertising campaigns or sales plans he created, but never this exuberant eagerness.

Ben showed me the enormous stack of material Mac Puccelli had given him to study. He went upstairs to begin reading the reports and documents immediately. I stayed at the kitchen table, absorbing first the relief that Ben finally had a job and then the realizaton that he would be traveling through Alabama and Georgia. He was so happy I couldn't tell him that the idea scared me to death. Just two weeks before, on March 11, in Selma, Alabama, James Reeb, a white minister from Boston, had been beaten to death by white men because he participated in a civil rights vigil. Eight days later, Governor George Wallace informed President Johnson that Alabama could not afford the cost of police protection for civil rights marchers. Less than a week after Wallace's statement a white Detroit housewife, Viola Liuzzo, was killed by a sniper in Alabama while transporting black voters in a registration drive.

Ben would be traveling all alone in Alabama with no marchers around him. To Negro people he would be an unknown white face; to white people he would be a Yankee integrationist. When I finally admitted my fears, Ben assured me there was no danger. He had the protection of the federal government behind him, he said. It was *too far* behind him for my comfort.

Soon after Ben started his new job, I remember envying Hazel Dale, when I took her daughter Melanie home to their big comfortable house after Melanie had played all day with Sarah. Hazel's husband, Russ, worked at the post office. He was home every night. This Negro family had seemed the epitome of warmth and security and closeness. With five sons and little kitten-faced Melanie, Russ Dale not only provided material comforts for his family but he participated in all the Cub Scout, Little League, and school activities to help his children and others. The Sunday afternoon I had taken Melanie home it seemed as if Russ Dale's involvement with his children had paid off handsomely. Several of the Dale sons came out, smiling and gentle, to help Melanie unload her family of dolls and to display gracious, confident good manners toward me.

It was Monday morning when Mattie Weaver, her round brown face taut with strain, left a knot of Negro women in the school playground to come toward me. She walked alone across the playground. Russ Dale had died yesterday, she said. Mattie, usually open, direct, and talkative, was strangely vague about the details. Finally, as I pressed her with questions, I understood why. Russ Dale and his son Petey had been beaten by teen-agers. Russ, who had driven his son to a hospital, had died at the door. "White teen-agers?" I asked Mattie. She looked away. "Yes," she said.

That moment I could respond only with: "What can I do?" Mattie said I could send food to the Dale family. She was taking casseroles and salads over. Did I want to make something that she could put in Hazel Dale's freezer for later in the week? Of course I did.

It wasn't until I was home, preparing food for this family, so suddenly and senselessly deprived of a father, that a most unexpected reaction set in. As I went through all the mechanics of slicing vegetables, sautéing, mixing what would be a meal for Hazel and her children, each moment built into a strong wish *not* to see Hazel. I could give the food to Mattie Weaver. She would take it to Hazel's house. Hazel had many friends; she wouldn't even notice I hadn't come.

Once again, an emotion too strong and too inexplicable demanded investigation. Why was I so reluctant—in truth, afraid—to see Hazel Dale? The teen-agers who had caused her husband's death were white. Yet Hazel was a rational and gentle person. I needn't be afraid she would reject me because I was the same color as her husband's killers.

But her husband was dead. If a group of Negro teen-agers had killed Ben, could I remain reasonable?

Since that day when I stood in my kitchen, grappling with my fear of facing Hazel Dale, much has been written about white guilt. I met it head-on when I realized it was not Hazel's reaction that frightened me, it was my own. A good man, a man I knew, had died and for no reason except that he was black. I had lived all my life as part of the majority who could have done something to prevent this. And I hadn't done enough. Now my shame at facing his widow was so strong that I wanted to run from it. I could have run and no one would have known—except me. In the end, it seemed that if I ran my guilt would only be greater.

Mattie Weaver who walked beside me that afternoon

didn't know how long and high the four steps to Hazel's house were for me. Once inside, there was no time for me to deal with my guilt.

Hazel Dale looked so small in the corner of the sofa, as if she had pulled all her emotions inside and then folded tightly around them. Her second oldest son, Craig, had led us into the large living room where Hazel sat motionless. I could hardly hear her soft thank-you-for-coming. Then Mattie, large, calm and efficient, asked if Petey, her eldest son, was "back yet" from the police station.

Earlier Mattie had told me the details of Russ Dale's death, and at first I assumed Petey was at the police station identifying the white teen-agers who had beaten him and his father. I knew that Russ Dale had taken his six children to a small park at the edge of our neighborhood for a family baseball game. He had driven home to start the charcoal fire for the evening cook-out. Fourteen-year-old Petey was left in charge of the younger children. While Russ was gone, three white teen-agers told Pete, "Niggers aren't allowed here. Go home." The children couldn't go home, of course, and Petey had the presence of mind to tell Craig, thirteen, to take the four little children, crying and frightened now, behind a tree while he tried to hold off the three white boys.

When Russ Dale returned, he found Petey, bloody and still being beaten by the white teen-agers. The smaller children ran for the car. So did Pete, dazed and stumbling. Russ tried to help him. The teen-agers now attacked them both. According to Craig, one of the white boys even reached in through the open car window to hit his father on the side of the head. Russ had driven Petey to a hospital emergency ward and had fallen to the floor, dead, while Petey's wounds were being treated.

But now as I listened to the conversation between Mattie and Hazel, something awful and unbelievable was revealed. The hospital had sent police back to the park and the three high school boys had been found and identified, but not arrested. Petey had not been at the police station identifying the white teen-agers who had beaten him and his father; instead, he had been held there all night by detectives who tried to get him to say *he* had started the fight!

Four years later, a newspaper article brought back my horror over Russ Dale's unavenged death when I read that two Negro youths, fourteen and sixteen years old, were charged with murder when a white store owner suffered a heart attack after they had taken $16 from his store. But that day, in Hazel's living room, I was shocked that any detective could look at Petey and believe he had started a fight with three high school boys. Petey was a slim, slightly built youngster, a violinist and chess player, not an athlete. His younger brother Craig was also small for his age and the other Dale children were under ten years old. Even without Petey's gentle shyness, it was physically ridiculous for him to start a fight when he had five smaller children to protect. Yet when the detectives brought Petey home and allowed the bruised, bereaved youngster to go to bed, they had told Hazel, "Just be glad the white boys' parents aren't pressing charges!" She had also been told that her husband's body must be picked up immediately by an undertaker.

Mattie nodded as Hazel spoke in a barely audible voice. I could only listen. My expanding outrage had no place in a house of mourning. Only later when Mattie and I stood on the sidewalk could I ask my angry questions. How could the police believe Petey had started the fight? His injuries alone proved much. Why was there no autopsy to determine the cause of Russ Dale's death? Hazel mentioned a large swelling on his head; she had considered a closed casket. Why had the police demanded that an undertaker pick up the body so quickly? Why hadn't Hazel pressed charges against the white boys?

Mattie Weaver looked at me out of old, old eyes with the

same ancient acceptance I had seen in black eyes before. There was nothing to be done, she said. Nothing could bring Russ Dale back.

Mattie and I parted that day on the sidewalk. There was, again, nothing I could do. Except go with Ben to Russ Dale's funeral. And wonder why these Negro people could nod to us in friendly acknowledgement of our presence. No one told me my kind "should behave themselves" as whites had done to blacks after Philadelphia's riot. No one asked me why my people were so violent.

Russ Dale's death removed any self-pity I felt as I said good-bye to Ben each Sunday now. A white man was still safer anywhere in America than a black man had been in our neighborhood.

Chapter Eighteen

Ben had never talked so much about his work as he did now. He told me of his trips to see school officials in Georgia, Alabama, and Florida and his occasional visits to other states when he was needed. His assignment was to explain the federal requirements for school desegregation and to try to persuade school superintendents to go ahead with "all deliberate speed" as demanded by the Supreme Court decision in 1954.

It was now eleven years since the Supreme Court decision; a Negro child in first grade then would now be out of high school. And, in many districts, Ben found that this was exactly what happened. Negro children waited for the decision to be enforced while delays ate up the years that could have been theirs. Some districts had complied, but most looked for every possible means of delay. Citizens who subscribed to law and order didn't mean *unpopular* law or *immediate* order.

Ben was also finding that he had no weapon except persuasion with which to enforce the federal law requiring school desegregation. Theoretically, the government could bring suit against a school district and if it could be proved that the district was deliberately refusing to desegregate, then eventually federal funds could be withheld. This would mean, however, months and even years of court battles. Ben explained that if the case was won, withholding money was still politically unpopular (as was proved when Chicago's school funds were withheld only to be released, immediately and without explanation). Meanwhile, all he could do was to tell school officials what was required by law.

"I feel like a policeman asking people to please not park in the no-parking zones," he said one week end. "They keep saying, 'Yup, one of these days we'll stop.' But those Negro kids get older and older waiting for the places that belong to them."

Ben was also learning—and teaching me—what else happens between the law and its enforcement. Some of the people he worked with in Washington were completely dedicated; some were solely interested in keeping their jobs with a minimum of effort. Color had little to do with the difference. Some black people were as cautious about rocking no boats as were some of the whites. And some whites charged with enforcing the Supreme Court decision sympathized, consciously or unconsciously, with the Southern schools and accepted all the tactics of delay. We finally understood why Ben had been hired without academic credits or professional experience. Mac Puccelli, the head of his department, was a sincere and determined man; he believed Ben's demonstrated belief in integration was more important than degrees on paper.

Some of the experiences Ben related on week ends were funny, others were deeply moving. He told me about the school superintendent in Lincoln County, Georgia, to whom he had said, "Well, integration shouldn't be a problem in a county named after Lincoln!" The man looked horrified. "Oh, Lord, not *that* Lincoln," he said.

In the Florida Panhandle Ben was constantly followed by

a white Volkswagen when he visited the homes of black families to encourage them to register at the formerly all-white schools. At each stop the car would be parked nearby and the white man inside held a newspaper in front of his face. The black families assured Ben passionately that they *liked* the all-Negro schools.

In Alabama there was no subtlety. Cars with official license plates parked outside Ben's motel door. One night, Ben said, Governor Wallace made a speech on television about federal people coming to town to force "race-mixing." "He was getting so specific," Ben told me, "I half expected him to give my name and room number." After the speech, school officials suddenly lost whatever spirit of co-operation they had shown before.

Ben had found that he could apply extra pressure through the Justice Department which could bring suit against school districts for "depriving a citizen of his civil rights" to register in the school of his choice. He began to visit black families in Alabama with a Justice Department man who was also checking on voter registration. Most of these visits, Ben told me, had to be made at night. Black families were afraid to be seen talking to federal men in the daytime.

One night Ben and the man from the Justice Department approached an unpainted, rotted shack that looked hardly able to stand. "But in the light from the doorway," Ben continued, "I could see a few spindly flowers that someone was trying to grow in the hard clay near the steps."

A shy, dark-skinned young man of about fourteen let them into a one-room cabin. Inside, the walls were covered with scraps from a wallpaper sample book and the floor with unmatched squares of linoleum. Each had been applied with a kind of undefeated neatness.

Next to the stove, in the center of the room, sat the oldest, tiniest Negro woman Ben had ever seen. She was surrounded by six children, each one with an open book. The light from the stove flickered across the faces of the children and over the dried-leather face of the old woman. Her voice was unexpectedly clear and strong when she answered the Justice Department man. Yes sir, she had gone to register for the vote two times already. It was a long walk—"near three miles"—and when she got there they told her they had "run out of the right papers." But she was going to walk back there tomorrow again.

When Ben asked if the children would use their right to register at the formerly white school, she nodded. Nat would. Ben said Nat, the young man who had let them in, looked at him fearfully and then at the old woman who might have been his grand- or great-grandmother. She twisted in her chair and glanced at Nat. "Yes, Nat's going," she said firmly.

Then Nat pulled himself up tall and repeated, "Yes, sir, I'm going." The six children sitting on the floor around the old woman never moved, except to look up at Nat. When Ben left, he said he heard her voice, going on with the interrupted lesson. "Now you read, Minty," he heard her say.

While Ben was working in the South, I was learning new things at our Northern integrated school. Spike was nine now, in third grade; Noah, seven, in first grade; and Sarah had started kindergarten. There was no question that my children were getting an excellent education. Noah was receiving the same wonderful basics from Mrs. Grant, the Negro first grade teacher I had instinctively chosen for Spike. Spike was with one of the older teachers who had been at Henry School when it was all white.

When Sarah's blond, elderly kindergarten teacher requested a transfer "to be nearer my home," I was actually pleased. The new Negro teacher was younger, warmer. Barbara commented cynically that the school had been close enough to the white teacher's home for ten years—until the school had become predominantly black.

The next episode involved Noah, our aggressive, outgoing youngest son. Mrs. Grant phoned to say that Noah had brought Ben's penknife to school. After picking it up from her, I was amused at the kind of rumor that could have started over "a first grader was caught with a knife at school." Not long afterward, I got a second phone call. The school nurse told me that Noah had been kicked in the stomach by another child, Jerry; the nurse had soothed Noah, but could I come get him?

At school, I found Noah happily basking in the attentions of the nurse. I was told Jerry's mother had been called and Jerry would be punished for kicking Noah. It won't happen again. Jerry was, I knew, a Negro child about a year older than Noah.

Something in Noah's attitude made me question him closely. He finally admitted that Tim (twelve, also Negro) had held Jerry while Noah tried to grab his lunch. That's how Noah had got kicked. I phoned Jerry's house and told his father what I now knew was the truth. "Yes, that's what Jerry said," his father responded. "Thank you for calling," he added, politely but distantly. For the first time I realized I had to guard against bias *toward* my children at school. I did not want them to learn to expect special privilege because they were white. It was only by comparing notes with Barbara that I found how subtle the bias could be.

Spike had turned out to be the same casual scholar I had been in school. He was curious, enthusiastic, happy, but inclined to think about Mongolia when the class studied Minnesota. We weren't worried. Spike read well and liked school. We could not blame the teachers; Noah had the same teachers and got A's. Spike's second- and third-grade teachers, however, seemed almost frantic over his inability "to live up to his potential." One teacher, an elderly white woman who had been at Henry School for many years, volunteered to pray for him. I repeatedly received notes, phone calls, invitations to conferences.

When I mentioned to Barbara the teachers' concern over Spike, she exploded. Her son Jimmy's grades dropped drastically between report cards. She had asked for conferences and finally managed to arrange one. The teacher (white) said not to worry; Jimmy behaved himself well.

Jimmy was in Noah's class. When Spike had this teacher, she had called *me* to explain the low mark Spike would be getting in math. It seemed incredible at first that Barbara had to ask—then wait—for a conference. Now, Barbara said, you could see the subtle difference: the teachers felt Spike had a potential to "live up to"—if Jimmy "behaved well," this was all the teacher expected from him.

I still believed there was some unintentional mistake. Then, a few weeks later, I met Barbara by accident on the school grounds. I mentioned that Jimmy had helped Noah with his reading the night before. The two boys had been playing together and Jimmy showed Noah how to "sound-out" some words in the instructions for a game. Noah was in the highest reading group; now I wondered if he might not be better off in a lower group where he could get extra help in phonics.

Again Barbara got angry. Jimmy was not in the top group. On impulse, we went to see the teacher. She greeted me by name; she didn't remember Barbara's name. I told her I had watched Jimmy Hamilton helping Noah to read. "Mrs. Hamilton and I both want to discuss our children's reading placement," I said. As often as Barbara tried to get the teacher's attention, as often as I said conclusively, "Let's put Noah in the lower group on trial," the teacher returned again and again to the subject of Noah.

I was now ready to believe Barbara. This teacher, who was white, did not dislike Negro children; she simply saw my child and Barbara's child differently. In our unplanned dual conference, her interest went instinctively toward Noah, not Jimmy.

This was only the first (and most easily measured) experience with white teachers whose deep unconscious attitudes consistently favored children like mine. Much later, in the upper grades, Spike asked me to please talk to one of his teachers who nagged him about his handwriting. He was trying his best. I had not yet met his teacher and when I walked into her room she glanced at me and became immediately flustered and obsequious. She barely hid her investigation of my clothes. I felt her eyes tick off the labels: Etienne Aigner pumps and handbag, my Braemar sweater from school days, the thick tweed skirt I had made myself. Her hands flew to her hair and she pushed papers into stacks on her cluttered desk, snubbed out her cigarette. I had her full attention and it was sadly apparent why.

I explained that Spike's handwriting was as bad as his father's. Oh, don't worry, she chirped now. She understood. With Spike's "fine background" she realized she had misjudged his potential. She had judged his "fine background" solely on my clothes. As I told Ben later, she had no way of knowing if this was my one sober day in a month or whether our family pushed dope for a living.

Her sudden re-evaluation of Spike's potential embarrassed me, and I asked, merely to prolong the conference and give it a semblance of meaningfulness, whether girls had better handwriting than boys. Yes, girls usually wrote better, she said. Then she shuffled through some papers on her desk. "But some boys write well too. And this," she lowered her voice, "is *even* a little colored boy." She showed me the paper, proof of this astounding miracle.

In the class this woman taught, 75 per cent of the children were black.

Most white parents at our school had no idea of the bias Negro parents fought. It was Barbara who told me that one teacher cast her Christmas play entirely with white students. This meant every white child in the class had a part; not one of the black children. When Barbara complained the teacher said the Negro children didn't speak well enough. Another white teacher, when asked to select children for a TV broadcast, also chose only white children, until it was pointed out that integration was the subject of the show.

Then one night a white teacher stationed at the door to direct parents to a Home and School meeting stopped me. Would I find the principal and tell her to call the police, she whispered urgently. She nodded toward a group of boys at the corner. She was breathing hard and genuinely frightened. They were up to something, she said.

I had just walked through the group. They were youngsters I knew, some of them the thirteen- and fourteen-year-old brothers of my children's playmates. We had all said hello. They had been talking happily. They were up to nothing. But they were all Negro boys. The teacher wouldn't believe me when I told her they were harmless children. Well, she said, if everyone's tires got slashed, it wouldn't be her fault.

I was afraid she would send her message through someone else. A Negro man I knew came along. I said, "Dr. Prentice, I've told Miss Jones those boys at the corner don't seem to be up to mischief. Do you agree?"

Dr. Prentice seemed to understand what was happening immediately. In his meticulous Harvard accent, he said to Miss Jones, "They are quite all right, I assure you. In fact, one of them is my son." Miss Jones flushed.

It was on school field trips, however, that our ever-present delusions of white superiority seemed most blatant and depressing. When Noah's class toured the Philadelphia Museum of Art, I guided the little group of children assigned to me. There were five black children and Noah. I searched desperately for some brown faces for the children to see. I could find none, except for a background figure in a colonial scene, a slave holding a tray of food. Then one of the children was missing. Searching for him, I opened the door to a back stairway. There he was, staring happily up at a large portrait of a brown-skinned, regal Moorish prince. Our entire class made the detour down those back stairs.

I realized if American schools failed to help make Negro children confident, productive citizens, then each badly educated child would affect my children's world. Spike, Noah, and Sarah would pay the taxes for welfare and for prisons. So I was delighted when a study of schools in our area was announced. Some schools near us were definitely below standard. I hoped an investigation would change this; a well-known firm of "educational scientists" was doing the research and analysis, paid for by a large foundation grant.

Our principal, Vangie Peters, introduced me to the director of the project one morning when I happened to be at school. The director was a white man with thinning, light brown hair and a busy, confident manner. Yes, he said, they were going to make education really exciting for my children. He toyed with a sheaf of papers in his hand and said proudly, "Imagine a science center where your children will be taken each week to work with the latest equipment?"

I was astonished he had gone that far in his thinking. The study was just beginning. The research was supposed to find out what the children in our area *needed*. From the textbooks I had looked through and some of the teachers I knew, I hardly expected the research project to uncover an acute need for a science center. But I said only that I was personally more interested in better basic education for underprivileged children than in more frills for my own.

The director waved his sheaf of papers and dismissed my innocence with a knowledgeable smile. "Oh, Mrs. Stalvey," he said, "you can't do anything for those children! Whatever you do for them, the home undoes!"

Three months later, after the team of "educational scientists" had collected their salary and expense checks for the "research," "community opinion-gathering," "scientific space-utilization," and the conducting of numerous neighborhood meetings, they made their considered recommendation . . . a science center!

I was appalled at the waste of money and the cynicism of the project directors. There had been one community meeting when I was positive they could not ignore the real problems. Dr. Kenneth Clark, the Negro psychologist, was the speaker. He pointed out that American schools had educated wave after wave of immigrant children even when no English was spoken in the home. I remembered that my mother, my aunts and uncles had learned English in school and then taught it to my German-speaking grandparents. The home had not undone what the school taught; the home had benefited from it. Dr. Clark went on to say that the job of the school is to teach children no matter what kind of homes they come from. "Anything else," he said, "is as ridiculous as expecting hospitals to treat only well people."

As Dr. Clark spoke I watched the director of the project. He was whispering to his assistant and shuffling papers. When Dr. Clark finished, the director announced the plans for the science center.

When I expressed my anger over the expensive and dishonest "study" to Barbara and Leland, Leland's wrought-iron face hardened even more. He walked from the bookcases in his living room to the chair where Ben sat. "Yes," he said, "they study us all the time. It's a whole lot easier than *doing* anything."

Chapter Nineteen

On June 2, 1965, a Negro deputy sheriff, O'Neal Moore, was killed in his squad car during what white newspapers called "a highway ambush" near Bogalusa, Louisiana. A white man was arrested for the slaying. Two weeks later, a thirty-eight-year-old black man, Willie Brewster, was shot in the back by white nightriders in Alabama. He died three days later. Willie Brewster had never taken part in any civil rights activities.

Television brought this news into black homes from Maine to California, just as it had shown black people the Alabama police using whips, dogs, hoses, and tear gas on Negro marchers at the bridge in Selma. They could watch men, and women and children too, stumbling, gasping, and being lashed by policemen on horses.

Then, on August 11, the Watts section of Los Angeles exploded in the midst of a 90-degree heat wave with a violence that made Philadelphia's riot seem as mild as a street dance. Once, people erupting in almost five days of burning and looting would have frightened me. Now I felt a sense of relief; the inevitable had happened—black people had fully released their anger.

I combed through the white newspapers, trying to separate rumor, bias, and speculation from fact. The most ominous *fact* was that thirty-four people had died in Watts—and that thirty of them were Negro. As in Philadelphia, the Watts riot was not an attack on white police or even a two-sided battle. No policemen were killed. Instead, the action was directed against white *property,* possibly the property of the unscrupulous businessmen Barbara Hamilton described to me, businessmen like my own father.

But most white people I talked with saw Watts as an unforgivable Negro act of violence. What enraged them was the $45 million estimate of property damage.

The phrase "Burn, Baby, Burn" became famous after Watts. Leland explained that, ironically, this phrase was commonly called out to preachers and musicians and it meant "to respond, to *feel*." Whites interpreted the phrase literally.

Few people, black or white, seemed to share my alarm that American citizens had been shot down in American streets for the crime of looting, a crime that carries no death penalty in our courts. The rumors of snipers and claims by police of "self-defense" were clearly refuted by the Negro death toll. I was deeply distressed that no one objected to these mass street executions.

As the summer of 1965 drifted into fall, my depression deepened until Joan and Paul Benson called from Omaha one Sunday morning to tell us they finally had their house. It had been built on a piece of land bought through a white friend of ours. There was, Joan said, another happy piece of news. Paul's voice broke in. "Nothing to get all that excited about," he said, but he had won a gold medal for his film on heart surgery. The medal was to be given him at a medical convention in Atlantic City and he would stop by to see us. It was, Paul said with elaborate casualness, not the Nobel

Prize; however, Joan's voice rippled over the phone wires, light with love and laughter. Perhaps not, but Paul was so up in the air about it he wouldn't even need a plane to get to Philadelphia.

The night before Paul was to be honored he sat in our living room and tried to talk of other things. But even his new house took second place. He was the first black doctor to win the award. In fact, the committee might not even *know* he was black. The film showed only his rubber-gloved hands. He could hope, at least, that he had won the medal on merit, not because someone decided the award "ought" to go to a Negro physician "this year."

Ben tried to reassure Paul by pointing out that the American Medical Association had recently *rejected* a change in its by-laws to prohibit racial discrimination in all state societies. The change had been voted down in favor of a mild statement against "prejudice." Ben said Paul could be sure his award was no "meaningless liberal gesture." He had certainly won the medal as a doctor.

Paul glowed as Ben spoke. For the first time since we had known him he dropped his cool, imperturbable façade. He was a happy, excited, proud man, and it was good to see him enjoying his triumph. Paul left our home that morning saying he'd be back that night with the medal and a bottle of champagne.

Sixteen hours later, Paul walked back through our door, his eyes avoiding mine, and tossed a small leather box on our hall table. He sat in the living room in the same chair he had bounced and beamed in the night before. Now he was hunched forward, his head down. He had forgotten the champagne. Then he began to talk in jerky sentences with long pauses in between.

Dr. Paul Benson had arrived at the cocktail party given for medal winners. At the door, the committee chairman stopped him. "Are you delivering something?" Paul's words came swiftly now as if he were ripping a bandage from a wound quickly to avoid the pain. "I told the man who I was." The committee chairman had stared at him for a minute. Then, Paul said, "he reached around and took the hand of the white man behind me." The chairman led the white man into the room and left Paul standing in the doorway. Paul looked up at us with a face I had never seen before; questioning, forlorn. Even during the house-hunt humiliations, nothing had changed him like this.

Neither Ben nor I spoke. My fury at the white chairman, a doctor himself, had no place here. Paul had always been the big, confident brown bear. Now the wounded bear was trying to get up and get on. I had to wait silently.

Paul wrenched a grin to his face, sat up straight, and said in a businesslike voice, "I'm a big fat nigger from Georgia and I shouldn't forget that." Then he rushed into a description of the rest of the convention. He had stood alone for a while at the cocktail party until another doctor introduced himself. That night Paul's prize-winning film was shown. "The chairman," he said, "introduced me with the same enthusiasm he must have shown over Medicare." Paul looked out at the few brown faces he saw in the audience. It seemed to him they were sitting up a little straighter.

If Paul could find something good in an experience that had stripped him of the dignity he had earned, I would not challenge him. But while he talked of other things to lift our mood, all I could think was that Paul had done everything white people said black men should do. He had obtained an education, raised a fine family, lived according to the highest standards of his church and his country. He "helped his own kind" through charity medicine and with fund-raising. He had made a nationally recognized contribution to science. Yet the committee chairman had treated him the same as he would have treated a black man on welfare with a criminal record. That night when we talked about Watts, Paul said, "That's not the way. People got killed."

Then what *is* the way, I wondered.

Paul didn't show us his gold medal that night. Joan showed it to me when I went to the Bensons' housewarming in Omaha a month later. Ben had insisted I make the trip. My increasing despondency worried both of us. What had begun, over four years ago, as a vague wish to "do something" had turned into a torturous education. But the more I learned, the less I felt I could do to change what I saw. A visit to Omaha, Ben felt, would give me some feeling of accomplishment. The Bensons finally had their house.

Joan and Paul met me at the Omaha airport. Joan was radiant. As I kissed her and hugged Paul, white people stopped, stared, and muttered angrily. Our Philadelphia neighbohhood seemed far away. Driving from the airport we crossed Omaha, drove through bleak marshlands, past "Industrial Site" signs until I wondered where the house could be. Finally, across from an abandoned farmhouse and surrounded by cornfields, stood a beautiful stone ranch house.

I learned later that this house had cost a great deal more than money. The owner of the land had changed his mind several times about selling it to the Bensons; several builders had refused the "controversial" job. After the Bensons finally found a contractor who would build for them, a cross was burned at the construction site. The contractor withdrew his men and the search for a builder began again. The house, however, was finished now and it was exactly what Joan had dreamed of. The living room was immense, four times the size of the tiny living room where the Bensons asked us not to help them. Each child had a big sunny bedroom to himself. Paul had an outsized chair in his study. Because I was so happy for them I tried to forget how easily white families acquired their homes.

As I sat unpacking in the guestroom and talking with Joan,

the doorbell rang. During our trip from the airport, Paul had said "someone interesting" would be dropping by. Joan had sighed with a loving disapproval. Paul had chuckled and asked Joan to keep his secret. I knew Paul liked to put people together in unlikely combinations, and so when the bell sounded I walked into the living room with Joan, prepared for anyone from a priest to a nightclub dancer.

I was not prepared for Marcus Garvey Moses.

Black men with bushy hair and beards are common now, but in 1965 Marc Moses looked as incongruous in that elegant room as a hand grenade in a bowl of fruit, and just as frightening. He was also dressed in black, pure black on which lint seemed afraid to settle. He was holding the youngest Benson child.

My reflexes alone got me across the room with my hand extended. He had kissed the child and was getting to his feet, unfolding like a carpenter's ruler until there seemed to be no end to him. He did not stoop like some tall men, but stood erect, relaxed, sure of his power. It was only when I got closer to this ferocious looking man that I saw the startled look in *his* eyes. He was surprised as I. A white woman, obviously middle class in my plain-dress-with-pearls, was apparently as foreign to his world as he was to mine. Marc took my outstretched hand as if it had thorns.

When Paul said laughingly, "I thought you didn't shake hands with white people," Marc looked decidedly uncomfortable. I replied lightly that he had had no choice; I had shaken his hand. This black palm tree of a man with his bushy hair and long, thin body had treated me courteously out of surprise. Feeling like a mouse trying to put a panther at ease, I wanted to make him comfortable. I need not have worried. Except for his instant of confusion, Marc Moses recovered immediately and began what can only be called my interrogation.

I had never felt so dehumanized in my life. Marc Moses'

anthracite eyes looked at me as if I were a machine, a white machine. He asked a question and then sat back, waiting to see if my gears hesitated or creaked or fell apart. His voice had the cold detachment of a professional.

He pressed the first button: "So you're from Philadelphia. What do you think of Cecil Moore's picketing at construction sites to get black men into the labor unions?"

I was surprised Marc knew this much about Philadelphia's problems. I answered that I approved of anything that would open up jobs for people and that the picketing seemed to have done this.

Next button. "How do you feel about black people defending themselves?"

I said, "Every American has the right to defend his home and family."

Once this blunt, impersonal attack might have angered me, but I had been tested by black people in so many slow, subtle ways that Marc's directness was welcome. He questioned me like the lawyer I later learned he was. And to him I was guilty until proven innocent. I wished Ben were here; he would like the efficient way Marc got straight to the point.

And so I sat in the Bensons' beautiful living room with its muted colors and soft fabrics while this totally black man hunched forward in his chair hurling questions and statements at me as if they were bricks.

"Martin Luther King is naïve," Marc said quietly. "Nonviolence is a chimera. When American troops in Viet Nam advance with no weapons except the singing of 'We Shall Overcome,' then I'll subscribe to nonviolence."

Was I expected to argue? This man was only telling me what he believed. I nodded. I could accept his feeling this way.

He went on. More statements, more waiting for my objections. He wove quotations from Aristotle, Thoreau, John Kennedy into tightly reasoned arguments. He spoke simply,

— 233 —

exposing his ideas to the test of clear language. Since then, much of what Marc Moses said that night has been repeated by black men who rose to prominence later, but in the Bensons' living room in my first meeting with someone who would later be labeled "Black Militant," it was all new. In 1965 I had not yet heard anyone say, "Black people are fighting in the wrong place. Why should we die in Viet Nam when we can't live in Mississippi?"

Marc's words were not delivered in the wild rhetoric of the impassioned orator, but his low, slow, meticulously enunciated words were more powerful than loud shouts. Almost gently, he said, "We will have to die to make the white man see us as human beings, but we will take some of you with us." His hatred, his anger, was not defiant and challenging; it was quiet as a religion. "There is no hope for the white race," he said with implacable conviction. "Their history and present actions only show they are becoming worse."

Suddenly it seemed that for the first time since the death of Malcolm X a black person was expressing feelings that seemed natural. Marc Moses was as bitter as I believed I would be if I were black and if the death and discrimination I had witnessed had happened to my family instead of around us.

I was growing more and more curious about Marc. He appeared to be in his middle thirties. How long had he been in Omaha? Why had none of our black friends here ever mentioned him? In Philadelphia I had met people as blond and blue-eyed as I who considered themselves Negro; I toyed with the idea of short-cutting Marc's test by saying I was black. But his great sincerity made it impossible for me to lie to him.

As if he had read my mind, Marc said, "How do you know you don't have black blood?" I didn't know, I replied. Had the Moors ever got into Germany? My grandparents were immigrants. But my husband had read that the longer a family has been in America the more likelihood of black blood. Ben's family had been here for generations, so perhaps he had some.

This appeared to be Marc's last brick. He sat back in his chair now. Paul grinned and said, *"Now* do you believe there are some sincere white people?"

Marc said, "No."

I said, "Good." If Marc had answered any other way it would have been a polite lie.

Now it was my turn to ask questions.

"What are you doing?" I asked. Marc looked at the floor. "Not enough," he answered. When I asked what he was doing for a living, he replied, "I'm a small-town lawyer for poor people." Did he have children? "No. I'm not married. I would not bring black children into the world as it is."

In 1965, white America's fears were directed solely toward the Black Muslims and I asked if he were a member. I knew that his name, *Marcus Garvey* Moses, came from the first black power advocate, a black man who tried in the 1920's to organize black people. Elijah Mohammad, present head of the Black Muslims, was once a young lieutenant under Garvey. Marc's father must have been a militant-thinking man, to give his son this name.

Marc said he was not a Muslim. "I could not follow their dietary laws." He smiled. "I like pork too well." But he added, soberly now, that he believed Malcolm X was killed by white orders and that whites had made a mistake in having him assassinated. "It's like cutting down a dandelion—it releases millions of seeds. Men like Malcolm X will multiply each time one is killed."

Marc made this statement in 1965, long before any of us heard of Stokely Carmichael, Rap Brown, LeRoi Jones, Eldridge Cleaver, Huey Newton or Bobby Seale.

When Marc got up to leave, Joan Benson kept her promise

to her children and called them to say good night. What I thought would be my last contact with this impressive man was ending as he became a tree for five little boys to climb. Paul's sons hugged and climbed over Marc in sleepy-eyed joy. Marc telescoped his long body and knelt to whisper to each little boy. Each child nodded seriously, kissed Marc on the patch of dark-brown skin above his black beard, and went to bed. Marc turned to Paul. "But someday soon," he said, "you've got to tell them there are tigers out there." Then Marc waved a long arm in my direction, said good-bye, and went quickly out the door.

The next evening, at Joan's housewarming party, I found out what Marc Moses had accomplished in Omaha. It was good to see Janet Adams and all the other black friends who had once taught me so much. With innocent enthusiasm, I began to tell Janet about having met "the most interesting person named Marc Moses." From the look on Janet's face I might well have said Benedict Arnold or Attila the Hun. It soon developed that to Janet and all the other people at the party my "interesting person" was their public catastrophe. Why? Because the angry things Marc said to me had also been said before City Council, School Board meetings, any place he could find to speak out. Marc Moses, it developed, was making large waves all over Omaha, and my black friends here were literally open-mouthed to find I considered him likable and valuable. Even Paul Benson admitted he had expected Marc Moses to be "more than even *you* could take."

I listened to the criticisms my friends made of Marc Moses, waiting to hear if he had violated any laws, damaged any property, told any lies. Paul only shook his head and said Marc was "too radical." Janet Adams, her patient face hardened for the first time I could remember, said, "Marc Moses antagonizes the white community and stirs up the Negro community in an irresponsible way."

In answer to both of them, I described hearing Cecil

Moore, the black lawyer, speak one night at a small Philadelphia church. I was one of the few white people there and, with Barbara Hamilton, I had watched sullen, angry-eyed people fill the room. Then Cecil Moore began to talk: "The white man has stood on our necks long enough. We'll shove him off if necessary."

I could feel tensions relax around me. Tired women who might have scrubbed floors and sinks and toilets in white homes that day beamed and said, "Amen." Cecil Moore was expressing what they felt and could not articulate. He was not "stirring people up"; these people had been angry and frustrated all their lives. I saw relaxed, hopeful, proud people leave that church. Marc Moses, I suspected, was doing the same thing for black people in Omaha.

Janet didn't agree. Marc Moses had turned down "help" from white people, powerful people willing to give him "important jobs." "So important that he would be afraid to say what he believed?" I asked.

Gradually my amusement at defending a man I hardly knew disappeared. I was suddenly aware that I had changed more than I realized. These people were my friends; they had given me my important first lessons, but I had moved on to a big city. I knew what happened to black children in Northern schools; I had seen an angry white mob threaten a young black couple; and I had faced the wife of a man killed by white bigotry. Education, praying, and polite pleas had not saved Russ Dale's life or the Buchanans' peace in Folcroft. To me, the time had come for black people to point with anger, to demand change, as Cecil Moore and Marc Moses were doing. But the people at the Bensons' party didn't agree; the "pupil" had now seen more than the teachers wanted to remember.

Yet I knew it was more than my city experiences. My old friends, Paul, Joan, Janet Adams, were middle-class people, educated, talented. Very humanly, they wanted to see hope for peaceful progress; they wanted to believe that other black people could advance along the same path they had. They had made their adjustments to life. Paul had swallowed his humiliation; Joan had her house; Janet Adams directed a new school project she felt would make important progress. Marc Moses frightened them. They must have struggled to hide their anger and he poured his out. They wanted to be hopeful and he reminded them that among poor people nothing had changed; that they had less freedom than they wanted to believe. I wished I could agree with my old friends rather than with a man I had talked with only once. But from what I had seen in the three and a half years since Omaha, I was afraid Marc was closer, much closer to the truth.

The next morning as my plane flew over the flat farmlands of Nebraska, I realized that finally the Omaha portion of my education was over.

Chapter Twenty

My trip to Omaha had lifted my spirits, but in an unexpected way. I told Ben about Marc Moses, his directness and courage, but also about the dislike Marc had apparently created in both the black and white communities. Now Marc seemed a lonely figure. I asked Ben if he thought I could write Marc a note wishing him good luck.

Ben felt it might be a helpful gesture, but he said, "You may not get an answer. Or you may get a cold, hostile reply." Anyone as bitter as I had described Marc to be might hit back at any white, Ben cautioned me, if only as a reflex.

I finally wrote Marc, telling him that Ben and I believed his speaking out was valuable, that we were sorry to learn he had little support among our friends and that we wished him luck. Even, I added, if good wishes from whites were unwelcome. Marc's reply consisted of three closely typed pages. The first pages showed the caution and hesitation of a man afraid of friendship. Then, near the end of the letter, he wrote, "You are one of the few people who has taken the time to say anything decent to me." If Marc Moses could admit this much, then perhaps he wanted—needed?—friends he was afraid to make.

An active correspondence began. Soon envelopes addressed in Marc's distinctive handwriting arrived once a week, sometimes twice. His small, meticulously formed script surprised me; a large, heavy scrawl would have seemed more typical of this blunt, outspoken man.

At first what Marc wrote had an impersonality, as if Ben and I were an audience. There was no demand that we agree. Ben said that perhaps Marc only hoped for someone to listen, someone who might not be outraged at his outrage.

"I expect to die fighting the white man," he wrote. "But I will fall down on my face, not on my back." He quoted what Claude McKay, the Negro poet, had written after the 1919 Chicago riots in which twenty-three black men had been killed, some stoned to death in alleys:

"If we must die, let it not be like hogs, hunted and penned in some inglorious spot. Oh, let us nobly die."

My replies to Marc consisted of my own anguish over what I had seen. Here at last, unlike Mattie Weaver who told me nothing could be done about Russ Dale's murder, was someone who shared my distress. It was a relief to express it.

Marc rejected docile acceptance. He wrote scathingly of Martin Luther King's policy of nonviolence. "When a man is nonviolent while women and children are brutalized as they were in Selma, then this man becomes an accessory to that violence." "Our fight is a man's job," he wrote. "Women should be kept out of demonstrations."

Marc also wrote about revolution; the kind of talk that was later to shake the country when other black men screamed it on television or to newspaper reporters. But Marc's words were there on paper, to read and re-read, and to be aware of what he didn't say.

"Your government fears talk of revolution because they know they've failed some of their citizens. If you've done right, you don't need laws to prevent *talk* of overthrowing you." But Marc never talked of overthrowing anyone. He wrote solely about self-defense, of "black people banding together to defend themselves from violent whites."

I was not conscious that our correspondence was changing, but looking back, I realize it was gradual. Once Marc's letters rang with wholesale condemnations of "this racist country." Now he began to write of his daily activities. Marc's clients were ghetto people. His office and home were in the ghetto, "so people can find me fast." I think now that he wrote, almost to himself, to clear his mind of what had happened during a long day.

"A nine-year-old came to the office today. He wanted to borrow a nickel to buy some ice for his swollen eye. A teacher hit him 'for being dumb' he said. I asked if he had told his Ma. He looked scared and said the teacher would beat him more if he told. We've *got* to get these child-beaters out of the school system." Marc wrote of the obese, fourteen-year-old shot in the leg by a young policeman who could easily have chased and caught him without firing. (The youngster had taken his brother's car, became frightened when a patrol car followed him, parked the car and ran, until he was struck by the bullet.) Marc described the trembling little Negro Girl Scout who was not allowed to identify the white man who molested her when she came to his door selling cookies. Her parents were told by the police that they would not accept a complaint.

Then Marc wrote of a far more serious case. An unarmed teen-ager had been chased by police, cornered in front of a ten-foot-high chainlink fence, and, as he was futilely attempting to climb it, shot in the back and killed. "The black community has too many unanswered questions," Marc wrote. "Witnesses say no attempt was made to save the dying youngster with proper medical attention." A fair investigation by city officials was vital, Marc said.

Marc sent us carbons of the letters he wrote to the mayor and the police commissioner. He sent us reports of his meetings with officials. His pleas were far from "irresponsible." They were instead calm, well-documented, with names, addresses, times noted. His goal was to get Omaha's officials to conduct a believable inquiry into the facts. "Ghetto people must feel they can receive justice," he wrote, "or an explosion is inevitable."

Marc sent us the official replies. His warning had been read as a threat. City officials had used more time and paper to reject the need to investigate than an investigation would have required. Evasion, fear, and perhaps guilt came through their odd reluctance to investigate the killing of a nineteen-year-old for suspicion of robbery. If the youth had been tried and convicted, the penalty would not have been death. An investigation, then the transfer of the policeman involved in the slaying would have calmed the community. It wasn't done.

Ben shared Marc's letters and he also shared my growing admiration of Marc. It was Ben who pointed out Marc's immense underlying hope. "With all his talk of revolution and dying," Ben said, "this man is preparing documents instead of weapons." But it was, Ben felt, such a pathetic waste for a man like Marc, who could contribute so much to society, to be forced to fight it instead.

When we read some of Marc's letters to Leland and Barbara, they agreed, but Leland said, "I've known a lot of black men like this. Do you know what happens to the angry, brilliant ones? They end up in a graveyard or a mental hospital." Both Ben and I protested. Leland said, "It's been happening since slave days. The strong, the brave, the brilliant black men get killed off, one way or another."

"What about you?" I challenged.

The hard black planes of Leland's face seemed to become even more rigid. He got up and stood behind Barbara's chair.

"I pray a whole lot," Leland said, smiling thinly, "and I've lowered my expectation of progress." But for the rest of the evening Leland's thoughts were somewhere else.

Over and over again I wrote Marc asking what I could do to help. I felt I wasn't doing enough. Surely he, who was so critical of white indifference, could suggest something more. Surprisingly, Marc wrote, "That Panel of Women is your biggest gun. There's nothing you can do in the ghetto, but talking to those whites in the suburbs is more important than joining a dozen civil rights groups. Remember, Malcolm X told all sincere whites to educate their own kind."

Marc's letters became less restrained as the months passed, but he ignored my questions about his childhood, his parents, his brothers or sisters. Yet he asked question after question about Ben. When had Ben left South Carolina? (At the age of nine.) Did Ben visit his relatives when he was in the South working on school desegregation? (Yes.) Finally Marc seemed to overcome his stereotype of Southerners, especially *male* Southerners. "It's hard to believe in a *good* Southern white man," he wrote, "but I have come to trust your judgment."

Marc's trust made me feel a new kind of hope. If two such different people, a bitter black lawyer and a WASP house-wife, could become friends, certainly others could. But Marc neatly minimized our differences. After one of his condemnations of "all whites," he added, "You know I don't mean you. You are not white; you are a person." This was clearly a compliment so I ignored my vague uneasiness over Marc's rejection of the truth.

Sometimes Marc's handwriting would wobble with fatigue, yet the letter would be interrupted by a late-night phone call from someone in trouble. "I'm so tired," he wrote, "maybe too tired to be effective. But there's no place else these people can go." Paul Benson had told us why. "Marc never gets around to sending bills even to people who *could* pay." And so the people who called Marc for help knew he would respond, even if they hadn't paid him the last time or the time before that.

Ben and I were never to know where Marc's dedication came from. We could only guess. Facts about his past came indirectly and in pieces. Marc wrote about trying to get *Little Black Sambo* out of the school libraries. "As the only black kid in class, I was never allowed to forget *I* was Sambo." When a domestic worker who had been fired and denied her four days pay because she was absent on the fifth day asked him for help, he wrote, "The woman's child was sick. I remember how often *my* mother had to leave one of us sick while she went to take care of Mrs. Cohen's kids—so Mrs. Cohen could go to her bridge club." Marc never mentioned his father. It was Janet Adams who told me that Marc's father was "as brilliant and as bitter as Marc," that he had worked as a laborer at the packing plant—and, when Marc was a child, had blown his brains out with a shotgun one night.

Janet and all our other black friends in Omaha were unhappy about our friendship with Marc. For a while, I tried to convince them they had misjudged him. I wrote Janet and Joan about the constructive things Marc was trying to do, citing the detailed reports he submitted to city officials. Joan never commented; Janet insisted Marc was a "dangerous influence." On the other hand, Marc condemned "the Toms and Jemimas who sell their own people out and do more harm than some whites." Janet Adams, he said, was a Jemima. If she cared about the children in the ghetto schools, she would find some way to get rid of the brutal teachers. I too was sickened by the Uncle Toms who reassured white people that "everything is just fine." I knew whites wanted to hear, and then quote, these reassuring remarks to other whites to soothe their own consciences. But Janet and Joan and Paul weren't Toms. They worked in different ways than Marc because they were different people. Couldn't anyone understand anyone else?

Ben felt I should stop trying to get people like Janet Adams and Marc to understand each other. "These days, black people don't have the time or the tranquility to *give* understanding," Ben reproached me. "When the house is on fire, there's no time for philosophical discussion. And I don't think that people like us—white people whose house is not on fire—should advise black people. Even if they seem to be acting strangely in their efforts to get out alive!" Ben reminded me, gently but with irrefutable logic, that Marc and men like Paul Benson had led quite different lives. We had met Paul's patient accepting father who had raised Paul in a segregated Georgia town. Perhaps the militancy of Marc's father, his having gone to an all-white school, his own ruthless observations, had shown Marc he was equal, if not superior to, many white men. In contrast, both Paul and Leland Hamilton had shown subtle signs of having to disprove self-doubt.

Paul had visited us after a trip to Atlanta, rejoicing over how politely he had been treated by salespeople, waitresses, cab drivers. I couldn't help saying that this "wonderful" treatment was what I had taken for granted all my life as a human being; that it was like being glad someone didn't slap you. Paul had looked at me silently for a while. "Yes," he said, "I see."

With Leland, his sincere but unthinking compliment to Ben revealed his doubt. "Some whites," Leland said, "think blacks should be treated equally. Ben thinks we really are equal." Impulsively, I had chided Leland, "Why didn't you say 'knows' instead of 'thinks'?" Leland stopped his usual ceaseless motion. "Your touchdown," he said uncomfortably.

"Marc Moses could never have made either of these statements," Ben said.

What I did not understand about Marc for a long time was his attitude toward women. Just as Marc did not choose to see me as white, he also seemed to write to me as if I were sexless, a colorless, neuter mind. He wrote about Ruth Mc-

Phetridge, the white president of the Urban League Guild who was trying to help him have a particularly brutal teacher fired. I remembered Ruth so well, with her sad aquamarine eyes and her mouth unnaturally hardened into its thin grim line. "She's very smart for a woman," Marc had written. "But she should not be this hard. Her husband should have protected her. It's man's work to fight."

It seemed beside the point to preach sex equality to Marc. I was more concerned with what might have happened to Ruth McPhetridge to make Marc see her as hard. But then Marc wrote one day about a couple picked up and beaten by police, apparently for no reason except that the man was black, his wife white. Marc directed his almost incoherent wrath, not at the police, but at the husband who "had failed to die rather than allow his wife to be brutalized."

Marc's misplaced wrath was so odd that it forced me to fit together all his strange attitudes toward manhood I had largely ignored before. It had seemed, at first, an archaic form of chivalry, a quirk, a harmless if outmoded attitude: Women must be protected at all costs; men must die to protect them.

It was by comparing Ben's attitudes with Marc's that I was finally able to gain a little insight into the problems of black manhood. Ben had never displayed anything like Marc's need to prove or defend his manhood. Ben was thoughtful, loving, protective, but also able to ask for and accept my ideas. Our relationship was that of equals. And Ben's masculinity never depended on superficialities. When the children were babies, he helped me with diapers and housework unselfconsciously, ungrudgingly. "Man's work" and "woman's work" overlapped for us. But, just as my grandmother had done, I ran the household for my husband's convenience; I knew from my own experience what "a hard day at the office" was like. Ben proved his manhood by going out each day to provide food, clothing and shelter for me and our children, just as my grandfather had done for his family. Ben and my grandfather took their manhood for granted.

And then I realized why they could. As white men, Ben and my grandfather could provide for and protect their wives and their families. Black men could not, neither financially nor physically. I remembered Janet Adams telling me "the fact of life" her father told her when she was old enough to leave the house alone. He said, "You must not antagonize white people. They are in control. There is nothing I can do to protect you." Janet said his statement was true and necessary. A (black) neighbor's daughter had been raped by white boys; her father was beaten for protesting. What would it do to Ben to tell Sarah he couldn't protect her? What would it do to our sons growing up with knowledge of their father's helplessness?

Nor could black men protect their families financially. Only a few of our black friends had had fathers able to earn enough so that their mothers could stay home. Dolph Priest's aggressive father had a degree in Speech, yet the best job he could find was as a men's room attendant. Dolph told us, "White men prefer to hire the docile, not-too-bright black men. It supports their stereotypes and precludes any chance of being overshadowed intellectually by 'a nigger'." Dolph said his father couldn't "yas-suh," and so had spoken out, got fired often, and "Dad ended up buying oblivion in a bottle."

"The smart black men," Dolph insisted, "figured out that when they couldn't find work they could provide for their families by leaving them. That way, the children were eligible for welfare. When I was a kid a lot of my friends used to go meet their fathers on streetcorners, just so they could see each other."

Negro women, however, had no problem finding jobs. Cooks and maids were always in demand. Most Negro women could easily earn more than their laborer husbands. And so the matriarchy of the black community was artificially molded by white barriers. The tired women, resentfully serving as both breadwinners and housewives, couldn't welcome their men home with the gratitude I felt for Ben. Nor, I suspected, could they give their husbands a feeling of manhood by responding physically after exhausting days.

Was this what Marc Moses had seen in the childhood he wouldn't talk about? Was this why he wouldn't marry and have children? Was this why other black men found destructive ways to try to prove their manhood?

Or suicidal ways? It would have been foolish for the black husband to "die first" defending his wife from a police-beating, as Marc demanded. And when James Meredith announced he was going to walk along a Mississippi highway I felt at first this was also a needless and dangerous form of exercise. Then it made sense. James Meredith had been the first Negro student at the University of Mississippi. His enrollment caused white riots. Thousands of troops and national guards were needed to get him in and he was guarded constantly. Until his graduation, he had to accept protection stoically. Perhaps now he needed to prove his manhood, if only to himself, by walking along a highway of his native state "to prove a black man is safe in America." His courage was all he proved. He was shot the second day of his walk, on June 6, 1966, by a white man hiding in the brush along the road.

When all networks confirmed the fact that James Meredith was only slightly wounded, I felt America had escaped through our traditional good luck. But the shooting of James Meredith was to produce two words that caused more tremors in the white community than had the riots in Watts. It has always seemed the height of irony that the cry "Black Power" was first shouted when the "power" of black people was at its lowest. James Meredith had just proved a lone black man could not walk safely along a highway, and Martin Luther King volunteered to finish the walk, joined however by whites. Stokely Carmichael, an unknown young man in overalls, a field secretary for SNCC, called out a phrase I have always believed was as innocent as a cheer at a football game. It was, I think, designed primarily to encourage tired people marching toward Jackson. But when this young man yelled "Black Power," the newsmen following Dr. King reported it and the white world rocked.

My first reaction to "Black Power" was that the young man had made a cruel joke. Talking of power to black people was like urging multiple amputees to play football. I suspected too that Stokely Carmichael had no idea of what he meant by those two words. Later, he must have felt exactly like Newton when the apple fell on his head. He had accidentally discovered a secret carefully kept since slave days; whites were scared of blacks.

I had already begun to wonder if fear played a part in white racial superstitions. It accounted for some of our prized myths. The "happy, loyal, singing, dancing darkie" so determinedly preserved in school texts and Shirley Temple movies calmed us. Seeing Negro people as human beings with feelings exactly like ours could be terrifying. We knew that if we had been treated as we treated them, our hearts would be full of murder. When Stokely Carmichael yelled "Black Power," we were, I think, unable to cope with our emotions. It was as if Steppin Fetchit had suddenly become a track star. Worse, it was as if he had yelled, "Stop Thief!" Guilty white society panicked.

At first I was only amused as black "leaders" were hauled before microphones and cameras to interpret (and apologize for) Black Power. But something else was happening. When Black Power became white news, black people all over America read about it. They learned that two little words had the power to shake up genuinely powerful white folks. The brown-skinned porter in Savannah or Seattle probably knew no more what it meant than had Stokely Carmichael, but it sure did roll nice on the tongue. It got black folks more attention faster than all the spirituals and sermons and sit-ins combined.

Marc's life was unaffected by the new Black Power; he continued to write of people who had no power at all. He described a visit by an old man who was trembling with a fierce impotent rage at the names he had been called by a white trolley conductor when he didn't move quickly enough. Marc advised him to write to the trolley company. The old man had hesitated. "Well," he said finally, "I don't write so good." Marc wrote the letter for him. "Mr. Marc," the old man told him, "I can only pay fifty cents a week on your fee." Marc wrote me that he felt so sorry for this man, ashamed and defeated by his lack of education and his poverty. "I told him there was no fee; that I was proud to write a letter for any man brave enough to stand up to the trolley company; that if young men were this brave, our problems would be over."

Marc said the old man stood up straight, put out his hand, and said, "Black Power, brother." When he left the office, Marc wrote, "he walked differently than when he crept in."

On July 3, 1966, a radio announcer on a Philadelphia station said that the National Guard had been called in to quell riots in Omaha. In that moment I wished, fervently and self-ishly, that we had never come to know Marc Moses. Marc's tall, bearded figure was quickly identifiable and widely disliked by the police. It would be two days before we knew that no one was killed in the Omaha riot, and during those two days Ben and I sat by the radio as if by a sickbed. All those black people had been shot in Watts; now someone we knew was in danger. This was no deplorable event to read about; it was too real and too close. Racial war was developing in my country and—Oh Lord—my sympathies were on the "wrong" side.

Ben suggested we telephone to Marc. I didn't want to. I

dreaded hearing some telephone operator tell us he couldn't be located.

The newscasts finally reported the rioting in Omaha was over. Two days later, Marc's letter, written during the riot, arrived. His small script was strewn on the paper as if thrown there between phone calls and visitors. "I am in my office," he wrote. "My friends say I should stay out of the area, but how can I? People have to be able to find me if I'm needed."

The insurrection, Marc wrote, had been triggered by the death of still another black teen-ager, "executed on the streets by the police for a minor crime." It was after his funeral that Omaha's black teen-agers exploded.

Marc's sentences were like random shouts during a hurricane. "The young men are causing the action," he wrote. "If only the mayor and the police director had listened last winter!" Marc had received a phone call from an official to "cool" the crowd. "I told him I had tried to cool the crowd last winter when it was still possible. Nothing and no one can cool these kids right now!" Then in printed capital letters, Marc wrote: THE MAYOR JUST SAID ON RADIO THERE ARE NO RACIAL OVERTONES TO THE DISTURBANCE. MY GOD!

Marc's next statement disturbed me. "These black kids are attacking only the white and the Jewish stores," he wrote. "The first target was the Jewish furniture store that sells junk to old people and then eats them up with 'interest and carrying charges.' " It had an anti-Semitic ring. At the same time I thought it might just be unfortunate phrasing written by a distraught man.

Marc's letter ended abruptly. The next segment was dated a day later. "There was some action outside my door," he continued. "A cop on a motorcycle who was gunning around like he was the Lone Ranger, skidded and got pinned under his machine. He asked a black man to call headquarters for help. The man did and stayed with the injured cop until help came. When the squad car roared up, cops jumped out and beat up the black man before he or the injured cop could say a word.

"When the war starts full-scale, whites are going to wonder what happened. Their cops are what happened," Marc wrote.

Marc, of course, was publicly blamed for the riot. Janet Adams wrote me, quoting her minister: "The prophets of doom are happy today. Their predictions have come true."

The black middle class rushed to condemn—not the conditions Marc warned officials about but Marc's having "stirred people up" by pointing out the conditions. I replied to Janet with the sad comment Sebastian de Chamfort made in the 1700's: "We leave in peace the people who start the fires and molest those who ring the alarm bell."

Marc had not, however, told us all that had happened to him during the disturbance. We got the details later as part of the most dreadful letter I had ever read. The day after the riot Marc had walked into a white-owned grocery store in the ghetto "to buy one miserable loaf of bread." The white grocer recognized Marc, panicked, pulled a gun, and threw a caustic liquid into Marc's eyes. There were many witnesses. Marc had called the police and pressed charges against the man. At the hearing a white judge ruled that, by walking into the store, Marc had provoked the attack. Case dismissed.

Marc's letter written after the trial was so full of rage that it was painful to read. Even more agonizing was that he had apparently expected a fair trial. Like Paul Benson, going proudly to accept his medal, Marc had sincerely believed that this time he would get equitable treatment. Now he wrote: "One thing is glaringly certain; I was wrong to call the police and expect justice in the courts." Marc's pathetic expectation of justice showed how deep and constant his hope had been. I felt sick watching it die.

A few days later Ben and I were invited to a Black Power discussion at the home of a black couple, Ann and Jack

Peterson. By now, talk seemed useless. But Ann explained that this group would be entirely black except for Ben and me and their white minister. The object was to explore and try to unify responses to Black Power. A man from CORE would lead the talk.

Marc's new defeats in Omaha depressed me deeply, but he was writing now of the need for "black unity." I wondered how anyone could unify a large group of individual human beings who had only physical appearance in common. But if Ann Peterson's friends were talking about "black unity," if she wanted us there, Ben felt we should go.

When we arrived at the Petersons' house with its large terrace and lighted swimming pool, we found we knew most of the black people there. Like Jack Peterson, most of the men were successful doctors. Also a lawyer and a biochemist were included. We knew these were old friends of the Petersons who shared a common childhood in Alabama and who now lived near each other in our neighborhood.

It seemed odd to be discussing social issues around a luxurious swimming pool, but the white minister from the Petersons' church appeared comfortable about it. He sat in a large wicker chair, his feet on a matching hassock. He was in his thirties, blond, with small, delicate hands. His wife, also blond, sat next to him on a straight chair. They seemed a pleasant couple. The white minister had been sent to the church recently when it had become predominantly black.

Ben knew the man from CORE, Bud Carver, who was to lead the discussion. He was tan-skinned and casual. He perched on the edge of a table next to where the white minister was stretched out with his chair and hassock. Bud Carver jangled change in his pocket as he began to speak in an earnest but low-key, calm voice. "Black Power," he said, "is many things to many people—voting power, economic power, unity."

The white minister was not looking at Bud. He was adjusting the cuff of his shirt. Bud, still jingling the coins in his pocket as a quiet accompaniment to his words, said, "Black Power, whatever else it may mean, is primarily a call for black people to work together instead of against each other."

The blond minister sighed loudly and raised his small hands for silence. "I've got to cut off the talk right here," he said. He had worked hard for civil rights, he continued, looking around the group for confirmation. Several people nodded. "But this Black Power nonsense is dangerous, destructive, and detrimental to your progress." The minister shook his finger at Bud Carver and said, "Black Power will lose you everything you've been given. Every white person resents those words."

My face felt suddenly hot and I knew I was blushing, partly from embarrassment at the minister's patronizing manner, but also from my resentment in being included in his "every white person." As calmly as I could and holding on to Ben's hand, I said that every white person did not resent Black Power—that while I could speak only for myself, I liked it. I said that Black Power took nothing away from me, that there was nothing for me to resent, but I felt it inspired pride in black people who needed pride desperately.

Ted, a thin, dark obstetrician, leaned forward in his chair and asked, "But don't you think we can accomplish more by not antagonizing most whites?"

Ben shook his head. In the South where, week after week, he talked with school superintendents about desegregation plans, the "politeness" of black people had accomplished absolutely nothing.

"But we made it without violence," the black biochemist said.

Suddenly, I found myself in an extraordinary position. I felt more black than the black people around me and it was because I realized in that moment that they probably had less contact with poor, uneducated Negro people than I had come to have through Marc's letters. All the people on this terrace were successful, talented, and highly educated. Was it possible that they didn't know how much other black people needed a pride they already had?

Everything Marc Moses had poured into me for the past ten months poured out as I tried to explain about pride. I told them about the old man who had shuffled into Marc's office, so ashamed because he couldn't write a letter; the children beaten by teachers for being "stupid." Could they imagine, I asked, how it might feel to be ashamed of their grammar, of their clothing, of what they had been told was their natural inferiority?

I spoke directly to Ann Peterson, our hostess, whose exceptional I.Q. helped her become the youngest graduate ever of a prestigious white school. "Ann, can you imagine how it might feel to be average, just average, and to be trapped in an eternal circle of bad schools and underemployment? And not to know how to break the circle—to watch average white people, no smarter than you, move ahead while you stay forever behind. Ann, wouldn't even a meaningless term like Black Power sound so beautiful, mean so much—even if you only mumbled it to yourself?"

"Yes," Ann said. "Yes, it would."

I was talked out now and wondering if I had been as patronizing as the blond minister. I was trying to explain black people to other black people. But then color seemed not to be the issue. I was trying to explain to secure people how insecure people must feel. The black people on this terrace had all been born with superior I.Q.'s, the mental and physical health, the aggressiveness and sheer resiliency to overcome all the obstacles of being black. Each person here was demonstrably superior to me. Perhaps it was easier for *me* to understand how average people of any color felt.

A black attorney, a graduate of Harvard's law school, said,

"But in the long run, Lois, don't you agree moderation pays off better than violence?"

I was astonished to hear myself say passionately, "Moderation has won nothing—nothing at all—for the average, ordinary black person. The Watts riot frightened whites into doing more than they did during 400 years of black patience."

Bud Carver, the man from CORE, interrupted to say laughingly, "You'll be accused of inciting to riot, Lois."

"No," I said. "The people here will not riot. None of us here has any need to. Those average black people will decide the next moves, not us."

Ann Peterson suggested coffee and the group broke up. The white minister announced jovially that he had to leave. He waved his hands at me from across the room as he and his wife hurried across the lawn.

Several people asked me how many other whites felt as Ben and I did. I said I didn't know, but believed most whites would when they had black friends to teach them. But Marc's "black unity" seemed farther away than I thought. The black people around Ann's swimming pool had earned the right to feel secure. I wondered if it was right to have asked them to imagine (or remember?) how insecurity felt. They were, or had become, so different from the people in Marc's world. Did they realize, however, how many white people lumped them all together? How awful if black unity was accomplished only when the successful, the accomplished black professional realized whites viewed them no differently than they viewed ex-convict Digger Pierce?

Bud Carver drifted over to where I stood, still jingling the coins in his pocket. Just then the biochemist's wife asked me if I thought there would be more riots. Bud Carver spoke for me when he said, "They're inevitable. The young people are filled up with anger. The explosions, I'm afraid, have only just begun."

When the woman turned away, Bud said to me, "You know, I'm lucky. I can blend into a middle-class group like this—yet in a riot all I have to do is pull off my necktie and start yelling and I'm on the other side."

He was lucky. I couldn't. Through Marc Moses, I had become a part of the other side emotionally. But there was no way I could ever be truly there.

Chapter Twenty-one

At first, the aftermath of Ann Peterson's Black Power discussion brought me only a vague, unidentifiable discomfort. I had written to Marc about the evening. He replied, praising me. "You have more soul than the so-called blacks in that group. You were speaking for me—but even more effectively. Those Toms listened to you because you're white."

Marc's praise didn't please me. Instead it added to my concern that I had begun to substitute Marc's thinking for my own. On August 3, 1966, when Martin Luther King was stoned by white mobs in a West Chicago neighborhood, I had felt a deep contempt for "those whites" whose sick twisted faces looked out from our TV set. Yet the 6,000 whites who rioted when 800 marchers demonstrated peacefully for open-housing legislation were like the Midwestern lower-class people I had grown up with. I saw them, though, through Marc's eyes as The Enemy. I hated them. My surge of loathing toward these white Chicagoans frightened me. Was I becoming like some of the white radicals I had met? One thin, porcelain-skinned woman at a meeting had talked with narrowed, glittering eyes about her "racist suburban neighbors." She had seemed far more motivated by hate (of her neighbors) than love (of justice). I had also watched a white man nodding hypnotically when a black speaker at a civic meeting uttered what to me were vague, meaningless clichés. This white man's attitude toward black people was noticeably obsequious and his need to earn their approval was pathetic. Had any of these unnatural responses begun to apply to me?

Only some of what I had learned from Marc helped when I appeared with the Philadelphia Panel of Women. I could answer the questions of the white suburban audiences we spoke to, but I grew impatient with their lack of information and their indifference. Several times, I felt my irritation had been too evident.

At times like that Debbie Levy, the Jewish Panelist, was my most important anchor. Debbie, blonde and blue-eyed, had seen her mother enter the gas chambers at Auschwitz. If Debbie could survive unspeakable horrors and still patiently answer stupid questions like, "Why are all Jews rich?" then I had to try to stifle my impatience. Debbie had told me long ago that she used her awful memories as a reminder that she must never stand aside, as the "good" Germans did, and let another group of people be persecuted.

It was Debbie who gave me an article written by a California rabbi. It may well have been one of the first to discuss black anti-Semitism. The article, "The Hands of Esau," by Harold Schulweis, had been published in the December 1965 issue of a Jewish magazine, *The Reconstructionist*.

Even though I believed anti-Semitism among black people must surely be a minor problem, I was impressed with the rabbi's ideas. He dismissed what I knew to be true: that non-Jews exploit ghetto people in exactly the same proportions as anyone Jewish might do. The memory of my own father proved this even if common sense had not. But the rabbi wrote that if even one Jew defiles Judaism by exploiting black people, it is the responsibility of all Jews to persuade him, by confrontation, by moral pressure, to live up to the principles of Jewish ethics.

I felt that this man's call for action among Jews was a wonderful example to other religious groups. It might inspire Protestants and Catholics to police the members of their churches who exploited poor people. I asked Debbie to give me several copies of the article. I wanted to send one to Marc Moses. He would be pleased, I thought, about Jewish concern.

I was anxious too to send another copy to an old friend in New York, Dave Goldstein. Months ago, I had written Dave, an advertising man, about Marc's criticisms of ghetto supermarkets. Dave's agency handled a large national supermarket chain and I thought he might like to know that some supermarket chains had a bad reputation among black people. According to Marc, the least fresh produce, the most undesirable meat was sent to stores in the ghetto. Dave's reply—large heavy letters scrawled with a broad-tipped pen—had been, "Don't get involved in hopeless issues like race! Where's your business head? Emptying the Hudson with a teaspoon would be easier!"

I thought the rabbi's article might be interesting to Dave. The same day I mailed a copy to Marc. Their answers came back to me about a week later in the same mail.

Dave had written: "You're wasting your time trying to help Negroes. They won't even help themselves. Jews faced the same prejudices and we survived. But Negroes won't train to compete; they can't take abuse. The rapes and narcotics are typical. They have no pride; no character."

Marc's letter began: "I approve of anything that will relieve us of Jews, those human parasites who prey on black misery, suffering and misfortune. Jews are so cold and heartless where black men are concerned that I wish Hitler had killed them all. None of my best friends belong to this thieving, cheating, scheming group of scoundrels."

I remember sitting at the kitchen table, holding these two letters and literally trembling with hurt and fury. How could two people I respected read a sincere, self-criticizing article by a concerned rabbi and react with age-old ignorance and bigotry? I felt the same overwhelming grief I had felt when I had tried futilely to make Janet Adams and Marc understand each other. But now, the grief seemed even stronger. It was, I thought, the kind of grief a child must feel hearing his parents, two people he cares about, quarreling.

This time the pain turned suddenly into rage. I wanted to lash out at both these men. Marc and Dave, I decided, deserved to see each other's letters. Neither knew the last name of the other and they would never meet, but I wanted them to see their own stupid virulence mirrored in the letter of another man. I switched the letters and added a bitter note of my own, with the carbons addressing both men. How, I wrote angrily, could they hate each other and yet see *me*—a white gentile—as their friend? It was my group—the Christian Caucasians—who had created Auschwitz and the Ku Klux Klan. "We WASPs must be clever indeed," I wrote bitterly, "if we can get the people we persecute to fight each other instead of us."

That afternoon after mailing the two letters, I angrily cleaned cupboards and dresser drawers, trying to work off emotion and to struggle through a problem I had ignored before. I could acknowledge having met anti-Semitism in some black people. I had replied to their remarks exactly as I replied to white anti-Semites. A Negro doctor at a dinner party once began to tell me that "the Jews control American industry and keep black people out." I had asked icily if Jews owned General Motors, U.S. Steel, Ford, or the railroads, airlines, the packing companies? He backed down.

I had also met some Jewish people with the same anti-black feelings I had found in some Christians. This was no surprise. Human characteristics were more or less evenly distributed among all people. It even seemed useless to try thinking of Jewish-Negro relations; this itself grouped people.

Yet Marc and Dave, two men I considered intelligent, had quickly and viciously grouped each other. Why?

I could concede to Marc that there were people with Jewish names who took advantage of black people, but Schwerner and Goodman were Jewish names, too. These young men went into Mississippi to work for black justice; they risked, and lost, their lives.

If Marc wanted to judge Jews as a group, he could judge them either on the evidence of some ghetto merchants or on Schwerner and Goodman.

There were, as Dave contended, black people "with no pride or character," rapists and addicts. But there were also people with so much character that they submitted nonviolently to clubs, tear gas, and rocks to find a peaceful solution to an American tragedy. If Dave judged black people as a group, how did he decide to judge them on the convicted rapist rather than on Martin Luther King? In fact, I reflected ruefully, we could all decide whether to judge Italians on the Mafia or the Pope; the Irish on Joe McCarthy or John Kennedy; Germans on Adolf Hitler or Albert Schweitzer. And we could all decide whether to judge WASPs on Dwight Eisenhower or Lee Harvey Oswald.

That day as I prepared dinner, clattering pots and pans in angry hopelessness, I remembered something Mrs. Jefferson, the woman who cleaned for me, had told me several months before. "I heard this lady I work for on the Main Line talking on the telephone about a Jewish lady who had just moved on her block," she said. "She was telling another lady they should just all ignore her, let her know she wasn't wanted. I got to thinking. If she hated Jews that much, she must hate my people even more. I quit her." If Mrs. Jefferson, with her South Carolina segregated education, could act out of such logic, then even more should be expected of law school graduate Marc Moses.

Ben had flown home that night after a meeting with a school superintendent in a small Georgia town. The meeting had been successful; a few black children would be enrolled in an all-white school. But to me Ben's progress was overshadowed by a new recognition of black-Jewish hate. Why, I asked Ben, did some people who had suffered persecution turn it on others?

The three lines formed between Ben's eyebrows. "Some human beings," he told me, "need to deal with their hurts by hurting others. Mrs. Jefferson's reaction and Debbie Levy's vow never to Do Unto Others what the Germans did to Jews are not typical among us humans."

He was right, of course. And I had also begun to realize as I thought more about it in the next fews days that frequently the Negro and Jewish communities touched each other like two matchheads. I remembered black acquaintances who had commented that "when neighborhoods integrate, the Jews are the first to flee." I had protested that the white *Protestant* families had run from these same neighborhoods as soon as the first *Jewish* families moved in. There were, therefore, seldom any white Christians left to flee from the Negro families. Jews had also been excluded for generations from Establishment industries and many had turned to small, self-operated businesses; the grocery stores, the pawn shops, the drug stores. Mass merchandising killed these family-run businesses except in the low-income areas that supermarkets deemed unprofitable. "The 'Jew-Store,' " Barbara Hamilton had once told me, "was a ghetto term but often it was owned by a man named Rossotti or Kelly." And so, Negroes saw Jews only as neighbors who fled or store-owners who stayed. Jews often knew Negroes only as the group who had "changed the neighborhood" or as suspicious customers whose incomes never met their needs. Neither Marc nor Dave considered any of this.

— 263 —

It was easier to stay strangers to each other, fulfilling the scapegoat's need for scapegoats.

I remembered a phrase in Dave's letter. "We Jews survived prejudice." He had believed black Americans should and could do the same. I had heard this before from Jewish acquaintances. It was sometimes said challengingly as Dave said it, but it was also asked sincerely as a question.

I knew just enough about Judaism to have an opinion, and Debbie Levy had confirmed what I believed, that the Jewish religion itself had enabled people to survive through its practical guides to daily living. For over 5000 years, Judaism had provided important training, independent of public education. Rules of health, behavior, family unity were all part of religious obligation. Even dietary laws were vital survival techniques in the days before refrigeration and pure food laws. When Jews were forced to flee from country after country, these religious laws helped them survive. Through Judaism, their children could be educated even when schooling was forbidden to Jews. The history and traditions passed on from generation to generation gave Jews a security, an inner pride, and a strong sense of identity. When the Spaniards or the Russians or the Germans expelled the Jews from their countries, Jews were usually able to choose their lands of exile and, to some extent, prepare for their exodus. In whatever new land they chose (nearly always a land with a European-oriented culture), other Jewish families were likely to be there, speaking a common language and able to give at least comfort and advice to refugees. And they were white. Debbie Levy told me of her brother who ignored the "No Jews Hired" policy of a chemical company and identified himself only after he had become their top technician. "No Negro could do that," she said.

Historically, the Jewish experience had little in common with what had happened to black people who were physically identifiable and brought to America against their will. African religions, if slave owners had allowed them to be practiced at all, were as useless in the climate and culture of the American colonies as ice-skates would be in the Congo. African culture and religion had been developed around co-operation (in climates producing bountiful, year-round food supplies) rather than around European-style exploration and conquest (to find better food sources). Africans, of course, had not been allowed to prepare for their kidnaping and enslavement. (Leland Hamilton had traced his ancestry and found that one forebear had gone one morning to the village well where he was captured and hauled aboard a slave ship that took him to South Carolina.) Whatever religious traditions might have brought comfort to men, women, and children crammed into the holds of slave ships were denied to these people, many of whom spoke different languages. (Today, in Nigeria alone, there are over 247 different tribal tongues.) An African chieftain or religious leader was as helpless in the depths of a slave ship as a Lutheran minister would be, kidnaped from his prayers and thrown in with a boatload of Swedes, Italians, Germans, and Russians and deposited in Ghana.

We know that, once in America, black tribes and families were deliberately scattered to prevent communication and unified action. Bantus and Watusis were separated from their kinsmen; a wife was sent to Georgia, her husband to Virginia, their children to Mississippi. Religious ties too were ripped.

For a long time in colonial days clergymen and slave-owners disagreed over the teaching of Christianity to the slaves. Clergymen were committed to the "conversion of the heathen"; slave owners struggled with the moral-vs.-economic problem of men, supposedly equal in the eyes of Christ, enslaving each other. I had never realized what compromise they arrived at until Marc Moses' fulminations against "the anodyne of slave religion" made me think. As I listened closely to the hymns and sermons in Negro churches, it suddenly seemed clear why black Christianity was so unlike the Christianity I had been taught.

In the small Milwaukee church I attended with Grandfather for so many Sunday mornings, Jesus' admonition to "turn the other cheek" was never overemphasized. Nor were the comfortable German-Americans sitting around us in any apparent hurry to get to heaven. Life down here was not that unpleasant. In Sunday School I sat in front of the picture of Jesus with His arms outstretched to white-, black-, and yellow-skinned children and sang "Jesus Loves Me, This I Know." It seemed He certainly must. My well-fed, well-cared-for life suggested that Someone up there did. We sang "All Hail the Power of Jesus' Name" and "Have Thine Own Way, Lord" sure of the Power and content with the Way the Lord ran things.

In black churches, it was entirely different. It was the black preachers who gave sermon after sermon on turning the other cheek and—since there was little choice—loving one's enemies. "Swing Low, Sweet Chariot" was a plea to be carried home where life had to be better than the tenements and cotton fields down here. "Nobody Knows the Trouble I've Seen" would have sounded as incongruous in my white church as "We Shall Overcome." And so I sang "Onward, Christian Soldiers" with confident fervor while the black child sang "When I Get to Heaven Gonna Put on My Shoes." She may not have had the shoes in which I marched "Onward as to war."

The difference, once I looked closely, was that the Christianity taught to American slaves and passed down over the generations, was a religion on which the colonial clergymen and slave owners had compromised, a Christianity designed to keep slaves docile and resigned. There were laws forbidding anyone to teach a slave to read or write, but no one prevented Miss Ann, the white slave mistress, from teaching "Blessed are the Meek" in the slave quarters. It was, in fact, encouraged. With strong emphasis on heavenly rewards for earthly behavior, suffering people could be persuaded to wait for heaven rather than revolt on earth. All men were equal unto Christ, said the clergymen. Yes, added the slave owners, but only after death.

In my church the punishment of hell rather than the rewards of eventual peace in heaven was used to keep me in line. For black people, hell was not that impressive. The contrast wasn't there. To a black child in an unheated Philadelphia tenement, eternal fire might have sounded downright delightful. And so while I was taught morality through Christian threats, black people were kept meek by Christian promises.

I could understand exactly what Marc Moses and Malcolm X meant by slave religion. But I wondered if Marc had ever realized that this corrupted form of Christianity was taught to slaves because most slave owners were Christians? Judaism forbids the owning of slaves, and it is a matter of record that there were few Jewish slave owners in America. If someone like Marc wanted further proof, he need only remember that slaves were given the surnames of their masters, those slave-names black militants replace with "X." There are very few black people in America bearing the names of Levy or Cohen or Goldberg. The names passed down through generations of black families, from slave-owner origins, are the clearly Protestant names, the Williamses, Browns, Joneses, and Lees.

Marc might remember, too, that there was one common bond between black and white Christianity. Like Marc and other black people, I was taught that the Jews killed Christ. How ironic if Marc's anti-Semitism had, after all, its roots in the slave-religion he loathed!

Much has happened since 1966 to bring black anti-Semitism to national attention. Yet I have not been able to add any new facts to what I felt as I tried to understand two friends who hated each other. I have attended discussions designed to mend Jewish-Negro relations. I heard a Negro speaker say bitterly, "God save me from Christian love and Jewish justice." And I watched as a rabbi leaped up to accuse the speaker of anti-Semitism.

But that September in 1966, as I waited for whatever reply Marc and Dave might make, the problem of black anti-Semitism was personal, not national, in scope. Dave's answer came a few days before Marc's. There were only two sentences written in his large, bold, black scrawl. "You had no right to send my letter to anyone else. Our friendship is ended." There was no reply I could, or ever did, make.

Marc's six-page letter began by discounting—forgiving—me for—everything I had written in my bitter note enclosed along with Dave's letter. "You are a woman—and so are inclined to sentimentality where Jews are concerned." The next five pages of Marc's letter embroidered the label he pinned on all Jews. As I read Marc's newest diatribe against "the Shylocks who drink black blood," I thought he sounded exactly like my father, openly bigoted, willing to debate stereotyped opinions, almost eagerly. But I had no heart to debate with Marc.

Instead, I debated with myself. Was I right to feel such severe disappointment in him? Who was I to demand perfection in anyone? Perhaps Marc had a right to some flaws. And he had so few friends; he was the focus of so much criticism.

These thoughts didn't change what I felt. Marc did need friends, but I couldn't be one of them any longer. I found I could neither ignore Marc's anti-Semitism nor accept it. To pretend either would be a patronizing hypocrisy. Expecting less sense of justice from Marc than I would expect from other friends was more a betrayal of both myself and Marc than my honest feelings would be.

I showed Ben the new reply I had written to Marc. This time Ben nodded, but he also put his arms around me. He may have known I had to reach a point like this and that, when I did, it would touch parts of me I was still not aware of.

I had written Marc that his attitude toward Jews made me wonder if we were both really working toward the same goals. That, for the first time, I realized I was not concerned only with the rights of black people. Rather, I was concerned that all people finally see and judge each other as individuals. I could understand, I wrote to Marc, that he could hate all white people, but singling out Jews as special scapegoats was, to me, as irrational as the labeling by color that he fought so hard to change.

With a tremendous sadness, I told Marc that if he could not accept Jews as individuals, then perhaps he had never accepted me as an individual either. His "Dear Sister" and his statements that I "thought black" had once pleased me, but now I wondered if he had turned me black in his mind to avoid revising his group label of whites. If he had had to do this to accept me as a friend, then I did not want to be accepted. "I am white," I wrote. "I will always be."

As I wrote these lines, a memory of Ruth McPhetridge, the white president of Omaha's Urban League Guild, was released somehow. The strange bitterness of Ruth had stayed somewhere in my mind all this time. Her full mouth with its unnatural tightness and her deeply blue, but bleak eyes had seemed one day to look back at me from my own mirror. I had wondered how she had become what Marc had described as "too hard for a woman." It was easier to do than I had dreamed.

Marc's reply to my letter was as close to an apology as he was capable of making. But it was not a retraction. "I did not write these things to upset you," he said. There were many fine Jewish people. He went on to describe all the good people he knew who were Jewish. Some of his best friends? Telling Marc about "the good darkies" so many white people described to me seemed useless.

— 269 —

I continued to exchange letters with Marc, but a certain spell was broken and that was as it had to be. Through Marc I had discovered a part of America I could have found in no other way. But Marc's activities and opinions had absorbed me long enough. It was time that I came home again.

Chapter Twenty-two

The unraveling of black and white relationships that began in the summer of 1966, when Stokely Carmichael yelled Black Power, accelerated by fall. I felt that the black pride that surged up at the sound of those two words finally allowed men like Carmichael to express their disillusionment with white liberal help. Now, even whites who could accept Black Power were told to step to the rear of the ranks and take orders instead of running the show. After years of dedication to nonviolence and integration, people like Stokely Carmichael were saying in disgust, "All right, you don't want us. Give us decent schools, decent housing, and stay as far away as you want. We want you even less."

This attitude distressed some white people we knew. Tina Kesson, the active, bubbly professor's wife who had chosen the neighborhood just as we had, seemed shaken by a SNCC benefit in late September of 1966. She had sold dozens of tickets, she said, for the benefit movie. Before the screening a black man with a beard told the predominantly black audience, "We don't need whites. Why don't you honkies go home?"

Tina and her professor husband had stayed, but the speaker's hostility disturbed her. She came over the next morning and filled my ash trays with partly smoked cigarettes. "But I thought they *wanted* integration," Tina said. "If they don't, what am I supposed to do?"

Talking with Tina forced me to examine my own feelings. Labor unions had fought their battles alone, I told Tina. Women had conducted their own fight for feminine voting rights. If black people wanted to continue their battle without white help, it might be because they preferred to owe nothing when they won.

Tina snubbed out another half-smoked cigarette. Maybe, she said, but she enjoyed her friendships with black people. It would be bad if they ended.

I tried to imagine how it would feel if every black friend we had now rejected us. It seemed that this could not change our beliefs. Through friends we had learned what happened to people who were black, but my concern could not be reserved for friends. It must apply to people I didn't know and whom I might not like if I did. Marc Moses' anti-Semitism had ended my trust in him as a friend, but he deserved—had the right of a human being to—justice. And of course, anti-black or not, so did Dave Goldstein. Wasn't justice the right even of the unjust?

Answering Tina's question in this way opened another personal inquiry. I still did not know what motivated my emotional involvement in civil rights. If it was because of some need for appreciation, for gratitude from black people, then the new black attitudes would alienate me. Barbara Hamilton had said, "Black Power neatly eliminated phoney white liberals who were more interested in their power than our progress." It would also eliminate whites who couldn't work without black gratitude. I said to Tina that Black Power might let us find out if we were interested in rights or self-righteousness and that I wanted to know.

The change to what is now called black militancy didn't affect what Barbara Hamilton and I were doing. We were both devoting most of our time to the Panel of American Women. The Panel reached white audiences and at least created discussion. Often I felt depressed by the persistence of the old myths and misinformation, but if they existed, the Panel was one step toward trying to change attitudes. As a white person, I had gone "home" to speak to my own kind. Barbara was willing to join people like Debbie, Claire Cassidy, and me.

Meanwhile, the Buchanans, the Negro couple who had moved into Folcroft, moved out. The all-white community had harassed them for three years. Chet Buchanan had said, "I can't let them win or no other Negro family will ever be able to move anywhere." But their daughter, Lucy, was growing up. They could see signs of damage from the awful tensions under which she had been raised. Betty Buchanan felt there was no choice. A seven-year-old child needed playmates. The Buchanans moved into our neighborhood. Even people who wanted to welcome them kept thoughtfully away for a while.

In October 1966 a Negro couple moved into Kensington, an all-white section of Philadelphia. For several days white mobs threw rocks and garbage at their house. According to the Philadelphia *Bulletin,* youths smashed police car windows and pelted policemen with bricks and bottles. More than a dozen policemen were hurt by the white rioters during nearly a week of violence, but none of the rioters was shot or beaten.

Just before the white Kensington riots, Ben began a new job. He would be working in Philadelphia instead of traveling through the South. At first it seemed safer. After Kensington, I wasn't sure. Ben got his new job through a black friend, Will Howard, who also worked for the government. Will was asked to recommend someone for Federal Contract

Compliance Director for Philadelphia and Pittsburgh. Will said he knew they were expecting him to recommend another black man.

"Wait," he said with a grin, "till they find out you're white and born in South Carolina!" Then he added seriously to me, "But I don't know any black man more sincere than Ben."

Ben's new job involved getting building contractors to obey the federal order that a "reasonable number of minority group workers" must be employed on any project paid for by taxpayers' money. The contractors, however, blamed the unions for the lack of Negro workers in anything above low-paying laborers' jobs. There were virtually no black men at all in the seven higher-paid building trades unions such as the plumbers, electricians, or sheet metal workers. These craft unions had been lily-white for generations. If Ben tried to get unions to integrate, he would be in an area even more sensitive than schools. The more I understood about Ben's job, the more difficult it sounded. Ben and one secretary were the team assigned to challenge the powerful trade unions and contractors. And wasn't Kensington the kind of community where union men lived? Very soon I was to meet one of these men, not through Ben but my children. I was to confront my own prejudice about blue-collar workers.

It happened when a tall man in grimey work clothes strode into his own living room and said gaily to me, "Sweet Jesus, how I hate niggers!" Incredibly, this man with his enormous grease-imbedded hands and his jutting chin seemed direct, honest, and unexpectedly likable.

I was in Woody Beecher's living room, talking to his wife Louise, because I had reacted to prejudices of my own. My daughter Sarah had brought their son Teddy, a thin, blond, seven-year-old classmate, to play at our house for several afternoons and on this afternoon, in May 1967, Teddy had asked Sarah to play at his house. While Sarah was changing her school clothes, Teddy talked with me in our kitchen. He was a wan, restless little boy, but manfully struggled to make conversation with a grown-up. "We've moving," he said, "so we can get away from the colored. They're bad, those colored." I asked him gently what the "bad colored" did. Well, lots of bad things and they were moving "where there ain't no colored at all."

Teddy had just walked home with my children and the two black playmates that Spike and Noah brought home that day. But Teddy's statement was given so parrotlike that it seemed useless to point out how he had laughed and played happily with the two "bad colored" just now. However, I decided to drive the children to his house and find out where they would be playing. If Teddy Beecher's family had some standards different from ours perhaps their standards of safety were different too. Sarah had recently played with a white child whose mother left them alone in a 16-story apartment building while she sat downstairs in the cocktail lounge. Ben and I did not want to shield our children from bigoted people, but it still seemed best to meet Mrs. Beecher before sending Sarah there alone.

The Beecher's home was part of a block of gray stone row houses three streets away from ours. As we drove up, Teddy pointed to his mother, a plump yellow-haired woman in plaid pants who was spraying a large rosebush in front of her door.

Louise Beecher smiled warmly. "Come on in," she said, "but excuse the mess. Can I make you some Instant?"

Teddy led Sarah to the back yard while I followed Mrs. Beecher into a living room much like the house I had grown up in. Like my grandparents, the Beechers apparently purchased furniture as it was needed. The sofa was sagging, but still intact. A new pink brocade chair was protected by a clear plastic cover. The middle-aged slipcovered chair next to a pile of *Field and Stream* magazines so obviously belonged to the man of the house that I avoided it. I sat at one end of the mohair sofa, across from an imitation fireplace.

Louise Beecher and I had hardly settled down with our instant coffee when a powerfully built man in blue work clothes burst through the door. In two strides he was in the middle of the room expressing his opinion of "niggers." He grinned and continued, "Hi. One of those niggers parked his car right smack in front of my house. Bugs me, it does."

Louise laughed. "That's Lois's car," she said, and introduced us. Woody laughed too. "No offense. They usually park their cars all over."

Woody apologized for not shaking hands with me. Just came from work. He operated "a dozer." Dirty work. He would wash up and have some coffee, he told Louise.

I had time only to ask Louise and be told a "dozer" was a bulldozer, that Woody was an operating engineer and he operated several different kinds of construction machinery. Woody came back into the room now, shook my hand with his huge hairy fist, and sank into the chair near the pile of *Field and Stream* magazines. He was a good-looking man with black hair and warm blue eyes with squint lines in the corners. I had noticed a maple gun case, glass-enclosed, locked, in a corner of the dining room. Those squint-lines could have come from the sun on construction sites or from aiming those guns at game.

Woody Beecher sat back in his chair, one leg resting over the side of it, and said he was sorry to have insulted my car, but "God, I can't wait to get out of this nigger-neighborhood."

I was about to say why we had chosen the neighborhood. But here was an opportunity to hear someone's honest comments on "race." Too often when people knew how I felt, the subject was either changed or became polite. It would be dishonest to pretend I agreed with Woody Beecher, but what would happen if I simply withheld my opinions and listened?

— 276 —

After his remark about the "nigger-neighborhood," Woody looked at me for a minute, expecting a reply. I smiled and said nothing. Louise said, "Isn't he awful?"

I kept smiling and said, "Well, he doesn't like the neighborhood."

"I sure don't," he said. "I drive my minister nuts talking this way, but that's how I feel, dammit." Louise explained that after the first "colored family" moved on the block, their minister had brought in a man from the Human Relations Commission to organize a meeting.

The Beecher's block was only three streets away from us, but I knew there were still pockets of whites in Mt. Airy who had *not* welcomed integration and who had stayed out of an angry stubbornness or because they could not afford to move.

"Listen," Woody said, "most of the people who went to that meeting have moved to the suburbs by now. I'm still here, but not for long. One nigger family I could stand, but there are too damn many now!"

I said, "Oh?"

The challenging bravado with which this man made his first statements about "niggers" suddenly changed into an earnestness. Woody Beecher sat forward in his chair, arms resting on his knees, looking seriously at me out of warm blue eyes that almost matched his blue work clothes. There was no glitter of hate, only concern.

"It's the Quakers," Woody said. "They're the ones who started all this integration business. The Quakers control the banks and the mortgage companies. They're the ones who make money on moving the niggers into white neighborhoods."

I did not have to pretend interest in the theory he began to develop. It was a fascinating, agonizing parallel to what people said about Jews or the Catholic Church or any other group they disliked. Woody had only changed the name.

Unexpectedly, Woody paused, then ended his tirade with:

"Well, maybe it's not only that. I guess I just don't like living with Negroes." Again he looked directly at me, his wide forehead creasing into lines. I was struck with his good looks, the kind of rugged open face you see in paintings of pioneers. He would look natural with his gun and game over his shoulder. I was also struck by his voluntary change from "niggers" to "Negroes."

Now Louise Beecher broke in. She twisted her rings and looked at them as she said, "I know we're not supposed to feel that way, but I don't like living with them either. I'm afraid of them."

Louise was bending toward me from her end of the sofa with the same serious earnestness as Woody's. She pushed her yellow hair back with one hand. She was afraid of the colored, she said again. "I was beaten up by a gang of colored girls when I was a kid. Now I look at all those black faces and I just get scared. I know it's wrong but I just can't help it. I know they're not all that way," Louise said quietly, shaking her head, "but when you read about all those Negro criminals in the newspapers . . ."

I felt a stab of anger at the white newspapers that always found ways to identify and feature Negro crimes with photographs and front-page positions. Yet the white youth who shot fourteen people from a Texas tower last August or the white killer of five innocent women in a beauty shop that November of 1966 had caused no talk of "white crime waves."

But Louise Beecher had gone on to describe her feelings at the meeting held by the Human Relations Commission when the first Negro family moved onto their block. Until now, I'd always believed these meetings were vital, that old and new neighbors should be encouraged to know each other. Now, for the first time, I saw these meetings through the eyes of someone like Louise.

Pamphlets were passed out, she said—"Your *New* Integrated Neighborhood." Louise shook her yellow hair and frowned. I shuddered. Of course! This was no "new" neighborhood to Louise. She told me they had lived there for fifteen years. This unfortunate title would only make them feel more insecure. Louise kept shaking her head as she talked. The man from the Human Relations Commission said they should visit their new neighbors—"socialize with them!" "I couldn't say anything at all. No one else did either. One of the colored families was there. I didn't want to say anything that might hurt their feelings. I kept thinking how I'd feel if I was them."

My flood of sympathy and respect for Louise Beecher was as sudden as it was unexpected. Of course she would feel unable to say anything. I could imagine one of the men I knew from the Human Relations Commission conducting the meeting. His poise and vocabulary and positive attitude would squelch someone like Louise Beecher. But she had the compassion to understand how the black family at the meeting must feel. "Imagine having a meeting held about you!" she said.

And so she had remained silent. She was a woman who knew she "shouldn't feel that way," yet no one had helped her feel differently.

I asked Woody if he had gone to the meeting.

"Hell, no," he snorted. Louise wouldn't let him. Then, in apology, he said, "Listen, it was just as well. I didn't want to hurt anybody's feelings either. I know they gotta live someplace, but Jesus, why did they all have to move in here?"

I answered, "Woody, there are so many places where Negro families can't buy. So it's natural for these families to move into whatever areas finally open up a little."

Woody waved a large hand. "Hell," he said, "they can move in any place!"

"Folcroft? Kensington? Would *you* move into a neighborhood where people threw rocks through your window?"

Woody nodded in sympathetic understanding. "Yeah. Okay, maybe they can't buy anyplace. And I know it's the real estate guys who make all the money if they can scare whites into moving. That's one of the reasons I stuck it out this long. But now there's this family next door with at least ten of the blackest kids you ever seen."

Later in the conversation, Woody would tell me about a "brave woman" (white) who was "taking care of her ten children all by herself"; about the "gangs of Negro boys just looking for trouble," and the (white) "teen-agers who oughta have more to keep 'em busy." Louise and Woody saw people differently and they honestly didn't know it.

Then Woody turned to me. "You're okay," he said. "You looked like one of those liberals. But you listen—not like my minister." I thought of all the people I hadn't listened to.

Woody Beecher apparently had a lot he wanted someone to listen to because he shifted his big body in the chintz chair and began to move his large hands in uninhibited gestures. "Yeah, I know it's wrong to be prejudiced. All right. I heard it enough; Sundays and on TV." Woody and Louise Beecher had been made to feel guilty. But was feeling guilty the solution? Apparently not, because Woody Beecher suddenly began to speak with angry eloquence. "What gets me so mad," he said, "is that—okay, integration has to come—but why in *hell* is it people like *me* who have to do the integrating?"

"Why is it," he continued, half out of his chair now and gesturing toward me, "that those people on the school board tell me *my* kid's school has to be integrated and they don't have any kids or grandkids in public schools? How come my minister sends his kids to private school if he's so big on brotherhood?

"And some of the guys from around here," he said, "who talked loudest about integration and who treat me like some kind of a Ku Klux Klan nut if I open my mouth have found some good excuses to move. Oh, not because the block is integrating," Woody said, twisting his mouth, "but because they all of a sudden found their house was too small."

Here, Louise laughed. One woman, she said, told her she couldn't stand the smell of Italian cooking next door. "She stood it for six years until a Negro family moved in on the other side of her!"

But that wasn't all, Woody said now, getting to his feet and standing before the imitation fireplace, too impassioned to sit still. "I'm a union man," he said, "and those newspapers write about how the unions should integrate. How integrated are the newspapers?

"My God, Lois, I'm no genius. I couldn't be a newspaper writer. If I was that smart I wouldn't have to worry about some colored guy getting my job. To tell the truth, it wouldn't take long for a colored guy to learn how to operate a dozer. Then what? I'd be integrated right out of my job.

"I read those speeches that the doctors and lawyers make at those Brotherhood banquets," Woody said, "but do you ever notice where they live—where their kids go to school? Check that sometime. And no one's gonna shove them out of their jobs. Christ, all I got is my job and my house and no college education. Those rich liberals on the Main Line or in Chestnut Hill don't have to worry about any of what I've got to worry about."

"You tell me," he said, "why they do all the brotherhood talking—and people like me are supposed to do all the integrating?"

He stopped and peered at me with his keen hunter's eyes as if I could answer him. I couldn't.

Now I knew that for all our living in the neighborhood, sending our children to the public school, Ben and I were not too different from the "liberal doctors and lawyers" Woody condemned. Ben's job wasn't threatened by hundreds of black men who could learn it quickly; our block was too sophisticated to be panicked, leaving us the only white family, and even if it did we had been allowed to know black people and gradually work through our fear of difference.

I remembered episodes that supported what Woody said: the prominent lawyer who had spent half of a dinner party telling me how long he had worked for civil rights and the other half explaining why, out of his forty office employees, he couldn't hire a Negro secretary—or file clerk—or receptionist; the rabbi of a synagogue in a changing neighborhood who praised the Panel and who, I learned later, had been the *first* to move from the neighborhood when it integrated; all the people who spoke out against "racism" and lived in the suburbs. Marc Moses had once said, "Notice where your 'liberal' politicians and supreme court justices live and send *their* children to school." Woody and Marc—what an unthinkable combination! Yet they both saw the same thing— from opposite ends of America's complex race illusions.

Then, unbelievably, I heard Woody Beecher say musingly, his anger gone, "Well—listen, Lois, I guess it'll all get worked out some day. There are a couple of decent Negro guys on the block. One guy was fixing up this old car for the Big Brother club he belongs to. There was this other colored guy up the street who is just as mad as I am about the lousy trash pick-up our block has been getting these days. Maybe me and the colored guy can start a petition and fight city hall a little. Matter of fact, we were kinda talking about it."

Woody had returned to his chintz-covered chair now. His large angry gestures had become the shrugs and head-shakings of a man thinking. He hunched his big shoulders beneath his blue work shirt and looked straight ahead as if into the future. "I'm not dead set on moving like Louise is. Some of these Negro guys are okay. Some anyway. And there's enough jobs for all of us. Just scares you when you first think about all those black guys waiting for your job. But there's enough construction work to spread around."

The change in this man who had greeted me by saying how he hated "niggers" was incredible. Then I remembered something I had read: when people fully express their negative feelings, the positive feelings begin to surface. It seemed almost too neat an explanation, but it was happening.

Woody Beecher was not a neurotic, hate-filled man. Rather he was a troubled man, feeling outside (and inside) pressures "not to feel that way" about black people. Yet people like me—and too many others I knew—had made the blue-collar Woody Beechers into our scapegroats. We had made them into something for *us* to sneer at, to feel superior to. We silenced them with our pious intellectual statements if indeed we spoke to them at all.

What if the Human Relations Commission had set up a meeting where people like Woody Beecher felt free to say what they really thought? A meeting of whites only, where whites could admit their fears and speak without being patronized by "experts" or silenced by the presence of black people? What if, instead of pressing for neighborhood "socializing" that seemed to invade even the privacy of a worried white man's home, they had put a man like Woody Beecher in charge of neighborhood communications? I could imagine Woody reassuring people that, "Hell, all niggers aren't bad." Wouldn't this be more convincing to his neighbors than a human-relations expert talking of "our common humanity" or "our commitment to social concerns"? Woody would not try to tell his neighbors that "all men are equal," but I thought he would be able to convince them they were "equal enough." If his white neighbors stayed, they could find out in time about "our common humanity" if they worked together on getting the trash picked up.

At the door, Woody said to me, "You know, I never thought about it before—but if Negroes could buy in the suburbs and all over, then they wouldn't all push into neighborhoods like this. Somebody's gotta open up the suburbs for them."

I said that this was what open-housing laws were all about; that when people could all move wherever they wanted, then there would be no panic blocks and no white or black ghettos. The Human Relations Commission was gathering names on petitions to send to Washington. Maybe he could take some around.

Woody Beecher looked down at me as if I were his son Teddy, unaware of the facts of life. "Oh, no," he said patiently, "you don't understand, Lois. The Human Relations people don't work for *us*. They work for Negroes. They wouldn't want me."

I never saw Louise and Woody Beecher again. Newark exploded two months later. When I drove past their house in August, I saw a Negro woman lovingly pruning the rosebush at the door.

Chapter Twenty-three

When Newark and Detroit erupted in July 1967, my first reaction was that people would now understand that if Watts was a cry for help, Newark and Detroit were screams. It took only a few days to find out I was wrong again.

White people we overheard in restaurants or on trolleys talked about law and order, but only for black people. They behaved as if there had been no white riots ever, no Little Rock, no University of Mississippi, no Folcroft or Kensington. People like Woody and Louise Beecher had their fears reinforced, their guilt over feeling prejudice washed conveniently away.

White news media reported the racial events in Newark and Detroit with little sifting of hearsay or hysteria. Even President Johnson said sternly on a special telecast, "There is no American right to loot, burn, or shoot a rifle from a rooftop!" He must have forgotten the Boston Tea Party and he was proved wrong about rooftop snipers. The Commission he appointed to study what really happened in Newark and Detroit would state later "most reported sniping incidents were demonstrated to be gunfire by either police or

National Guardsmen." But no one would know this for over a year.

During the terrible two weekends in July as I read the confusing, sometimes self-contradictory articles in white newspapers, I knew we could get an eye-witness report from Mike Le Bec, a black newscameraman friend who surely covered both events. This time I didn't want to hear the truth; what I could piece together from the white newspapers was sickening enough. By reading beyond their strange preoccupation with property damage, I had found that fifty-nine Americans had been killed—fifty-four of them black. In the Boston Massacre of 1770 five Americans died when the British tried to enforce *their* law and order; in South Africa's Sharpesville Massacre in 1960, the United States condemned the street slaughter of sixty-eight black Africans. Yet now, in the Newark and Detroit Massacres, it was the property damage and rumors of snipers, not the death toll, that made up the headlines. Mike Le Bec would know what the newspapers had not reported and I didn't want to hear it.

We had met Mike in early spring of 1967 through Dolph Priest. As a reporter for the Negro-owned newspaper, Dolph had given Mike assignments long before Mike joined an international news service as one of the first black cameramen in America. Dolph was at our house one evening when Mike phoned, trying to locate him. I impulsively asked Dolph to invite Mike over. Through Mike Le Bec, Ben and I were to learn of American life that horrified even black militant Marc Moses.

When Mike Le Bec arrived at our door that first evening, he looked exactly as I expected a newscameraman to appear. Except for his light brown Negroid face and his crinkly bushy hair, he might have been the Hollywood version of a news-chasing photographer. He was dressed in well-worn but expensive sports clothes, a cashmere sweater, tweed slacks, burnished loafers. He walked into our house carrying his tall muscular frame with a loose athletic assurance. Apparently in his forties, his hair showed a touch of gray and I noticed a long scar on his left cheek. Later we learned this had come from a beating by police when he photographed the events in Selma, Alabama.

As the evening progressed, Dolph urged Mike to show us his South Philadelphia film. "Here?" Mike said. "Don't worry," Dolph told him. The film was in his car. He brought it in and set up his equipment. With his camera, Mike had penetrated a part of the ghetto no white person could ever have entered. We learned later that it had taken weeks before even Mike was trusted. He had stayed in the neighborhood, letting people talk to him. Finally, he was allowed to see what their lives were like, the lives of the old and the ill, people pushed by the mistakes of urban renewal, the nit-picking of welfare rules, and the blank walls of human indifference into their last resting places.

Mike's film showed an old man, hobbling through his own waste on bandaged feet, warming some mess over a gas ring. He said quaveringly, "If I could only get me just a little education in something, I could keep me a job." Another remnant of a man sat licking a turkey back for nourishment; Mike's flat voice explained that his heart was so bad chewing was too much exertion. This man was entirely dependent on his neighbors to bring him food. Another lay stupefied in bed; his arm gone, torn off in an industrial accident; he had been waiting five years for his claim to be settled. He lived on dog food.

An old woman talked as she struggled down a flight of stairs to a bathroom. She and the five other families using it kept it locked she said, because "the landlord won't put no front door on the building." There was no seat on the toilet; she flushed it with a plunger. She paid $70.00 a month for her bedroom and kitchen. "But there's worse places," she said.

Then wistfully, "But how I pray the Lord for just a little more heat—just a little more."

Once I would have told myself there were ways out of this misery—public help of some kind. Now I knew that no human being would live as these people did unless they had exhausted all their resources, intellectual and emotional. There was a time when I would have wanted to rush in with whatever food and clothing I could take. By now I knew it would make little difference to the dozens of people in Mike's film. It wouldn't even buy me a comfortable conscience.

After that first evening, Mike became a frequent visitor. He was unmarried and his last-minute assignments when news broke in various parts of the country made planned social life impossible. There was always room for an extra plate at our dinner table. Our children adored and adopted him. He listened patiently and soberly to their long stories; they called him "Uncle Mike" and profoundly confused an occasional white visitor.

Mike seldom talked of his news-service assignments. He took the filming of a Chicago murder scene or an airplane crash as calmly as a milkman works his route. Mike was a self-proclaimed loner, covered by layers and layers of observed and digested human miseries. If Dolph Priest was a cynic, Mike was a post-graduate of cynicism, accepting realities and adapting them to his survival.

Mike had become a cameraman, he told us one night, through luck and a little extortion. He had been born and raised in a ghetto not much better than the one he filmed, but "Dad was healthy; worked as a janitor. Mother was a domestic." In high school a white teacher had lost a son Mike's age and Mike's interest in mechanical gadgets reminded the teacher of his dead child. "Mr. Fitz found an old camera for me. I fixed it. He bought me film out of his own pocket." Photography became Mike's abiding love and for years he supported himself repairing cameras and learned his own craft. During World War II he applied for the army photography school and was told they "didn't have one for Negroes." He fought in an all-black infantry unit. After the war he came back to his repair job and to photographing whatever interested him in his spare time. During the 1963 picketing of construction sites organized by Cecil Moore to open building trades jobs for black men, white TV cameramen noticed that the tall brown-skinned man with his camera could get closer to the action than they could. Local, then international news services began buying film footage from Mike.

"One day," Mike said, "I figured that a news service ought to have its own black cameraman. But if it could buy my films it would never hire one." So Mike stayed away when the next racial news broke. He grinned. "I got frantic phone calls. I was suddenly an employee and an 'instant member' of the cameramen's union." Mike was now working on getting a black crew; a black sound man, assistant, and reporter.

Mike saw little of his film on American TV; most of it, he explained, was taken for European use. Some of the more violent scenes he had shot in places like Selma were seen only overseas. I didnt know which disturbed me more, that we didn't see everything or that Europeans did. Mike also told us about the game he played with Northern police. In any news event involving them he turned his camera on the most violent policeman he saw. "Clubs stop in mid-air," Mike said.

Mike told us, too, about the frequency with which he was followed by police who saw only a black man driving an expensive sports car with photographic equipment in the back seat. "To the average cop," Mike said, "I have obviously stolen the car." Many times that spring when Mike left our house we would hear later that he had been stopped, searched, and questioned on his way home. Mike always made it sound humorous—the policeman who stuck a gun in his back as Mike was unloading his equipment in front of his apartment ("He was sure he'd caught me red-handed!") and the policeman's widening eyes as he scanned Mike's credentials. ("Jeez, I didn't know they had black ones!")

But one night as Mike was leaving our house he checked and found he had forgotten his wallet. Mike spent that night in our guest room. It no longer seemed like a joke to me. An American man could not cross Philadelphia without his "passport."

About three weeks had passed since the Newark and Detroit Massacres when I answered the door late one night and found Mike standing there. Congressmen had already begun to make tasteless jokes about a proposed rat-control bill and I had had time to find out that few white people were shocked by riot deaths. A small news article had recently quoted a National Guard official who criticized guardsmen for "firing without orders" and recommended new riot training; the Philadelphia papers ran it on a back page.

Mike had no jaunty smile when I opened the door that evening. He touched my arm as a greeting and went to sit in the yellow chair he had occupied so often. He had first been in Newark, he said, and then Detroit. From there he had gone directly to a friend's deserted cabin in the woods. He had stayed there alone, drinking mostly.

Much of what Mike finally told us that night has since been documented by the Civil Disorders Commission, but not all. No one documented the horror on the face of a hardened newsman. At first Mike only stared at the floor and told us fragments of his own feelings. "I've seen a lot. I never thought I'd see anything like this." During World War II Negro troops had been assigned to burial details; Mike had handled fragments of human bodies and retched his way through to what he felt was an impenetrable shell. "But this got to me. In both those cities there were women and kids killed. Right here. In America."

Mike said he didn't even know what he photographed; he

wasn't even sure he hadn't just stood there not touching his camera.

He straightened up in the yellow chair and took a breath. The National Guardsmen had gone crazy with panic, he said. In Newark he had seen them spray an occupied housing project with bullets. "There were kids inside and you could hear them screaming—babies crying and women shrieking. But some rumor spread that there was a sniper in there and a young guardsman—a kid himself—let loose with a machine gun."

Mike stopped and shuddered and then continued. "Some of the white cops and guardsmen tried to stop each other. In Detroit—Lord, I guess it was Detroit—a young white cop came over to me with tears streaming down his face. He tore his badge off and threw it down in front of me; he was quitting the force. He said, 'My God, I can't do these things! I can't be part of this.' Then he just stumbled off."

In Newark, Mike saw a guardsman shoot in the air to warn a group of looters away from a liquor store. "In about a minute a jeep full of guardsmen zoomed up looking for the 'sniper.' The first guy tried to tell him he had fired the shot, but they were too busy shooting at the roofs. He just gave up and walked away.

"Some of these cops and guardsmen were so scared you could smell it," Mike went on, "but some of 'em—you could look in their eyes and see how they loved shooting people they'd hated all their lives. The yells about 'niggers' were almost as thick as the bullets."

Any movement at any window was fired at. Mike heard screams in one building and ran in to find a child in diapers with a bullet through her eye. Negro women were running through bullets to find children, while from windows children leaned excitedly out, watching. "They thought it was television," Mike said, "not real life, I guess." In Detroit, a four-year-old girl died when someone behind her lit a cigarette; a National Guard tank machine-gunned the window because of what they thought was a "flash of gunfire," killing the child and severing the arm of her young aunt.

Mike was bitter about "snipers." If there had been any, he said, they could have picked off a hundred cops. Instead, "those police and guardsmen were shooting all over the place like maniacs. It's a miracle they didn't kill more of each other!" He saw bands of police and guardsmen creeping up on each other in the darkness or around corners of buildings. Several times only a split-second recognition held the gunfire. He had also seen jeep-loads of guardsmen smash windows labeled SOUL BROTHER, and do their own looting.

Now I asked Mike about a newspaper statement I could not understand. White newspapers reported that snipers had attacked a hospital in Detroit. What had happened?

Mike shook his head back and forth as he answered me. "The National Guard did the shooting in the hospital," he said. Black men from the neighborhood had heard a rumor that the injured were being treated brutally by white doctors and interns. They had gone in to find out. A group of guardsmen followed them in.

"I was there when it happened," Mike said in an expressionless voice. Mike had heard the rumors of indifferent medical treatment too. "The place looked like an army field hospital during a battle," Mike said, "except the floors weren't absorbent earth. And those tile floors were so slippery with blood that the doctors were wearing galoshes."

Mike's hands wiped continually at the front of his shirt as he went on. Brutal interns? Mike said they were mostly overwhelmed and desperate. But he had seen a policeman carrying a black child of about ten. The policeman said to a doctor, "Here's another half-dead one for you." The doctor had taken the child and skidded its body across the blood-slick floor of a room. Mike pulled his fingers through his bushy hair and said, "The child's body slid across the room and stopped at a pile of other bodies on the floor. People were just lying there, stacked up. And a couple of them were dead." The men from the neighborhood who had come in to complain simply looked—and then tried to help. But the National Guardsmen came rushing in.

Mike was looking directly at me now. But his eyes, their whites yellow with red veins, were seeing something else. "My God," he said, "there never was anything like what happened then." The guardsmen began to shoot. Injured black people stumbled in and out of the packed rooms, screaming. Mike had flung himself to the floor when the shots began. When the guardsmen finally left, Mike had no trouble walking out of the hospital, but when he got to his hotel people grabbed him. They wanted to take him back to the hospital. Mike confessed he was so dazed he couldn't understand the excitement he created in the lobby. Then he looked down. The front of his clothes were soaked with blood from lying on the hospital floor.

Mike got in his car. He never stopped driving until he got to Pennsylvania, to his friends' cabin.

Chapter Twenty-four

Someday, when we look back at the Newark and Detroit Massacres, we may find that they marked a crucial fork in the road where black and white Americans moved swiftly down separate paths. Black friends of ours who had been moderates became angry; those who had been angry became frantic. Yet white people seemed unable or unwilling to accept what had happened in the two American cities.

In the public library a white woman said to me, "I was for them before this! All that destruction of property! And after all the tax money we've poured into their slums." Until Karen Paine, black, brilliant, and wrathful, paced my living room a few days after Detroit, I had wondered too why Detroit, of all cities, had erupted. Detroit had made maximum use of its poverty money, employment was high, and there were more black people in its city government than in most cities. Then, realizing what had happened to Karen Paine in the five years of our friendship, I thought I could understand why some poverty programs failed.

Karen paced the floor, her anguish making her literally incoherent. Once she had been a laughing, hopeful woman, proud that her newly earned master's degree in social work would make her useful. Her lightly waved black hair had swung becomingly above the soft, pastel-colored clothes she wore. Now Karen was still beautiful in her tight Afro hair style, but the colors of her African dashiki were as sharp and bitter as her words.

"The Nazis killed Jews fast," she said. "Now America is speeding it up with us." These were her few coherent sentences; others had gone on endlessly until even Karen obviously forgot how she had started them. She seemed to be talking until she might hear something that made sense to her.

Each of the five jobs Karen had held since we had known her had ended forlornly. The first two were in privately funded projects that were dropped when the money ran out. Karen quit two others because of what she proclaimed was "institutionalized insensitivity to people." In her present job with a poverty project, she seemed desperately aware she could never help as many people as quickly as she wanted to. She took on too many tasks, completed few. Her words, once insightful and articulate, were now snarling and inconsistent. Once, after hearing her, Leland had said, shaking his head, "Ecclesiastes seven, seven." "Surely oppression maketh a wise man mad," Barbara finished for him.

Karen was also being used by white groups who wanted a "militant speaker." The last time I heard her speak I sat among upper-income suburbanites who listened without expression as Karen let out her rage in desperately vague jargon. Suddenly I had the terrible realization that Karen was their entertainment, an experience they could boast of having submitted themselves to—a new-style minstrel show.

Karen, as obviously ill as she was, had been hired for a responsible position in a ghetto training program by white people who may have needed black faces or, perhaps, the chance to prove that "they" were incompetent. And Karen seemed unaware that the system she talked of destroying had already destroyed her.

It had not destroyed black men like Dr. Kermit Yerkes, a fair-skinned Negro Ph.D. in charge of the arts program at the day camp my children attended. Half of the campers were black children, yet Dr. Yerkes told me first he "hadn't noticed" that all the faces in the enormous montage lining the arts room were white; then he "couldn't find any pictures of Negroes in the arts." When I brought him pictures from *Ebony* magazine Dr. Yerkes never found time, he said, to add them to the montage. Barbara Hamilton explained the self-loathing that made men like Dr. Yerkes reject their own group. Dr. Yerkes was eventually appointed head of an important slum project.

He would work with another black man we knew, Harold Portius, a giant whose white hair loomed up out of nearly every large community event, black or white, in Philadelphia. He had once heard a Panel of American Women and telephoned me, asking if I would lunch with him; he would like to help the Panel get some important dates. During our luncheon, he spent most of the time telling me how he had "bit and scratched his way up," how he had outsmarted several "black leaders," and how his power came from being able to "get every black in this town tearing up the streets if I snap my finger." Finally I asked about Panel appearances. Harold Portius patted my hand across the table. "We'll talk about that some evening at dinner." He smiled. When I said, "Fine. Come anytime. My husband would enjoy meeting you," Harold Portius suddenly remembered he was late for an appointment. Reliable sources told us later that Harold Portius "controlled" a huge privately-funded poverty program and I lost whatever optimism I had had.

While we knew of the black people whose desperation or self-hate or selfishness diluted poverty programs, we were exposed at the same time to whites who believed they were speaking to "their own kind" when they talked with us. In a coffee shop shortly after the events in Newark, an elegantly dressed blonde woman draped her mink coat casually back over the stool next to me at the counter and began a conversation. Our small talk wandered to her son who, she said, was graduating from Penn Charter, a famous local private school. But he was having trouble getting into "the right" college.

"The headmaster told me that if my son were colored, he'd have no problem," she said indignantly. "They get preference these days! Isn't it deplorable," she said, "how the colored are pushing white children out of college?"

I could hardly believe she was serious. I said that numerically it couldn't be much of a problem; there just weren't enough Negro children to displace any significant number of whites, even if all Negro children could afford college.

The woman ignored my comment. "Why, they're pushing us out everywhere," she continued. "Look what they did in Newark! Doesn't all that killing and raping they did there just make you sick?"

It seemed useless to argue with this woman but I felt I had to mention that twenty-one of the twenty-three people killed in Newark were black and that no rapes were reported.

"Why, that's a lie!" she said in sudden fury. Then her eyes narrowed into slits. "I hope your daughter marries a big black one," she added.

Her incongruous reply startled me so much I answered with what had leaped into my mind: "Oh yes. Far better than marrying your son."

But as I walked away I felt she was both pathetic and frightening. Her son had not made a prestigious college; she had had to suspend logic to find a scapegoat. She was apparently angry at me for threatening her fantasy. Had the headmaster actually told her this fable about Negro students? Did he need a scapegoat too for his expensive preparatory school that hadn't successfully "prepared" in this case? The frightening aspect, however, was the woman's rage at me for disagreeing.

This was happening too often lately. At a dinner party I had chatted with a man named Herbert Miller, a charming, genial man in his fifties, pink-skinned, white-haired, gregarious. When someone brought up the subject of civil rights, his pink face turned red. "They" should be put in concentration camps, he said. "Black Power, hell!" he snarled. "I've bought a gun and I've told all my neighbors to do the same. All my life I've been a liberal, but those black loudmouths have gone too far." His wife looked down at her plate in embarrassment, but Miller's eyes glittered and his big shoulders worked in some physical need to express his fury. "I made it on my own," he said, "and no black bastard is going to take it away from me."

I knew his history. He had "made it on his own." He had come from a poor family, been taken in as an apprentice plumber, had been left a small inheritance by an uncle, and with a bank loan, became a plumbing contractor. If he had been black, there would have been no apprenticeship, no bank loan, no business. I made the mistake of trying to explain why a black person couldn't have duplicated his feat; how Ben was even now working to get unions to accept black apprentices.

Herb Miller looked at me across the linen and silver of the dinner table. The hushed venom in his voice was more frightening than if he had shouted. "You are full of crap," he said softly. "Everything you say is *crap.*"

I did not understand what literally pulled me to my feet. I walked out of the dining room to the coat closet. No one else had heard the hate in Herb Miller's voice or seen his eyes. At the door I told Ben and our hostess that I had had a sudden blinding headache. Even as Ben drove me home I couldn't describe the fear that made me get up from that table.

Perhaps it was that I didn't want to verbalize—to make real —what I saw in the eyes of a prominent successful white man. Herb Miller was not like blue-collar worker Woody Beecher with his honest questions, his attempt to understand. Herb Miller had no economic need to hate or fear. He had only some frightening undefinable inner reason.

There were other disturbing omens as 1967 moved toward 1968. In late October Marc Moses came from Omaha to visit us. He saw Mike Le Bec's film of the poor people in South Philadelphia. Marc, even with what he had seen all his life in Omaha ghettos, was made speechless by seeing poverty he had never imagined. He had left the room abruptly and paced our yard in the dark. He left the next morning.

In November 1967 Philadelphia's school children organized a march to the Board of Education to emphasize their requests for black history. According to conservative white administrators inside the building, the demonstration was orderly. Suddenly the police charged into the children with clubs. On television, I saw a film of three policemen beating a black girl who had already fallen to the ground. Incredibly, the announcer's voice talked of the "unruly rioting students." In spite of voices contradicting what the cameras clearly showed, I was sure everyone would finally be aroused at policemen clubbing students. At first the president of the Board of Education condemned the actions of the Police Commissioner. Then, mysteriously, everything quieted down.

Dolph Priest had been there with the students. His usual reporter's stoicism finally broke. Dolph admitted that even he had not believed the police would dare attack the students. He had been wrong.

By the time fall turned into winter and 1968 arrived, the only progress I saw anywhere was through Ben's new plan for enforcing federal contract compliance, an approach that was soon to be named the Philadelphia Plan by the media. For fifteen months, Ben had listened as construction firms promised the "affirmative action" in hiring minority group workers that government contracts required. "Part of the affirmative action," Ben told me, "is for contractors to insist that the unions supply black workers." But with all the talk of training programs and efforts, the work crews in the high-paying trades remained almost 100-percent white. Meanwhile, Ben had talked with black craftsmen and learned about the tricks used to keep them out. Apprenticeship tests were seldom publicized in black communities. If young black men did appear, they were made to feel unwelcome, given no instructions and told coldly that they had "flunked." Black journeymen described how they were given undesirable, short-term jobs when their names came to the top of the union lists. "A few days work and I'm back at the bottom of the list again," a black crane operator told Ben. A seventy-year-old plumber, his skin the color and texture of old cowhide, told the moving story of his struggles to get training, then his futile attempts to get into the union. Finally, totally defeated, he had opened his own plumbing firm and operated it successfully for forty-five years. "But if it'll help the young fellas," he told Ben, "I just gotta try again!" Ben was now convinced that the only way to insure genuine affirmative action by the contractors was to hold up their money by refusing to approve contracts.

Ben tried to explain the Philadelphia Plan to me. "It means that as a contract-compliance officer, I will have to be shown how many black electricians, plumbers or sheet-metal workers the contractor will actually have on the job. Look, the government demands other specifications like a certain gauge of steel or quality of lumber. The contractors find ways to keep those promises. Well, they've been promising equal employment for years. Now we're just withholding approval until the contractors come up with people—instead of promises."

It was fascinating to watch what happened next. Construction firms that had glibly promised to hire minority group workers suddenly sent long letters written by attorneys explaining why it couldn't be done. Firms to whom Ben had once sent lists of qualified black craftsmen telephoned in haste for "new copies." A union president wrote Ben a passionate, but contradictory letter saying, "You have acomplished (sic) the Capitalists Work. By busting the Unions. The communists will be happy." Unions and contractors alike threatened to "go to Washington" to get their funds released. Despite the threats, my husband held out for firm job commitments for black craftsmen.

I teased Ben, saying happily, "See! I knew your natural stubbornness would be an asset in something!" But I was delighted with his obvious satisfaction in his work. His years in advertising now seemed a waste.

Ben wasn't sure just how far and how long the politically elected officials in Washington would back him, but the Philadelphia Plan was having some excellent local side-effects. The board of education, the mayor's office and several religious groups announced their own Philadelphia Plan; they would deal only with firms *demonstrating* equal employment. And some construction firms who were aware of Ben's strict enforcement had begun to prod unions to find black craftsmen before their own contracts came up for review.

Later, the Philadelphia Plan was to be declared "illegal" by the Comptroller General thirteen days after the election of a Republican president. An outcry from the black community plus rumblings in Pittsburgh and Chicago in the summer of 1969 would cause a reinstatement of a revised Philadelphia Plan, its strict enforcement untested as of this writing. But in the early months of 1968, it looked as if Ben had succeeded in creating a small crack in the lily-white building trades. It was amusing at first to hear that most black craftsmen thought Ben himself was black and, finding he was not, believed, "Well, his wife is!" Finally, I realized the poignancy behind these rumors. To men who had fought futilely for so long, it was incredible that anyone could be as determined as Ben without some special self-interest.

In March 1968 President Johnson's Commission on Civil disorders released its report and I thought I saw another sign of progress. The Commission, headed by Governor Kerner of Illinois and composed of respected unimpeachable men, had weighed the evidence and pointed to "White Racism" as the cause of America's problems. The horrible massacres in Newark and Detroit were documented with names, places, times. What Mike Le Bec had told us was now in print for everyone to read. Americans would finally know the truth and white Americans would react, either out of compassion or self-interest. However slowly, people would begin to change.

I said all this to a white neighbor, Simon Thornhill, a quiet man in his sixties who had worked in civil rights since his teens. He had given me comfort so often when I no longer felt hope. He would point out gently from his long experience that "each generation can only accomplish less than it wants to, but the accumulation of the generations counts." But this time I predicted to him that things would move faster. The Kerner Report would make real changes.

I remember the expression on Simon Thornhill's lined face, a gentle sadness I did not understand until later. He said he would bring me a book. It was a red book 667 pages long. In the beginning it said, "relations between whites and Negroes in the United States is our most grave and perplexing domestic problem. . . . Racial misunderstanding has been fostered by the ignorance and indifference of many white citizens." The book described the unequal schools, the expensive white flight from Negro neighbors, the mistreatment by police. As a summary, the governor of Illinois had written: "The report contains recommendations which, if acted upon, will make impossible a repetition of the appalling tragedy which brought disgrace to Chicago in July"—"of 1919." This book had been written before I was born. Governor Kerner was a twelve-year-old boy in Springfield, Illinois, when another Illinois governor, Frank Lowden, appointed a committee to study the Chicago riots of 1919 in which thirty-eight people had been killed. The only major difference in the report Governor Kerner was to duplicate fifty years later was that, in 1919, fifteen whites had been killed along with twenty-three Negroes. In 1919 Chicago's Negroes fought back.

A prestigious committee of men had investigated the 1919 riots. I wondered how they would have felt if they had known that a woman yet unborn would read their words and know that no one had listened. Would my grandchildren fifty years from now read the 1968 Civil Disorders Commission report with the same kind of sadness?

It was Barbara Hamilton, sensitive as always to the feelings of others, who recognized my inexpressible dejection. She worried about me, she said. She thought it would help if I talked to Leland. Ministers, she teased me gently, know more than just the Bible verses. I rarely thought of Leland as a minister, but of course he was someone I could talk to. He was undoubtedly accustomed to the vague, confused, painful emotions I had struggled to express, emotions I didn't want to add to Ben's burdens.

As we sat around the Hamiltons' kitchen table on a rainy March afternoon, Leland seemed no longer the husband of my best friend and no longer the pacing black leopard. With Barbara pouring coffee for all of us, Leland easily became the fatherly, patient listener he must have been for hundreds of troubled parishioners. To him my unfinished sentences, my vague scraps of thought, seemed to be intelligible. His wrought-iron black forehead creased in sympathy for what I could hardly comprehend myself. When I finished, with the admission that I felt tired and discouraged, Leland stirred his coffee and paused. He wanted to tell me two things, he said, one in which *he* was an authority, and one in which only I could be the expert.

"I know about discouragement," Leland said, "and I've learned not to be frightened by it. I've come to believe, Lois, that profound hopelessness is often a necessary catharsis. Only when you can accept the facts of what didn't work, can you go on to find what does."

"But," he said, "there is another area in which you alone must decide how you feel. I want to tell you about something that happened a few weeks ago. We organized a picket line around the ghetto office of a crooked car dealer. A young white woman was part of the picket line. After several hours of walking she came up to me and handed me her picket sign. She said, 'My feet hurt. And you know, all this is really more your problem than mine.'"

Leland looked at me, warmly and directly. "This woman was honest, Lois. And she was right. It *is* our problem. If your feet hurt, Barbara and I love you too much to demand you carry our picket signs."

An unexpectedly wonderful feeling of release went through me. Someone like Leland was telling me I could go "home" now; that I had done all I could. Until that moment I hadn't realized how much I wanted to go "home"—to stop watching pain, to stop struggling with problems too big for someone like me to solve. I thought of a summer party in Omaha, our Rockbrook neighbors, everyone friendly, untroubled. It was like being told I could go back to sleep.

I remembered Joan and Paul Benson's words. They had put it even more strongly. "Don't help us or your children could get hurt." We hadn't listened and I wasn't sorry. But I had done everything I knew to do; I had tried so hard and accomplished so little.

And, of course, that was where the short, delicious dream of quitting ended. My children had not been hurt—yet. They would be if I gave up now. The problems erupting in America had been clearly outlined in the 1919 Report. My parents and grandparents had ignored them. They had passed the problems on to me. Whatever I left undone would be passed on to Sarah and Noah and Spike, compounded, impacted, pressurized from more years of festering. I was already afraid that my country—*their* country—was moving toward a long-postponed disaster. Perhaps nothing Ben or I did could stop it, but someday, our children would ask us what we had tried to do. For them, we had to do as much as we could, as long as we could.

"No," I said to Leland, "the woman with the picket sign was wrong. It *was* her problem too and mine."

Leland grinned. "Well," he said, "she came back later and picked up her picket sign again."

It would be good if I could write that my profound hopelessness did indeed prove to be a catharsis and that I found, at last, something valuable that I could do. Events in America's history were not arranged for my personal encouragement. My talk with Leland took place in early March 1968, just as Martin Luther King was being asked to go to Memphis to help garbage workers in their strike for better conditions. The next attempt I made to do something—anything—ended in abysmal failure on a rainy night at the end of March.

It was, I think now, Dolph Priest's unadmitted desperation that made him bring two South Philadelphia gang leaders to our house. Dolph had been spending night after night talking with the black thirteen- to nineteen-year-olds who made up the many gangs in the city. He admitted, "Sure, it's like giving aspirin for cancer, but these young kids are where it's at. They feel black adults failed."

Dolph had explained to us that gang life was not all "rumbles" and useless violence. These gangs were the "family" of children whose parents had to work and who had no time for family life. In gangs, children used the creativity that had been squashed by ghetto schools. There was real talent there, Dolph told us, organizational ability, discipline, loyalty. If all this could be steered into constructive channels, a lot could be accomplished.

Dolph had been trying. He changed his immaculate, fashionable clothes for jeans and shirts. He walked and talked with the ghetto kids for months. The future, Dolph said, was in the hands of these kids. They had grown up during the days of the promises. Some had been born at the time of the 1954 Supreme Court decision that schools must be integrated. These kids were fourteen years old now. They had seen Malcolm X slain and they had found that none of the promises were kept. Their schools had the same decaying buildings and the same brutal teachers their parents remembered; the jobs waiting for them were the broom-pushing types their parents still held.

Finally, one night Dolph admitted he didn't know what could keep these young "bombs" from exploding in some crazy act of violence against the white community. These kids were filled with a self-hate which they turned on each other and which could easily be turned on whites. "None of these youngsters has ever talked with a white person except a cop, a social worker, or a teacher, all figures of authority with some punitive hold over them. Maybe I can bring one of these kids to meet you and Ben," Dolph said.

The young men Dolph brought to our doorstep one March night never met Ben who was in Washington. Dolph introduced them by their gang names, Pighead and Tuna. Pighead was light-skinned, tall, with an enormous mound of crinkly hair. Tuna was shorter, very dark-skinned, and his head shaved to the scalp. They both wore long army surplus coats, which they refused to remove. They did not look at me.

In the living room the two teen-agers looked around with elaborate contempt. Pighead squinted at some of the pictures on the wall while Tuna sprawled in a chair. "So we're here, man. So what?" Tuna said to Dolph.

Dolph answered beseechingly, "She's different. Talk to her. Give yourself a chance to find out."

"If she's different," Tuna said, "that's too bad, baby. She's white, and that's *her* problem, not mine."

For the first time since I had known Dolph I felt more cynical than he. These young men trusted no one. Even the police exploited the gangs' hostilities. Dolph had told us recently that several policemen had deliberately dumped a black teen-ager in the territory of a rival gang, then sat in the squad car while the youngster was brutally beaten. Police, Dolph had added, occasionally created "rumbles" with false stories of rival gangs' "plans." Why would these two young men believe anything I said. To them I looked as much like the enemy as Pighead's Afro hairstyle made him look dangerous in the eyes of most white people.

Dolph tried to fill the silence. "Pighead is an artist," he said. Dolph pointed to one of the Hogarth prints on our living room wall. "Look," he told Pighead, "that Hogarth drew it like it was—all the social mess in his time."

Pighead stood in front of the etching while Tuna drummed his fingers on the arm of his chair, bobbing his head in a complex rhythm so that I saw light catch several light-brown scars on his scalp.

Dolph said that Pighead was still in high school. The principal there had never let anyone try for scholarships. He had told Dolph, "None of this garbage could make it, so why announce it? Half of 'em couldn't read the information if I posted it!" Dolph exposed the principal and as a result Pighead was applying for a scholarship at Moore College of Art.

While Dolph talked Pighead studied the pictures on our walls. Tuna continued to drum with his fingers and gaze contemptuously around the room. Suddenly Tuna jumped up.

"Let's cut out, man," he said to Pighead and walked to the door. Pighead followed him.

"Talk to her," Dolph said, "At least talk to her!" I had never before heard a frantic note in Dolph's voice.

At the door of the living room Tuna whirled around. "Why?" he screamed at Dolph. "Why in hell why?!"

Then he faced me, his arms held in front of him, wrists together, hands clenched. "Lady, you may be okay," he yelled, "but it's too late for talking!" He pointed his finger at Dolph. "He don't believe it's too late. He don't believe it."

Tuna walked back into the room. He turned to Dolph and then to me. "No more time for talking," he said. "Time only for *dying*." He whirled to Pighead, standing behind him. "Your drawings, man. All that gonna get you is a cop find out and he bust your hands instead of your head. You ain't goin' no place—and you know it just like I know it. We're dead men—dead men. One way or another—dead men."

I stood now, watching Tuna uncoil his feelings and use them like whips on all of us. I had not spoken a dozen words since he entered the room and now I wanted to tell him something he could not hear. I wanted to say to him, "Don't be so frightened," because Tuna was not shouting in anger, he was screaming in fear.

Beneath his shaved head his eyes looked as if they were full of flames, but his mouth was trembling. Then he took a step toward me and pointed back to Pighead standing at the door. "Know where he came from? His ma was raped by a honkie bus driver at the end of the line. Pighead is half honkie. That's why he don't see it like it is. It's always been the end of the line for him."

"See these?" Tuna demanded, thrusting his hands toward me to show dark crisscrossed lines on his palms. "Put there by my third-grade teacher with a steel-edge ruler." When I stepped forward Tuna backed away in some instinctive fear, but he kept yelling.

He turned his head. "See that ear, lady? Can't hear out of it. Cop busted it for me when I was twelve." He hit the scars on his shaved head. "See here and here and here. Cops, lady, your cops."

"All those signs on the trolleys, lady, that tell you Don't Be a Drop-out?" He pointed to a dark line near his eye. "Well, here's a present from the principal of the school I wasn't supposed to drop out of. And on the back of my head, lady, is another scar from when my fourth-grade teacher broke a window with my head. You know why they stopped hitting me finally in sixth grade? *Because I got big enough to hit back.*"

Tuna rubbed his head. "I shaved this so I can remind my brothers of all their scars. And remind them why the teachers stopped beating us."

His voice was rising higher in pitch and his eyes glittered. His mouth had stopped trembling. I thought of the people like Herb Miller whose eyes glittered in the same way when he said I was "full of crap." It was like watching a slow movie of two trains headed toward each other on a single track.

Tuna was saying now, "Lady, they're killing us every day, one way or another. But I'm not dying cheap. I'm taking ten of your kind with me."

He began the first syllable of a four-letter obscenity and then, incredibly, stopped himself. He was out of control but he could still hold back from using a bad word in front of a woman. Tuna rushed to the front door that Pighead had opened. Then he turned around once more and strode back to me. I reached out to him in some crazy attempt to offer comfort. He looked down at my hands.

He shook his head. "Lady, it's too late. Jesus Christ, don't you know it's too late?"

Tuna ran out into the dark.

Four days later, on April 4, 1968, Martin Luther King was murdered in Memphis and I thought Tuna was right.

Chapter Twenty-five

When Martin Luther King was murdered, the shock stripped away pretenses and, for the first time, I saw white fear. At first I saw it in public figures, then I saw it in myself.

On television, that Thursday night, the message from white officials was a quick, panicky sympathy and a quicker caution to black people to remain quiet. Most of the strained white faces seemed to be saying: "We-deplore-the-loss-of-a-great-man . . . and now *please don't riot.*" Mayors of large cities "mourned-with-the-black-community," and then requested all police and national guardsmen to report for duty. White network newscasters interviewed stunned, hollow-eyed black officials from civil rights groups. No matter where the newscasters began, they moved quickly to the nervous questions of what "they," the Negro community, would do in the streets.

Our telephone never seemed to stop ringing. Mike Le Bec called to say he was being sent to Memphis by the news service, that we must "lay in a stock of food. Anything could happen tonight." Barbara Hamilton phoned. Leland had gone immediately into the streets to listen to the grief and rage of the black crowds. Negro disc-jockeys switched instantly to tapes of Dr. King's speeches.

Then, very late that night, I realized I would have to send my children to their mostly-Negro school in the morning. And I knew I was afraid.

When white bombers killed four Negro children in a Birmingham church, when "my" kind attacked the Buchanans' house in Folcroft, I had been surprised that the black children at our school still treated me as a friend. But the mood was different now. America's symbol of nonviolence had been violently killed. Spike was in sixth grade; his classmates were not small children. Dolph Priest had phoned to say despairingly, "Lord knows what will happen when the schools open tomorrow." After an evening deploring the white fear that showed so clearly through its thin veneer of sympathy, I was feeling the same emotion. I mourned Dr. King's death, but I was afraid to send my children to school.

Once again as in Omaha, I sat up with my fear for my children. This time, around dawn, I suddenly remembered the Negro children who had braved the crowds in Little Rock. Ben had asked the black grandmother in Georgia to send her children to the white schools. Right now in Chicago, some Negro mother was sending her children, who were as precious to her as mine were to me, past crowds of white adults screaming, "Kill the niggers!" If Negro mothers had found the courage to submit their children to "my" people, perhaps it was time I learned how it felt.

In the morning Ben told me he believed we owed our children the truth. If they were to grow up during America's racial conflicts, they needed to be told, as clearly as possible, what happened. At a sad Friday morning breakfast we tried to explain.

"Dr. King has been killed," Ben said. "This was a terrible thing. Your Negro classmates will be feeling as sad as we do. Some might also feel afraid and angry. Dr. King has been killed, people believe, by a white man. Sometimes when people feel sad and angry they feel angry at anyone who is anything like the person who caused their sadness. If some of your classmates feel angry at all white people today, you must try to understand."

I could not send Sarah, Noah, and Spike off alone. I walked to school with them. This time the atmosphere was unmistakable. No one laughed or ran or shouted. Even the kindergarten children walked slowly, soberly. The schoolyard was as quiet as a church.

At noon, ten-year-old Noah came home crying. His best friend, Jimmy, said they weren't friends anymore. "He doesn't want *any* white friends *ever,*" Noah sobbed. I told Noah that Jimmy would feel differently some day.

Spike, conscientious and concerned at the age of twelve, took me aside. "All the Negro guys say they're not talking to anyone white today except the teachers. What do I do now?"

I asked how he felt about this.

"Well, I can understand how they feel," he said.

Maybe then, I suggested, that's what he should say to them.

"But if they're not talking to me?"

"Say it anyway," I told him. "They'll hear."

After school, Noah came home still tear-stained, but with his "other best friend," Kent. Kent's brown face was full of concern for Noah. "Don't worry, Mrs. Stalvey," he said, "I talked to Jimmy. I told him, didn't he notice that some of the most polite drivers on the Expressway were white. All white people aren't bad, I told him." Kent's dark-brown arm was around Noah's shoulders. He smiled persuasively. "Don't you worry now," he said.

Nothing bad happened at our school. Perhaps it was impossible for the black children to hate someone they played baseball with yesterday. There was a sadness and a brief turning away, but there was no turning *on* the white children. The principal, Vangie Peters, had wisely devoted the school day to a memorial program for Dr. King. She had also sensibly ignored the white minister's wife who wanted her to scold black children for the few angry names they called at whites.

For several days after Dr. King's murder white people seemed to be shocked out of their indifference. Letters to newspapers, calls on radio talk shows, a sudden increase in sales of the Kerner report, made it appear white people were concerned. Barbara said, "If something good doesn't come out of this awful killing, I will have trouble believing God exists." On the day of Martin Luther King's funeral, the Panel was scheduled to speak at a white upper-class suburban church. As we had done so many times before, Barbara, Debbie Levy, Claire Cassidy, and I drove together to the place where we were to speak. We were subdued and sad, but convinced that sharing our shock and sadness with a church group was an appropriate way to spend the funeral day.

As we entered the church, the first thing I saw was the large stained-glass window at the rear. There, in bright colors, was the familiar picture of Jesus and the little children that I had looked at all during my days in Sunday School. The familiar text was there: "Suffer the little children to come unto Me." But the Negro child and the Oriental child I remembered so well were gone. On this stained glass window, Jesus suffered only white children to come unto Him. When I heard Barbara's quick intake of breath, I knew she had seen the window, too. A stout blonde woman in a red wool dress offered the opening prayer. After the Amen, she looked at Barbara. "Our colored people have lost their leader and we offer our sympathies."

When we had each given our speeches, the program questions began. An elegant, middle-aged woman rose. She pointed her finger at Barbara. "Why don't you do something about your crime rate?" she demanded in cultured, but angry tones.

I put my hand on Barbara's arm and felt her shaking. She

couldn't reply, but I could. With all the horror I felt, I said to the woman, "While a great black man lies dead from a *white* assassin, let's just talk about *our* crime rate *first!*"

The program chairman jumped up quickly with an innocuous question, but other women, all expensively and elegantly dressed, continued to frame their fearful question, only more tactfully. "I know it's silly of me," one of them confessed girlishly, "but I'm afraid to go into the city." "Why do all Negro children carry knives?" another asked. Not once during the questions had anyone in the audience mentioned Dr. King. After the program, women crowded around Barbara telling her, as audiences always did, how much they loved their cleaning women. "Just like one of the family," was invariably added. I stayed near Barbara, fearful of how much more she could take. I heard her ask several women, "Why does your window of Jesus have all white children?" One woman said, "You people are so sensitive!" Another said, "Why, the picture was always that way!" When I asked the pastor he looked at me, smiled benevolently, and began talking to a woman next to me.

Then, the day after our appearance at the suburban church, I got a letter from a white woman in Cape Town, South Africa, who had written me long ago asking for information to form a similar panel there. Now, in a letter dated March 29, 1968, she wrote that "our Government has introduced a bill into parliament forbidding interracial political contact. We are not sure how much time we have left to organize a panel." The law would provide fines and imprisonment. She would let me know of "developments." I never heard from her again.

Here in America I could sense white fears building up all around me. A friend, working on her Ph.D. in political science, phoned to tell me about the "horrible" car accident she had in an all-Negro neighborhood. No, no one was hurt and she had only dented a fender in a collision with another car, driven by a Negro woman. "But I was so terrified," she said. "All those black faces looking in at me in my car. They could see I was scared and they looked as if they hated me."

I couldn't understand what she thought she saw. Another friend, also white, had had an accident only a week before. She had struck a black child who dodged in front of her car. She too was in an all-black neighborhood. Yet she had told me of the amazing helpfulness of the people who gathered around. In fact, the child's father had reassured her his youngster was not hurt and had brought her an aspirin. Why had these two women had such different experiences? Was it because hostility is as contagious as compassion?

Other white people had begun to talk differently, too, including people who had marched in Selma, collected funds for CORE and SNCC. The parents of Spike's white sixth grade classmates suddenly found strange or vague excuses to transfer their children to private schools. "Seventh grade is when dating starts," Principal Vangie Peters told me bitterly. A man who had been an officer in CORE until it was decided that only black people should hold positions of leadership now shrugged off the public school problem with, "Well, we may just have to write off this generation of Negro kids." His wife said later that, "Oh, any black person can get a job. Why, I can't even find a reliable maid or gardener." I suggested we solve the servant problem by encouraging *our* children to become domestics. The man and his wife glared at me, then changed the subject, demanding to know why I wasn't working for the campaign of Senator Eugene McCarthy.

Another white woman informed me her parents were stopped by the police at the edge of the Negro ghetto in Boston the day after Martin Luther King's murder. They were forbidden to enter. It did not disturb her at all when Ben brought her to the admission that black people were not allowed *out* of Boston's ghetto that night. This woman had been active in civil-liberties committees. "But this is different," she said.

It was after these experiences that I sat among the guests at Ben's birthday party late in August and realized that most of our remaining good friends were black. It had not been apparent at first; the room had been full of people, our friends. Mike Le Bec had gotten Leland to laughing uproariously over his first days as a cameraman; Dolph Priest had suddenly discovered a host of mutual acquaintances with Barbara. Even Karen Paine, now even more bitter than Marc Moses, seemed relaxed and happy that evening as we cut Ben's birthday cake. I tried to look at all the people around me with uneducated eyes. Light-brown Mike, Leland with his wrought-iron blackness, Dolph Priest's shining brown skin, the soft mink-color of Barbara's face. How could these faces cause fear?

The children in our neighborhood proved that racist fears and antagonisms were neither natural nor inevitable. I had watched, moved and thrilled, as my own children ignored color differences. Once Barbara had taken my blonde daughter Sarah and her dark-brown Paula to a movie. The two little girls had informed the parking lot attendant that they were sisters. They were convinced they had gotten away with their pretense. Often my children would relate incidents at school, describing a child as "tall, always wears a green jacket, has braces on his teeth." I listened, fascinated, that only occasionally would they mention the color of his skin. Sarah had brought home a picture she drew of a little brown-skinned girl in a swing. "That's me," she said. When I mentioned that her skin wasn't brown, she replied casually, "I know, but I couldn't find my pink crayon." My children had placed color in the minor role it should long ago have held. Why couldn't adults? After nearly eight years of trying desperately to understand white hostility, I felt no nearer than when I started.

And then I remembered my fear of sending my children

to school on the day after Dr. King's murder. I had not been afraid of Barbara's children or Karen's or Dolph's. I had been afraid of the black children I didn't know. It was easy to be afraid of strangers and to be afraid when we feel guilty as I did when a white man killed Dr. King.

Sitting in my living room, with familiar black faces around me, I thought I had finally found a hint of the answer. Weren't we whites perhaps still harvesting the guilt and the fear planted by colonial settlers? Out of greed, they had imported African people in such frantic haste until there were more blacks than whites in many early American communities. Historically, this was when laws forbidding education of slaves and social contact developed—when fear gripped men who knew they had gone too far. Since then, across the centuries, our legacy of fear and guilt remained fresh when the chains of discrimination replaced those of slavery. Was there not, however, something even deeper in our inherited obsession with color? Slave-owners needed the myth of black inferiority to justify themselves; the human need for status preserved this white illusion, but also, hadn't we used these unknown, different-looking people as a way to handle our nameless fears? Whites who could not face their own violent emotions, their surging frightening impulses to kill or rape, could project them onto people who were the color of the night during which bad dreams occur. We could project, accuse and punish—and exorcise our inner demons.

That evening, when our friends helped celebrate Ben's birthday, it seemed that white neurotic need was the only logical explanation I had ever found for the gross stupidity of white hatred. Facts—the Kerner Report and the 1919 Report before it—were useless. Logic was powerless against deep unconscious fantasy needs that converted so easily into unreasoning terror.

Chapter Twenty-six

Fear, guilt, and unconscious needs were not the simple solution I had once hoped to find for hate between people. Instead, as America neared the presidential election of 1968, I wanted to believe I was wrong. Unconscious fear could cause good people to do terrible things; guilt was more easily exploited by unscrupulous men than hate. On October 15, 1968, a disturbing article appeared in the Philadelphia *Bulletin*. It stated that the City Hall switchboard was deluged with phone calls from residents of an all-white area who had heard gunshots when police apprehended a (white) burglar. The white citizens believed that a "militant invasion" had come in retaliation for the neighborhood's opposition to school integration. Another small article ran the following week. Two white high school girls confessed they had slashed their hands with broken glass and then told school authorities they had been attacked by black students. When police found their original lies conflicted, the girls, fourteen and fifteen, admitted the ruse was designed to escape punishment for being tardy. Even children had learned to exploit white fear.

Early in November, my own fear took a new form. It began

at an informal evening at a neighbor's home. Sitting next to me on the sofa was a slender man in his late forties with gray-streaked blond hair. His name was Kurt Mayer. He was a sociology professor and a colleague of our host. He spoke little, but I heard what sounded like a slight German accent. As the casual conversation continued, someone talked about the army. Kurt said he had been "in the army," too. I asked Kurt quietly if he had been in the American Army. He gazed at me for a moment with light blue eyes that seemed tired. He had been in the German army, he said, and turned away.

The surge of revulsion that took hold of me was unlike anything I had ever experienced. Every Jewish friend I had ever had seemed to be in the room with me. This man had been a Nazi. It was only because I was trying to suppress my impulse to run that I forced myself to talk with him. Could I force myself to see him as an individual instead of as a member of a group as unquestionably evil as the Nazis?

"Were you a member of the Hitler Youth Group?" I asked him quietly so that only he could hear me.

Kurt Mayer shifted his body, turning to face me across the sofa. Again, he looked at me silently out of tired eyes. With a sigh, Kurt began to talk.

"Yes, I was a member of the Hitler Youth Group. Every child joined. It was like joining your Boy Scouts. We were, of course, taught to idolize Adolf Hitler. To us he was a saint, a savior. And when I was seventeen I joined the Nazi army."

I listened as silently as I had once listened to blue-collar worker, Woody Beecher, and with the same initial distrust. Kurt continued, "In the army we heard rumors of brutality toward the Jews in the cities, but we didn't believe them. If these rumors were true at all, we thought, they were isolated incidents involving petty ignorant officials."

Hitler, Kurt had believed, would not allow Jews to be harmed. Kurt smiled wryly, and I noticed that his long slender fingers were constantly in motion, twisting, twitching, going to his face. "Some of our best friends, of course, were Jews," he said, "but if Hitler thought it was best for Germany that the Jews leave, then it must be best. Still Hitler would not, we told ourselves, be unjust."

Kurt was talking louder now and I was conscious that other people were listening. His face took on a wistful, clouded look. When the war was lost and he came home, he found out what had happened to Germany's Jews. "Even then," he said, looking out of blank eyes, "I couldn't accept it. There are several months that I have never been able to remember. I don't know what I must have seen during those months."

A young woman with a Jewish name had been listening to our conversation. She broke in from across the room. Her voice sounded sardonic and bitter. "What did you *think* was happening in Dachau, Auschwitz, Buchenwald?"

"My parents," Kurt said, "lived ten miles from Dachau and they say they did not know what went on there."

I had always felt disgust for the "good Germans" who insisted they did not know what was happening. They were, I believed, liars. They did not want to know. Now I thought of all that I had not known about black people, of all that white Americans still denied; the massacres on the streets of Newark and Detroit, the hidden murders like the slaying of Russ Dale, the casual shooting of black teen-agers by police, the black children condemned to living death by brutal demeaning teachers.

"These things," I said to the young woman, "are happening now—in America, in Philadelphia—*less* than ten miles from where I sit this minute. It is easier than any of us believes to live ten miles from Dachau."

The young woman glared at me with more hatred than she had shown toward Kurt. She lifted her chin and pointedly turned away from me. Everyone else in the room quickly resumed their conversations.

I was almost afraid to ask Kurt, but I said, "Do you believe America could create actual concentration camps for black people?"

Kurt Mayer said, "No." There were three reasons why it couldn't happen, he said. First, other countries would put enormous moral and economic pressure on America if we established concentration camps. Then Kurt frowned and spoke more slowly. "Second," he said, "America has no long history of anti-Semitism as Germany had. And third, there is no religious difference between black and white Americans to make a 'Holy War' of the conflict." Then Kurt paused. "These are not very strong reasons, are they?" he said.

I said, no, they were not because if relatively small, weak countries like Rhodesia and South Africa could withstand world pressures over their racial oppression, strong, self-sufficient America could withstand them, too. To a large extent we already had. If America's history of anti-black prejudice was not as ancient as Germany's anti-Semitism, it was only because America was a younger country. Our anti-black feelings had existed since George Washington owned slaves.

The rebuttal to Kurt's third reason was the most apparent of all. Our "Holy War" was even broader than religion. "Protection of white womanhood" and "race-mongrelization" were rallying cries with ecumenical appeal. And who, Catholic, Protestant, or Jew, could reject the "holy cause" of *law and order?*

And I remembered something most of us Americans choose to ignore; that in my lifetime this government had forcibly taken American citizens of Japanese descent from their homes, confiscated their property, and interned them without trial in concentration camps.

I told all these things to Kurt, hoping this sociologist would know how to contradict me. "I am afraid you are right," he said.

— 321 —

A few days later, Karen Paine, her brown face molded into inarticulate despair, flung a paper at me. Her Afro hair style was fuller, bushier now, and she dug her fingers into it as she sat, head down, while I read what she had thrown on my lap. It was a newsletter from a California congressman, George E. Brown, Jr., dated May 27, 1968. In the mimeographed newsletter, Congressman Brown wrote of his concern that the House Un-American Activities Committee had recently suggested "detention centers" be used for "those planning guerrilla-type operations." HUAC had stated that the Internal Securities Act of 1950 "provides for the detention of persons when there is a reasonable ground to believe that such person probably will engage or probably conspire with others in acts of espionage or sabotage."

It was the *probably* that appalled me most. This law, passed during the reign of Joe McCarthy, could be used to intern people who, in someone's opinion, probably would engage in or conspire to commit espionage or sabotage. What if *probably* were in the hands of the people who called City Hall convinced that the police gunfire they heard was the "black militant invasion"? Or in the hands of the frightened white ladies the Panel spoke to on the day of Dr. King's funeral? Or the clenched hands of the important businessmen who felt "they" should all be in concentration camps and those of us who didn't agree were "full of crap"? If whites were already this terrified and vengeful, what would happen if a crazed, desperate youngster like Tuna committed some wild act?

"In Germany," Karen said quietly when I looked up at her, "they made the Jews wear yellow armbands. It will be easier here. We can't take our identification off."

I wish it had been bitter, half-crazed Karen instead of Leland who gave me a slim sheaf of neatly mimeographed papers stapled together into a booklet—its title: *Black Sur-*

vival Guide. Leland, who always seemed calm, made this dismal booklet even more depressing. He had been handed it on a ghetto street corner by a well-dressed black man who would not explain the credit line: "Distributed by the Black Community of Philadelphia." "What does it matter, brother," was all the man would say. Leland felt we should have a copy.

In this 16-page booklet there is no passionate talk of revolution or even of retaliation. It deals only with survival. The instructions are matter-of-fact and specific. The subtitle of the booklet is: *How to Live Through a Police Riot*.

The booklet begins with: "This booklet tells what you *must* do if you and your family want to survive. If you think they will not be after you, you're wrong. They will be going after anything that is BLACK—WHOEVER you are, WHEREVER you live, WHENEVER they get the word. Even if you think these statements are false, foolish or ignorant, *please do not throw this booklet away*. Put it wherever you can get to it in case you have to change your mind in a hurry."

The first pages explain how to know when a white attack is coming: scare propaganda in the news media "to prepare whites psychologically," police attempts to provoke "An Incident." During the attack, black families are urged to "stay together, away from windows," "put out all lights." "No one is safe indoors or outside. Police will shoot wildly at everything." After the attack, when utilities are cut off and food stores closed, black families are instructed to use emergency shelter provisions "as outlined in the Civil Defense bomb shelter list." To black people, we are now The Bomb.

Last month Ben brought a co-worker home to dinner. This man (white) had taken dangerous assignments in the South, his family was one of the few white families left in his neighborhood, his predictions and judgments had always been absolutely sound. I told him of my talk with Kurt Mayer, the

California Congressman's newsletter, the *Black Survival Guide*.

He put down his fork at our dinner table. He looked at me with sober blue eyes. "I don't want to know about it," he said. "The plain truth is I don't want to think about it."

Epilogue

A book must end; an education must not, and there must be a better ending for my country than I see now. For myself, one question I asked for eight years was answered the night Richard Nixon was elected President. He talked of a sign he had seen during his campaign, which read: Bring Us Together Again. The wave of sadness and yearning I felt at hearing those words finally explained my personal anguish over hate between two groups of people. "Bring us together again" were the words I wanted so desperately to hear as a child, from my parents who had parted in anger. I never heard them and my father is dead. Somehow this deeply hidden childhood wish had got mixed in with my hope that black and white Americans could understand each other. It had produced the personal pain when they did not. My parents' misunderstandings destroyed my home; black and white misunderstandings can destroy my country.

Perhaps recognizing the parallels made me able to accept certain somber realities. Eight years ago my first black friend, Grace Christopher, said she was afraid she could not raise her son in America; Mrs. Kozarik, the immigrant woman in

Rockbrook, said, "Most Americans don't care about others." I cannot tell either of these women I have proved them wrong. Instead, I wish, as Dorothy Parker once wrote, that "I knew a little more or very much less."

I wish I knew how America, the one country created by people from all over the world, could realize its potential as the natural bridge between Europe and Africa. Our people have their roots in both these continents, and we are the human links through which the world could be joined. If the blood of the hyphenated Europeans—the Italian-Americans, the Swedish-Americans, and my own German-American blood—had mingled, as it should have long ago, with the Americans who were involuntary immigrants from Africa, we would *look* as Americans should look. We would, some of us, be dark brown, and some of us pink, but most of us would be the *golden color* that would at last distinguish the genuine American.

But I am afraid that time and the astonishing American luck we took for granted have run out. For if white Americans have already begun to fear the black citizens whom we so greatly outnumber, then we are too vulnerable. Somewhere, right now, there is surely an insane black man ready to commit an act as unspeakable as those of Lee Harvey Oswald or Sirhan Sirhan or James Earl Ray. And somewhere there is a skillful white demagogue becoming aware of how effortlessly he could exploit white fear and convince the white majority it is "necessary" to intern those we fear. He could persuade us so easily to trade our morality and our freedoms for our "safety" and his power. And we would be, all of us, ten miles from Dachau.

When I say these things white people often look alarmed. Some ask, "What can I do?" I find I cannot tell them. The wall between two groups of Americans was built with millions of stones and I have finally come to believe it can only be removed by millions of white people each taking one stone away. Surely you and I know which stones we are personally capable of removing in our school or neighborhood or office or factory. And until I have done all I know to do, I cannot advise others.

Yet whatever I do may not be enough. There would then be agonizing alternatives from which my family must choose. If concentration camps for black Americans became a reality, I could not close my eyes and become a "good German." I would do everything, with all my strength and as long as I could, to prevent this horror in my country. Yet I must not pretend, even to myself, that I have the courage to enter those camps with friends like Leland and Barbara and their children. Nor am I brave enough to fight in some underground resistance. If I cannot die or fight with violence or stand silently by, then there remains only the coward's course of running.

When Ben and I discuss the sad alternative of leaving America, we know we must flee to a country immune to the tempting and contagious disease of white superiority. Africa seems the safest refuge for us. We have found more justice in black hearts than in white. Perhaps only in Africa can we hope that Spike, Noah and Sarah need never fight the same battle their parents lost.

The dreadful end of my education may be the acceptance of Grace Christopher's words. I may have learned only that we must flee, not to something better, but to some place where we can wait until America is again a country in which to raise children.

AFTERWORD—1988

Over the years, so many readers have written asking what has happened to me and to my family. I take special pleasure in answering. When the book ended in 1970, I could only *hope* that I had made the right choices for Spike, then 14, Noah, 12, and 10-year-old Sarah.

At age 15, Spike made his own choice: to attend our enormous public high school where he would be the only white student in his classes. During the first week, my racist fears surged. Three years later, he graduated with good memories and a good education.

During his first year at Penn State, I could finally ask my grown-up son if he might have preferred growing up with "his own kind" in a "good suburban school." I cherish his answer.

"Mom, the suburban kids up here are maybe three months ahead of me academically. I can catch up. But they'll never be able to catch up with what I know about all kinds of people."

Noah, at Northern Arizona University in Flagstaff, was shocked and angry when he first confronted an unfamiliar prejudice. He raged, "The cops up here treat Lee (a Navajo friend) the same bad way they treated Steve (a black friend) in

Philadelphia!" Noah is now a juvenile probation officer in Flagstaff, especially concerned with minority offenders. Noah and Debi plan to send their daughter Amanda to an integrated public school.

Sarah, at the University of Florida, chose a black roommate during her first year there. She wrote me, "If my white friends don't like this, then maybe they aren't the people I want as friends." She is now completing her graduate studies to become a counselor to elementary school children and is already battling bigotry when she spots it in schools.

In 1974, I tried to battle bigotry in education by writing another book, *Getting Ready* (Morrow/Bantam). In it, I described the damage I had seen being done to my children's classmates who were not white.

In 1976, I began to teach at the Community College of Philadelphia, a mostly black school. As a writing instructor and advisor to the college newspaper, I wanted to test my belief that teachers could build—or destroy—a student's self-esteem. Black friends predicted I would "last maybe a month" with my "radical" theories on teaching ill-prepared students to write and to use the freedom of the press. Two years later, with the support of CCP's (white) president, Allan Bonnell, our previously all-white newspaper had a black editor and I had the satisfaction of proving that students can blossom when teachers believe they can.

In 1984, with a nudge from Noah's wife, Debi, I began teaching a summer course, "The White World of Racism," at Northern Arizona University. Again, I had a theory. If white, black, and Native American students spent five weeks together, learning the history of racism, its present dynamics, and, most importantly, learning to know each other, then perhaps permanent personal change could occur. Now, each summer, I look forward to the miracles I see in that classroom as suspicion turns into sensitivity, and fears turn into friendships. Familiarity, as I have come to believe, does breed commitment.

Recently, I conducted a seminar for a group of college athletes, the kind of black (and white) students who were eased through high schools unprepared for college. Because I learned long ago how badly some students were cheated, I hope I helped them regain their self-esteem and learn the academic survival skills their parents were unable to impart. And so, opportunities to continue my education seem always to be there.

"Barbara Hamilton" and I have remained close friends. She is now dean of faculty at a mostly white college. We no longer talk about racism, I realize. We talk about our work and our children.

When I reread this book and think of all that Barbara—and black friends then and since—have taught me, I cannot help but feel I still owe a debt for that education. Yes, the wall between blacks and whites is thicker than I knew, but I keep finding my own personal stones to loosen and pull away. I still hope to prove Mrs. Kozarik wrong. Americans, when we know the truth, *do* care about others.

LOIS MARK STALVEY

January 1988

Marian Anderson
My Lord, What a Morning
Introduction by Nellie Y. McKay

American Women's Autobiography: Fea(s)ts of Memory
Edited, with an introduction, by Margo Culley

Frank Marshall Davis
Livin' the Blues: Memoirs of a Black Journalist and Poet
Edited, with an introduction, by John Edgar Tidwell

Joanne Jacobson
Authority and Alliance in the Letters of Henry Adams

Kamau Brathwaite
The Zea Mexican Diary
Foreword by Sandra Pouchet Paquet

Genaro M. Padilla
My History, Not Yours:
The Formation of Mexican American Autobiography

Frances Smith Foster
Witnessing Slavery: The Development
of Ante-bellum Slave Narratives

Native American Autobiography: An Anthology
Edited, with an introduction, by Arnold Krupat

American Lives: An Anthology of Autobiographical Writing
Edited, with an introduction, by Robert F. Sayre

Carol Holly
Intensely Family: The Inheritance of Family Shame and the
Autobiographies of Henry James

People of the Book: Thirty Scholars Reflect
on Their Jewish Identity
Edited, with an introduction, by Jeffrey Rubin-Dorsky
and Shelley Fisher Fishkin